# AUSTRALIAN Signpost MATHS

AF595874

1

Alan McSeveny Rachel McSeveny Diane McSeveny-Foster

**Pearson Australia**
(a division of Pearson Australia Group Pty Ltd)
459–471 Church St, Level 1, Building B, Richmond, Victoria, 3121
PO Box 23360, Melbourne, Victoria 8012
www.pearson.com.au


First published 2024 by Pearson Australia
2027 2026 2026 2025
10 9 8 7 6 5 4 3 2 1



Publishers: Sophie Matta and Rachel Elliott
Project Manager: Michelle Thomas
Production Editor: Laura Rentsch
Editor: Katie Millar
Designer: Anne Donald
Typesetter: Integra
Proofreader: Laura Rentsch
Rights & Permissions Editor: Alice McBroom
Cover art: Michael Barter
Illustrator: Michael Barter
Publishing Services: Jit-Pin Chong
Printed in Malaysia by Vivar

ISBN 978 0 6557 0875 9
Pearson Australia Group Pty Ltd ABN 40 004 245 943

**Attributions**
We would like to thank the following for permission to reproduce copyright material.

**123rf.com:** Amorozov, p. 21 (didgeridoo); Coprid, p. 21 (paper rolls); Nanastudio, p. 21 (gift); Photoshkolnik, p. 21 (barrel); Terekhov, p. 21 (suitcase); Zoraa, p. 21 (cube).

**Alamy:** Trevor Chriss, p. 93 (pin holder).

**Shutterstock:** Azure1, p. 21 (cheese); Irin-K, p. 21 (soccer ball); CKP1001, p. 21 (party hat); Ifong, p. 21 (ice cream); Koosen, p. 21 (glass); Mega Pixed, p. 21 (dice); Umberto Shtanzman, p. 21 (earth); Vladnik, p. 117; Zovteva, p. 21 (tent).



**Acknowledgement of Country**
Pearson respects and honours Aboriginal and Torres Strait Islander Elders past, present and future. We acknowledge the stories, traditions and living cultures of the Traditional Custodians of the lands on which our company is located and where we conduct our business. Pearson is committed to honouring Australian Aboriginal and Torres Strait Islander peoples' unique cultural and spiritual relationships to the land, waters and seas and their rich contribution to society.

Aboriginal and Torres Strait Islander peoples are advised that this text may contain images, voices and names of deceased persons.

# What is Australian Signpost Maths?

Australian Signpost Maths is a mathematics program providing direction and support for teaching and learning. The series covers the content and skills presented in the Australian Curriculum (v9) Mathematics F–6.

A Student Book and an online Teacher Resource are provided for Foundation.

For Years 1 to 6, a Student Book, an online Teacher Resource and a Mentals Book are provided for each year level. The online Teacher Resource provides a wealth of support for teachers.

The content has been carefully sequenced within each year level and across the F–6 series to take into account students' expected mathematical development. However, from the rich and varied material provided, teachers can develop individual learning programs to meet the needs of each student.

The Student Books are designed to support explicit teaching methods. Many group activities are provided in Activity, Investigation and Fun spots within the Student Books and the online Teacher Resource.

To maximise the benefits of the program, the Student Book, the online Teacher Resource and the Mentals Book should be used together.

Student Books

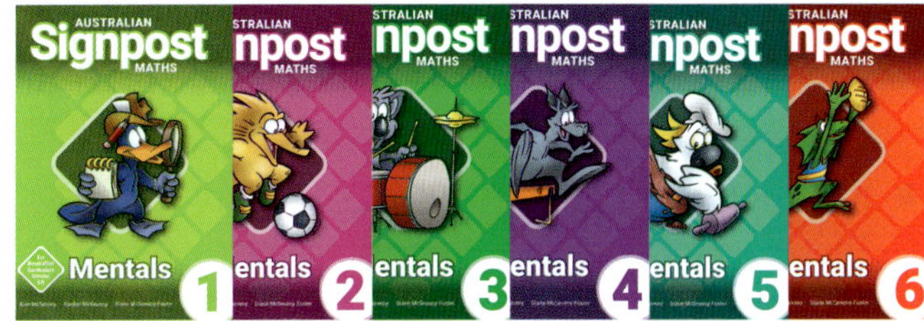

Mentals Books

Teacher Resource

# Structure of Australian Signpost Maths

In the F–2 books, the worksheet pages cover all of the elements: Number sense and algebra, Measurement and geometry and Statistics and probability. These are presented in a recommended order. Each unit of 4 pages usually begins with Number or Algebra. The Contents cross-reference allows teachers to quickly find the pages where each concept has been covered.

Within the program, explicit teaching, critical and creative thinking, language development and identification and treatment of weaknesses are given high priority.

### Identifying and addressing areas of need

Five progress tests are designed to identify each student's areas of need, and the follow-up program after each of the tests is designed to address these needs. A reference to the relevant worksheet page is given for each test question. A remediation record page is used to track the student's progress.

These testing resources can be found in the online Teacher Resource.

Parallel progress retests are provided for further testing after remediation has taken place. See pages 130 and 131 of this book for more information.

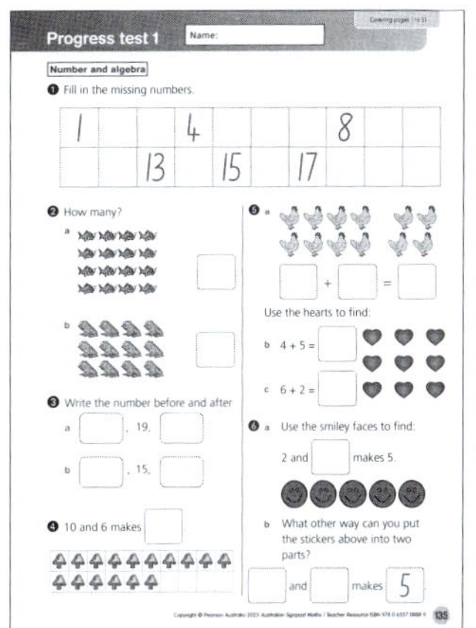
Progress test 1 Name:

Number and algebra

1 Fill in the missing numbers.

2 How many?

3 Write the number before and after.

4 10 and 6 makes

5 a Use the hearts to find:

b 4 + 5 =

c 6 + 2 =

6 a Use the smiley faces to find:

2 and makes 5.

b What other way can you put the stickers above into two parts?

and makes 5

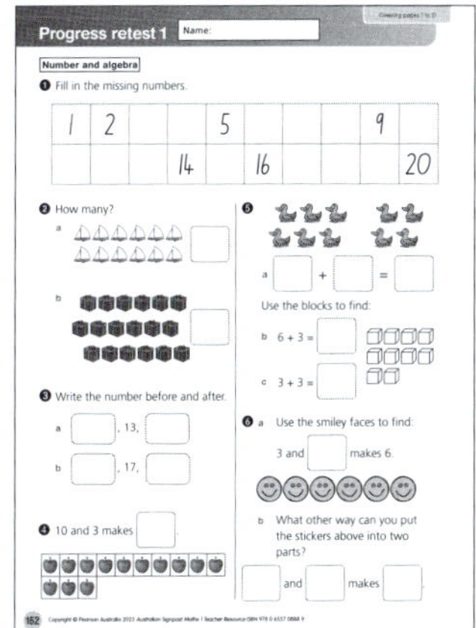
Progress retest 1 Name:

Number and algebra

1 Fill in the missing numbers.

2 How many?

3 Write the number before and after.

4 10 and 3 makes

5 a Use the blocks to find:

b 6 + 3 =

c 3 + 3 =

6 a Use the smiley faces to find:

3 and makes 6

b What other way can you put the stickers above into two parts?

and makes

## Special features of Australian Signpost Maths

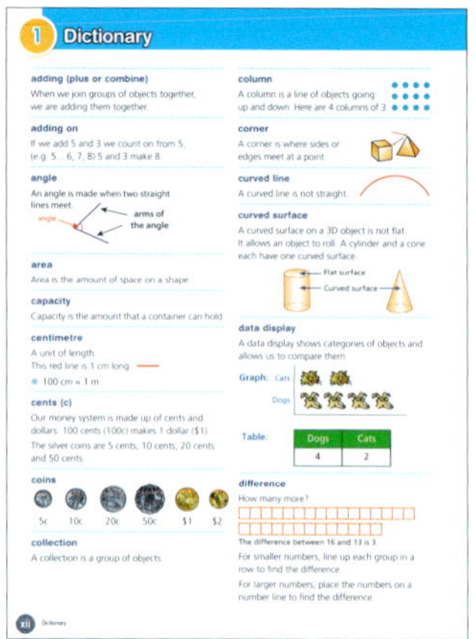

- **The traffic light icons**

  These are found on the top right of each worksheet page in the Student Books. They allow students to assess their own progress and give feedback to the teacher.

  - ☐ **Green:** I found this work easy.
  - ☐ **Orange:** I found some work on the page difficult.
  - ☐ **Red:** I don't understand the work on this page.

- **Dictionary**

  Terms used in the Student Book and terms that should be understood at this level are recorded here to provide a reference for students and teachers. This is found on pages xii–xvi of this book.

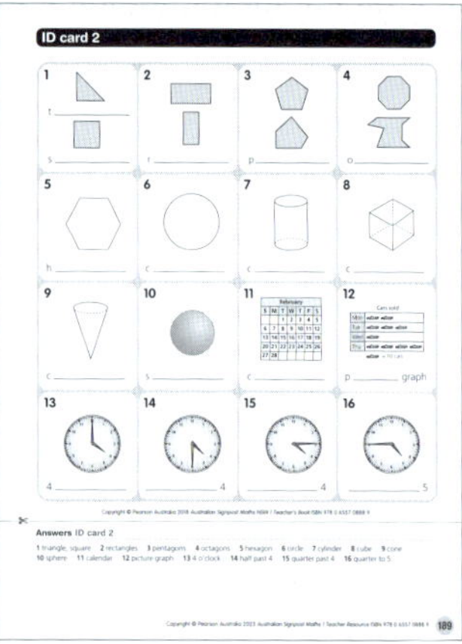

- **ID cards (Years 1 to 6)**

  These cards review the language of Mathematics by asking students to identify common terms, shapes and symbols. They are designed to be reused and are found in the online Teacher Resource and in the front of the Mentals Books.

- **Progress tests**

  These allow the teacher to identify each student's strengths and needs. Cross-references for each question direct teachers and students to the pages where that work is introduced. Tables are provided to record the follow-up that takes place and parallel tests are provided for retesting. These tests can be found in the online Teacher Resource.

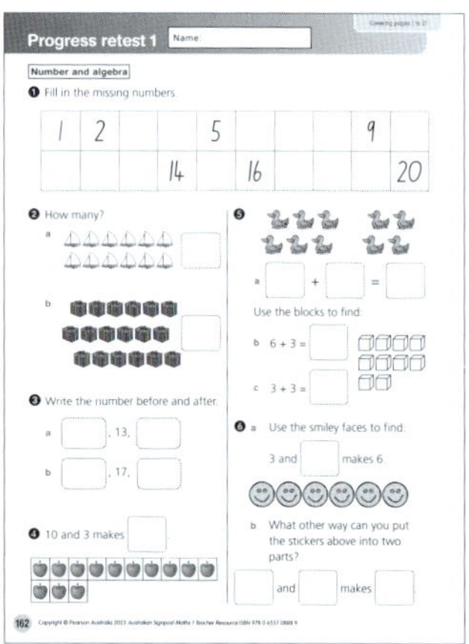

- **Year 1 Consolidation booklet**

  This 30-page booklet is found in the online Teacher Resource. It is designed to reinforce work completed in class and provides practice of important skills and addition and subtraction facts. The booklet can be used when there is limited supervision or when a student finishes classwork early.

- **Answers**

  These are supplied in the online Teacher Resource.

- **Blackline masters (BLM)**

  References are made to the blackline masters in the teaching suggestions provided for each student work page.

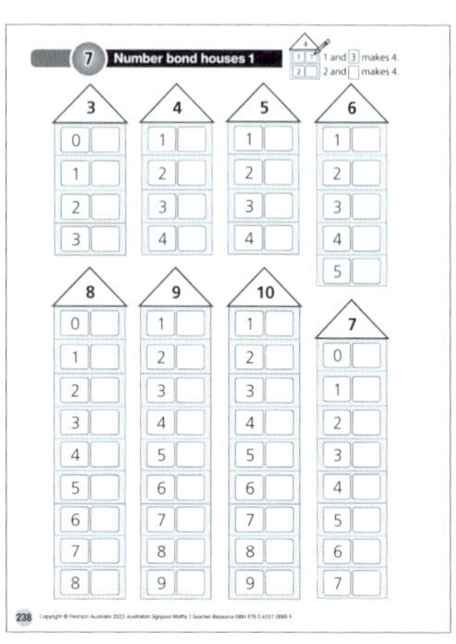

- **Differentiation**

  Each student work page has a Teacher Resource page to support it. Cross-references direct the teacher to pages where the concept is introduced and developed. These references may be from the Student Book for the previous year, the current year or the next year.

  The Teacher Resource support pages provide additional learning activities for students who need remediation or extension activities. The blackline masters provide activities to support students of various learning abilities.

- **Cartoons**

  Cartoons are used to motivate and instruct.

## Australian Signpost Maths icons

Signpost icons are used throughout the book as cues to the essential nature of exercises and activities, and as a guide to ways of engaging with them. These icons often indicate alternative or more concrete approaches to dealing with concepts.

This icon highlights **important rules and concepts** occurring throughout the book. It often appears with worked examples.

Investigations allow students to **explore and discover** maths concepts.

Activities provide **applications and enrichment**. These activities usually involve the use of concrete materials and partner or group work.

These enjoyable activities are used to **motivate and involve** students in mathematical pursuits. They usually involve games and puzzles.

## Structure of the Australian Curriculum, F–6 (v9)

**Numeracy elements**

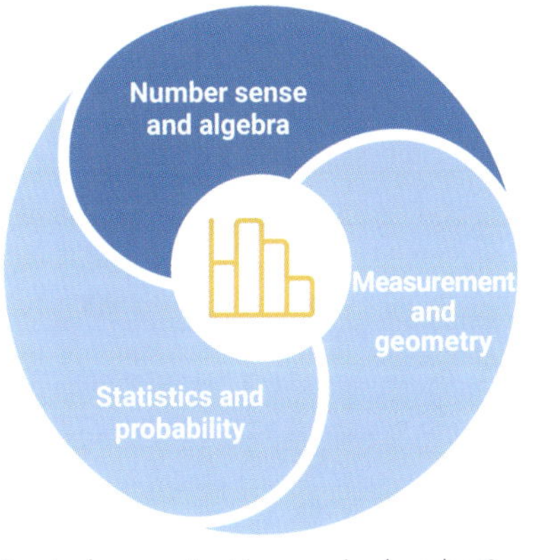


Curriculum content is organised under 6 interrelated strands: Number, Algebra, Measurement, Space, Statistics and Probability.

**Sub-elements for Number sense and algebra**

- Number and place value
- Counting processes
- Additive strategies
- Multiplicative strategies
- Interpreting fractions
- Number patterns and algebraic thinking
- Understanding money

**Sub-elements for Measurement and geometry**

- Understanding units of measurement
- Understanding geometric properties
- Positioning and locating
- Measuring time

**Sub-elements for Statistics and probability**

- Understanding chance
- Interpreting and representing data

The Curriculum strives to develop in students proficiency in Mathematics, highlighting Understanding, Fluency, Reasoning and Problem solving.

### Mathematics content of the Australian Curriculum

Go to v9.australiancurriculum.edu.au and you can find:

1 **Content descriptions** like AC9MFN01

2 **General capabilities** (found by clicking one of the symbols shown)

3 **Elaborations** which provide teaching suggestions.

* It is important that you download the **General capabilities** document from 'Downloads' in the top navigation bar of the website homepage. It contains the tables that list the progression level expectations for each Year, F to 10. It also provides the content of all progression levels.

* The **Learning areas** download gives a summary of Content descriptions and Elaborations. **Cross-curriculum priorities** can also be found there.

# Contents and syllabus overview

**KEY**

| Colour | Strand |
|---|---|
| Blue | Number / algebra |
| Green | Measurement / space |
| Orange | Statistics / probability |

| Page | Unit | Title | Strand | Number / algebra | Measurement / space | Statistics / probability | Content area | Numbers / money | Addition / subtraction | Sharing / grouping | Patterns | 2D shapes / 3D objects | Position / direction | Length / area / mass | Capacity / volume | Time / duration | Data displays |
|---|---|---|---|---|---|---|---|---|---|---|---|---|---|---|---|---|---|
| 1 | Thinking skills | | Critical and creative thinking is covered throughout. | | | | | | | | | | | | | | |
| 2 | 1A | Number revision | | ■ | | | | ● | | | | | | | | | |
| 3 | 1B | Number revision | | ■ | | | | ● | | | | | | | | | |
| 4 | 1C | Numbers to 20 | | ■ | | | | ● | | | | | | | | | |
| 5 | 1D | Shapes and patterns | | | ■ | | | | | | | ● | | | | | |
| 6 | 2A | Adding two groups | | ■ | | | | | ● | | | | | | | | |
| 7 | 2B | Addition sentences | | ■ | | | | | ● | | | | | | | | |
| 8 | 2C | Combinations up to 10 | | ■ | | | | | ● | | | | | | | | |
| 9 | 2D | Data displays | | | | ■ | | | | | | | | | | | ● |
| 10 | 3A | Numbers 11 to 20 | | ■ | | | | ● | | | | | | | | | |
| 11 | 3B | Numbers to 20 | | ■ | | | | ● | | | | | | | | | |
| 12 | 3C | Analog time | | | ■ | | | | | | | | | | | ● | |
| 13 | 3D | Reading the time | | | ■ | | | | | | | | | | | ● | |
| 14 | 4A | Numbers to 20 | | ■ | | | | ● | | | | | | | | | |
| 15 | 4B | Friends of 10 | | ■ | | | | | ● | | | | | | | | |
| 16 | 4C | Position language | | | ■ | | | | | | | | ● | | | | |
| 17 | 4D | Position language | | | ■ | | | | | | | | ● | | | | |
| 18 | 5A | Addition facts | | ■ | | | | | ● | | | | | | | | |
| 19 | 5B | Partitioning | | ■ | | | | | ● | | | | | | | | |
| 20 | 5C | Identifying objects | | | ■ | | | | | | | ● | | | | | |
| 21 | 5D | Objects in our world | | | ■ | | | | | | | ● | | | | | |
| | | Progress test 1: Administer test then address weaknesses. | | | | | | | | | | | | | | | |
| 22 | 6A | Groups of 10 | | ■ | | | | ● | | | | | | | | | |
| 23 | 6B | Counting by tens | | ■ | | | | ● | | | | | | | | | |
| 24 | 6C | Counting by tens | | ■ | | | | ● | | | | | | | | | |
| 25 | 6D | Units of length | | | ■ | | | | | | | | | ● | | | |
| 26 | 7A | Subtraction | | ■ | | | | | ● | | | | | | | | |
| 27 | 7B | Subtraction | | ■ | | | | | ● | | | | | | | | |
| 28 | 7C | Numbers to 100 | | ■ | | | | ● | | | | | | | | | |
| 29 | 7D | Informal units of length | | | ■ | | | | | | | | | ● | | | |

**KEY**

| | |
|---|---|
| ■ (blue) | Number / algebra |
| ■ (green) | Measurement / space |
| ■ (orange) | Statistics / probability |

| Page | Unit | Title | Strand | Number / algebra | Measurement / space | Statistics / probability | Content area | Numbers / money | Addition / subtraction | Sharing / grouping | Patterns | 2D shapes / 3D objects | Position / direction | Length / area / mass | Capacity / volume | Time / duration | Data displays |
|---|---|---|---|---|---|---|---|---|---|---|---|---|---|---|---|---|---|
| 30 | 8A | Odd and even numbers | | ■ | | | | ● | | | | | | | | | |
| 31 | 8B | Addition to 20 | | ■ | | | | | ● | | | | | | | | |
| 32 | 8C | Half past | | | ■ | | | | | | | | | | | ● | |
| 33 | 8D | Half past | | | ■ | | | | | | | | | | | ● | |
| 34 | 9A | Counting on | | ■ | | | | | ● | | | | | | | | |
| 35 | 9B | Counting on | | ■ | | | | | ● | | | | | | | | |
| 36 | 9C | Analog time | | | ■ | | | | | | | | | | | ● | |
| 37 | 9D | Analog time | | | ■ | | | | | | | | | | | ● | |
| 38 | 10A | Addition to 20 | | ■ | | | | | ● | | | | | | | | |
| 39 | 10B | Larger numbers | | ■ | | | | ● | | | | | | | | | |
| 40 | 10C | Informal units of length | | | ■ | | | | | | | | | ● | | | |
| 41 | 10D | Measuring length | | | ■ | | | | | | | | | ● | | | |
| 42 | 11A | Numbers to 100 | | ■ | | | | ● | | | | | | | | | |
| 43 | 11B | Subtraction to 20 | | ■ | | | | | ● | | | | | | | | |
| 44 | 11C | Comparing capacities | | | ■ | | | | | | | | | | ● | | |
| 45 | 11D | Informal units of capacity | | | ■ | | | | | | | | | | ● | | |
| 46 | 12A | Addition sentences | | ■ | | | | | ● | | | | | | | | |
| 47 | 12B | Addition | | ■ | | | | | ● | | | | | | | | |

Progress test 2: Administer test then address weaknesses.

| Page | Unit | Title | Strand | Number / algebra | Measurement / space | Statistics / probability | Content area | Numbers / money | Addition / subtraction | Sharing / grouping | Patterns | 2D shapes / 3D objects | Position / direction | Length / area / mass | Capacity / volume | Time / duration | Data displays |
|---|---|---|---|---|---|---|---|---|---|---|---|---|---|---|---|---|---|
| 48 | 12C | Addition by counting on | | ■ | | | | | ● | | | | | | | | |
| 49 | 12D | Comparing capacities | | | ■ | | | | | | | | | | ● | | |
| 50 | 13A | Numbers to 120 | | ■ | | | | ● | | | | | | | | | |
| 51 | 13B | Numbers to 120 | | ■ | | | | ● | | | | | | | | | |
| 52 | 13C | The hexagon | | | ■ | | | | | | | ● | | | | | |
| 53 | 13D | Picture graphs | | | | ■ | | | | | | | | | | | ● |
| 54 | 14A | Subtraction | | ■ | | | | | ● | | | | | | | | |
| 55 | 14B | Subtraction | | ■ | | | | | ● | | | | | | | | |
| 56 | 14C | Comparing the mass of objects | | | ■ | | | | | | | | | ● | | | |
| 57 | 14D | Mass | | | ■ | | | | | | | | | ● | | | |
| 58 | 15A | Counting back | | ■ | | | | | ● | | | | | | | | |
| 59 | 15B | Subtraction | | ■ | | | | | ● | | | | | | | | |
| 60 | 15C | Indirect comparison of length | | | ■ | | | | | | | | | ● | | | |
| 61 | 15D | Data displays | | | | ■ | | | | | | | | | | | ● |
| 62 | 16A | Doubles | | ■ | | | | | ● | | | | | | | | |
| 63 | 16B | Doubling and near doubling | | ■ | | | | | ● | | | | | | | | |
| 64 | 16C | Months of the year | | | ■ | | | | | | | | | | | ● | |
| 65 | 16D | Months and seasons | | | ■ | | | | | | | | | | | ● | |

**KEY**

| | |
|---|---|
| ■ (blue) | Number / algebra |
| ■ (green) | Measurement / space |
| ■ (orange) | Statistics / probability |

| Page | Unit | Title | Strand | Number / algebra | Measurement / space | Statistics / probability | Content area | Numbers / money | Addition / subtraction | Sharing / grouping | Patterns | 2D shapes / 3D objects | Position / direction | Length / area / mass | Capacity / volume | Time / duration | Data displays |
|---|---|---|---|---|---|---|---|---|---|---|---|---|---|---|---|---|---|
| 66 | 17A | Patterns | | ■ | | | | | | | ● | | | | | | |
| 67 | 17B | Combinations for numbers | | ■ | | | | | ● | | | | | | | | |
| 68 | 17C | Object hunt | | | ■ | | | | | | | ● | | | | | |
| 69 | 17D | Recognising 3D objects | | | ■ | | | | | | | ● | | | | | |
| 70 | 18A | Difference | | ■ | | | | | ● | | | | | | | | |
| 71 | 18B | Difference between groups | | ■ | | | | | ● | | | | | | | | |
| 72 | 18C | The pentagon and octagon | | | ■ | | | | | | | ● | | | | | |
| 73 | 18D | Analog time | | | ■ | | | | | | | | | | | ● | |
| 74 | 19A | Place value | | ■ | | | | ● | | | | | | | | | |
| 75 | 19B | Numbers to 120 | | ■ | | | | ● | | | | | | | | | |
| 76 | 19C | Place value | | ■ | | | | ● | | | | | | | | | |
| 77 | 19D | Finding the nearest ten | | ■ | | | | ● | | | | | | | | | |
| 78 | 20A | Subtraction by counting on | | ■ | | | | | ● | | | | | | | | |
| 79 | 20B | Finding the difference | | ■ | | | | | ● | | | | | | | | |
| 80 | 20C | Numbers to 100 | | ■ | | | | ● | | | | | | | | | |
| 81 | 20D | 3D objects | | | ■ | | | | | | | ● | | | | | |
| 82 | 21A | Equal groups | | ■ | | | | | | ● | | | | | | | |
| 83 | 21B | Using groups | | ■ | | | | | | ● | | | | | | | |

Progress test 3: Administer test then address weaknesses.

| Page | Unit | Title | Strand | Number / algebra | Measurement / space | Statistics / probability | Content area | Numbers / money | Addition / subtraction | Sharing / grouping | Patterns | 2D shapes / 3D objects | Position / direction | Length / area / mass | Capacity / volume | Time / duration | Data displays |
|---|---|---|---|---|---|---|---|---|---|---|---|---|---|---|---|---|---|
| 84 | 21C | Capacity and volume | | | ■ | | | | | | | | | | ● | | |
| 85 | 21D | Capacity and volume | | | ■ | | | | | | | | | | ● | | |
| 86 | 22A | Numbers to 120 | | ■ | | | | ● | | | | | | | | | |
| 87 | 22B | Skip counting patterns | | ■ | | | | | | | ● | | | | | | |
| 88 | 22C | Area | | | ■ | | | | | | | | | ● | | | |
| 89 | 22D | Comparison of areas | | | ■ | | | | | | | | | ● | | | |
| 90 | 23A | Equal groups | | ■ | | | | | | ● | | | | | | | |
| 91 | 23B | Using groups | | ■ | | | | | | ● | | | | | | | |
| 92 | 23C | Angles | | | ■ | | | | | | | ● | | | | | |
| 93 | 23D | Angles in our world | | | ■ | | | | | | | ● | | | | | |
| 94 | 24A | Skip counting | | ■ | | | | | | | ● | | | | | | |
| 95 | 24B | Number patterns | | ■ | | | | | | | ● | | | | | | |
| 96 | 24C | Months of the year | | | ■ | | | | | | | | | | | ● | |
| 97 | 24D | Gather and display data | | | | ■ | | | | | | | | | | | ● |
| 98 | 25A | Number patterns | | ■ | | | | ● | | | ● | | | | | | |
| 99 | 25B | Counting by 2s, 5s and 10s | | ■ | | | | ● | | | ● | | | | | | |
| 100 | 25C | 2D shapes | | | ■ | | | | | | | ● | | | | | |
| 101 | 25D | Properties of shapes | | | ■ | | | | | | | ● | | | | | |

**KEY**

| Colour | Strand |
|---|---|
| Blue | Number / algebra |
| Green | Measurement / space |
| Orange | Statistics / probability |

| Page | Unit | Title | Strand | Number / algebra | Measurement / space | Statistics / probability | Content area | Numbers / money | Addition / subtraction | Sharing / grouping | Patterns | 2D shapes / 3D objects | Position / direction | Length / area / mass | Capacity / volume | Time / duration | Data displays |
|---|---|---|---|---|---|---|---|---|---|---|---|---|---|---|---|---|---|
| 102 | 26A | Problems with equal groups | | ■ | | | | | | ● | | | | | | | |
| 103 | 26B | Number relationships | | ■ | | | | | ● | | ● | | | | | | |
| 104 | 26C | Calendar | | | ■ | | | | | | | | | | | ● | |
| 105 | 26D | The calendar | | | ■ | | | | | | | | | | | ● | |
| 106 | 27A | Sharing | | ■ | | | | | | ● | | | | | | | |
| 107 | 27B | Sharing | | ■ | | | | | | ● | | | | | | | |
| 108 | 27C | Money | | ■ | | | | ● | | | | | | | | | |

Progress test 4: Administer test then address weaknesses.

| Page | Unit | Title | Strand | Number / algebra | Measurement / space | Statistics / probability | Content area | Numbers / money | Addition / subtraction | Sharing / grouping | Patterns | 2D shapes / 3D objects | Position / direction | Length / area / mass | Capacity / volume | Time / duration | Data displays |
|---|---|---|---|---|---|---|---|---|---|---|---|---|---|---|---|---|---|
| 109 | 27D | Giving directions | | | ■ | | | | | | | | ● | | | | |
| 110 | 28A | Grouping to share | | ■ | | | | | | ● | | | | | | | |
| 111 | 28B | How many groups? | | ■ | | | | | | ● | | | | | | | |
| 112 | 28C | Comparing areas | | | ■ | | | | | | | | | ● | | | |
| 113 | 28D | Area using units | | | ■ | | | | | | | | | ● | | | |
| 114 | 29A | Looking for tens | | ■ | | | | | ● | | | | | | | | |
| 115 | 29B | Relating addition and subtraction | | ■ | | | | | ● | | | | | | | | |
| 116 | 29C | Relating addition and subtraction | | ■ | | | | | ● | | | | | | | | |
| 117 | 29D | Comparing mass | | | ■ | | | | | | | | | ● | | | |
| 118 | 30A | Bridging to 10 | | ■ | | | | | ● | | | | | | | | |
| 119 | 30B | Bridging to 10s | | ■ | | | | | ● | | | | | | | | |
| 120 | 30C | Bridging to 10s | | ■ | | | | | ● | | | | | | | | |
| 121 | 30D | Money | | ■ | | | | ● | | | | | | | | | |
| 122 | 31A | Subtraction strategies | | ■ | | | | | ● | | | | | | | | |
| 123 | 31B | Addition facts (extension) | | ■ | | | | | ● | | | | | | | | |
| 124 | 31C | Left and right | | | ■ | | | | | | | | ● | | | | |
| 125 | 31D | Subtraction facts (extension) | | ■ | | | | | ● | | | | | | | | |
| 126 | 32A | The halfway point (extension) | | | ■ | | | | | | | | | ● | | | |
| 127 | 32B | Making more patterns | | ■ | | | | | | | ● | | | | | | |

Progress test 5: Administer test then address weaknesses.

| Page | Unit | Title | Strand | Number / algebra | Measurement / space | Statistics / probability | Content area | Numbers / money | Addition / subtraction | Sharing / grouping | Patterns | 2D shapes / 3D objects | Position / direction | Length / area / mass | Capacity / volume | Time / duration | Data displays |
|---|---|---|---|---|---|---|---|---|---|---|---|---|---|---|---|---|---|
| 128 | 32C | Following directions | | | ■ | | | | | | | | ● | | | | |
| 129 | 32D | Gather and organise data | | | | ■ | | | | | | | | | | | ● |
| 130 | Identifying and addressing areas of need | | | | | | | | | | | | | | | | |
| 132 | 1 Number lines / chart | 2 Number bond houses | | | | | | | | | | | | | | | |
| 134 | 3 Number bonds (addition) | 4 Addition and subtraction facts | 5 Addition facts to 20 | | | | | | | | | | | | | | |

# Contents cross-reference

## Measurement and space

| 1 | Measurement (AC9M1M01-03) | Pages |
|---|---|---|
| | **Length** | 25, 29, 40, 41, 60, 126 |
| | **Area** | 88, 89, 112, 113 |
| | **Capacity** (internal volume) | 44, 45, 49, 84, 85 |
| | **Mass** (weight) | 56, 57, 117 |
| | **Time** (describing, comparing, sequencing, calendar) | 12, 36, 104, 105 |
| | Months and seasons | 64, 65, 96, 104, 105 |
| | Telling time on the hour, half hour and quarter hour | 12, 13, 32, 33, 36, 37, 73 |
| **2** | **Space (AC9M1SP01-02)** | **Pages** |
| | **2D shapes** (circle, oval, triangle, square, rectangle, quadrilateral, hexagon, pentagon, octagon) | 5, 52, 72, 92, 100, 101 |
| | Angles, sides and vertices | 52, 72, 92, 93, 100, 101 |
| | **3D objects** | 20, 21, 68, 69, 81, 85 |
| | **Position and directions** | 16, 17, 109, 124, 128 |
| | Left and right | 16, 17, 124 |
| | Giving and following directions | 109, 124, 128 |
| | Ordinal numbers | 39, 75, 99, 105 |

## Statistics and probability

| 1 | Data (AC9M1ST01-02) | Pages |
|---|---|---|
| | Collecting data | 61, 97, 129 |
| | Using data displays | 9, 25, 53, 61, 97, 121, 129 |

# 1 Dictionary

### adding (plus or combine)

When we join groups of objects together, we are adding them together.

### adding on

If we add 5 and 3 we count on from 5, (e.g. 5... 6, 7, 8) 5 and 3 make 8.

### angle

An angle is made when two straight lines meet.

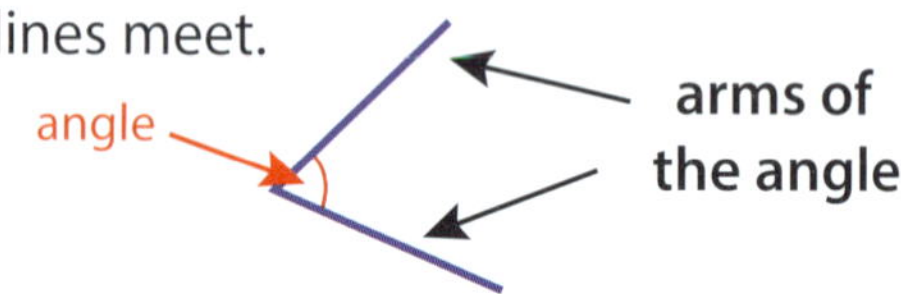


### area

Area is the amount of space on a shape.

### capacity

Capacity is the amount that a container can hold.

### centimetre

A unit of length.

This red line is 1 cm long.

- 100 cm = 1 m

### cents (c)

Our money system is made up of cents and dollars. 100 cents (100c) makes 1 dollar ($1).

The silver coins are 5 cents, 10 cents, 20 cents and 50 cents.

### coins

5c 10c 20c 50c $1 $2

### collection

A collection is a group of objects.

### column

A column is a line of objects going up and down. Here are 4 columns of 3.

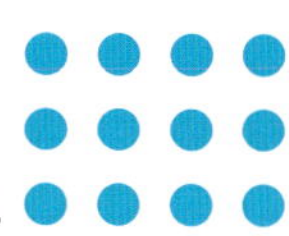

### corner

A corner is where sides or edges meet at a point.

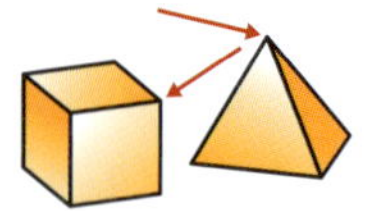

### curved line

A curved line is not straight.

### curved surface

A curved surface on a 3D object is not flat. It allows an object to roll. A cylinder and a cone each have one curved surface.

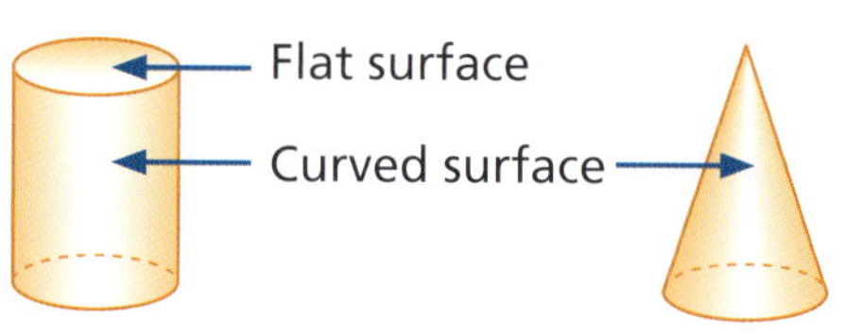


### data display

A data display shows categories of objects and allows us to compare them.

**Graph:**

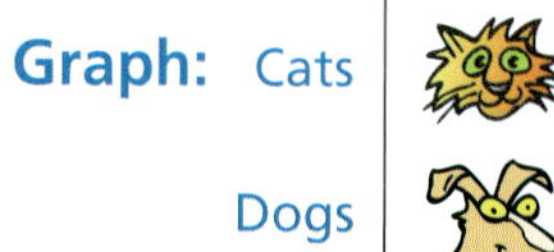

**Table:**

| Dogs | Cats |
|---|---|
| 4 | 2 |

### difference

How many more?

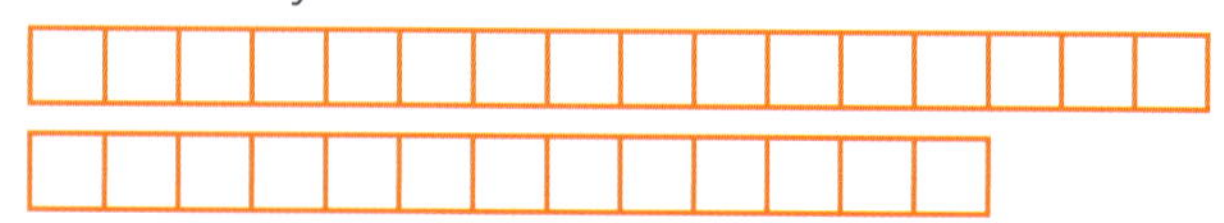

The difference between 16 and 13 is 3.

For smaller numbers, line up each group in a row to find the difference.

For larger numbers, place the numbers on a number line to find the difference.

## dollars ($)

Our money system is made up of cents and dollars.

100 cents (100c) makes 1 dollar ($1).

The gold coins are $1 (1 dollar) and $2 (2 dollars).

The notes are $5, $10, $20, $50, $100.

## double

Double means the same thing twice.

Double 4 means 4 + 4 = 8

## edge

An edge is where two faces of a 3D object meet.

## equal groups

Groups that have the same number of members.

## equals sign =

The equals sign means "makes" or "is equal to" or "is the same as" (e.g. 2 + 3 = 4 + 1).

## estimate

A good guess.

## face

A flat surface that has straight sides (e.g. the side of a box).

## flat surface

It is not curved.
It allows an object to slide.

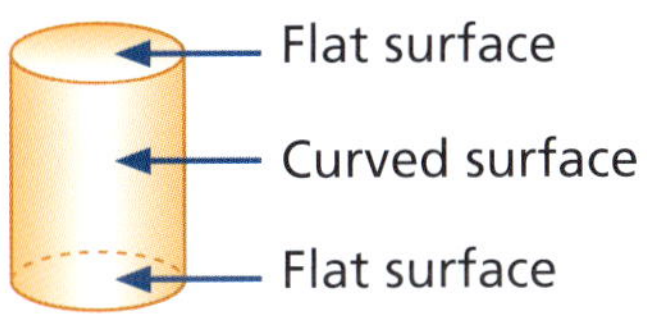


A cylinder has 2 flat surfaces, one on each end, and one curved surface.

## friends of ten

Numbers that add together to make 10.
The friends of 10 are 1 and 9, 2 and 8, 3 and 7, 4 and 6, 5 and 5, 6 or 4, 7 and 3, 8 and 2, 9 and 1.

## graph

See *data display*.

## half

One of two equal parts.

One half of the rectangle is coloured.

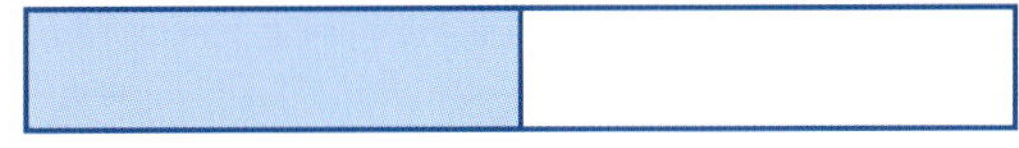

## halfway point

The halfway point is the middle position.

## hefting

To compare masses by lifting them with your hands.

## left and right

Left 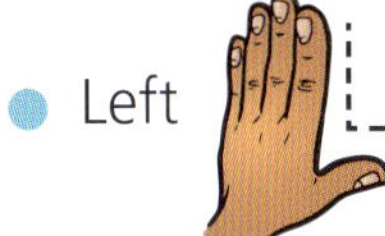 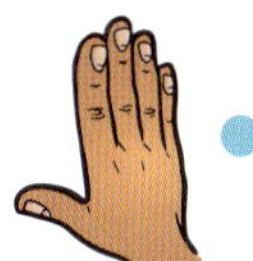 Right

The left hand makes an "L" for left.

## length words

| | | |
|---|---|---|
| distance | long | tall |
| deeper | longer | taller |
| higher | short | thicker |
| lower | shorter | thinner |

## mass words

| | | |
|---|---|---|
| heavy | light | weigh |
| heavier | lighter | weight |
| heaviest | lightest | balanced |

## notes

## number bonds

Pairs of numbers that add to make a specific number (e.g. 0 and 4, 1 and 3, and 2 and 2 all make 4).

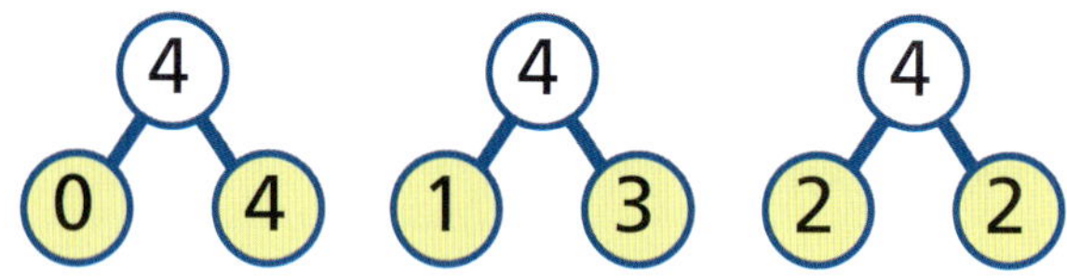

## number line

A number line is a line that shows numbers in order. Number lines can be used for many things (e.g. counting, adding and subtracting).

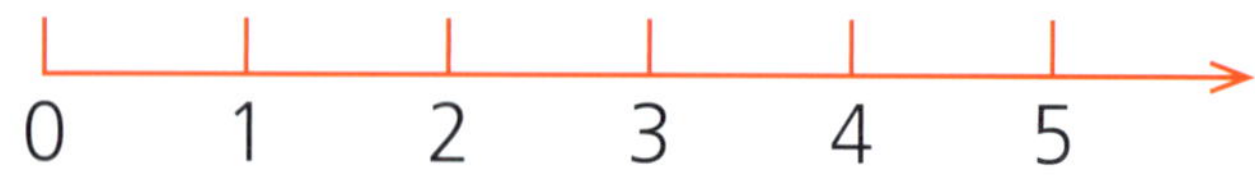


## number sentence

A number sentence uses numerals and symbols (e.g. 4 and 6 makes 10. This can be written as 4 + 6 = 10).

## numeral

A numeral is a written number symbol such as 7, 18, 92, 120.

## odd and even numbers

Odd numbers end in 1, 3, 5, 7 or 9 (e.g. 49).

Even numbers end in 2, 4, 6, 8 or 0 (e.g. 32).

## ordinal number

Ordinal numbers describe the order or position of something (e.g. 1st, 2nd, 3rd, 4th, 5th).

## partitioning

Partitioning is when a group of objects is broken up into two parts. The more objects there are in the group, the more different combinations can be made.

(e.g. The number 8 can be partitioned as 7 and 1, 6 and 2, 5 and 3, or 4 and 4.)

## pattern

A pattern is a group of numbers, objects, shapes, colours, sounds or actions that are repeated over and over again.

## place value

The position of each digit of a numeral holds a different value.

## place-value blocks

These are used to represent numbers.

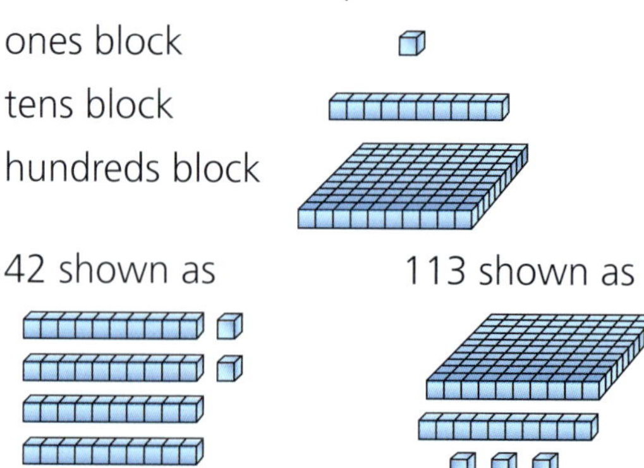


## reflection (or flip)

A mirror image.

## **right** and **left**

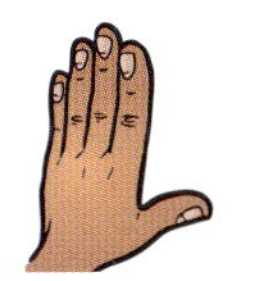
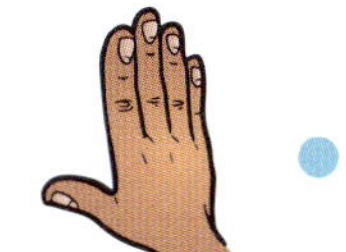

- Left
- Right

## row

A row is a line of objects going across. Here are 2 rows of 5.

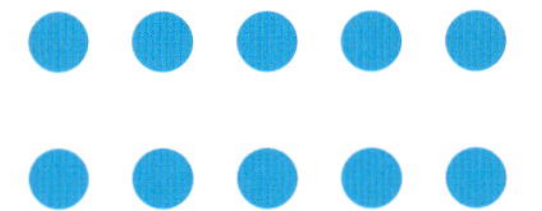

## sharing

When sharing, we make sure that each share is the same size.

2 people could share these 6 balls. Each person would get 3 balls.
If two groups are not the same, we can make fair shares by moving items from the larger group to the smaller group.

## slide

Moving a shape in any direction without changing the size or orientation.

## straight line

A straight line has no bends or curves.

## symmetry

A shape has symmetry when one side is the mirror-image of the other. It can be folded so that the two halves match, exactly.

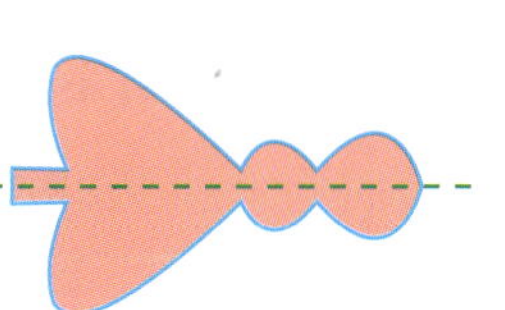

## take away (subtract or minus)

When we remove objects from a group we call this "take away".

## tally marks

Tally marks are used to keep count. Groups of 5 are used.

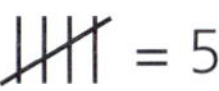

## three-dimensional (3D) objects

3D objects are three-dimensional.
They have length, width and height.

**spheres** (ball-shaped objects) are curved and round.
They can roll.

**cubes** (box-shaped objects) have 6 square faces.
They can slide.

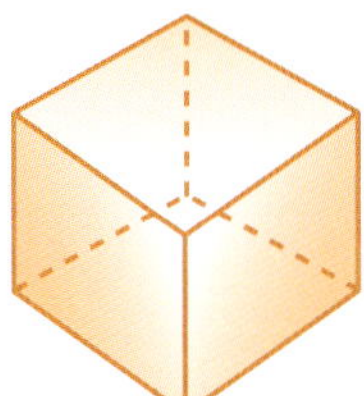

**cylinders** (can-shaped objects) have 2 flat surfaces and 1 curved surface. They can roll and slide.

**cones** (cone-shaped objects) have 1 flat surface and 1 curved surface.
They can roll and slide.

**prisms**
A prism has rectangular faces joining two identical bases at both ends.

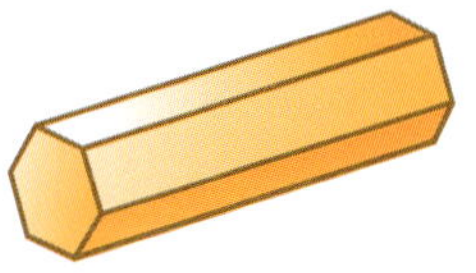
hexagonal prism

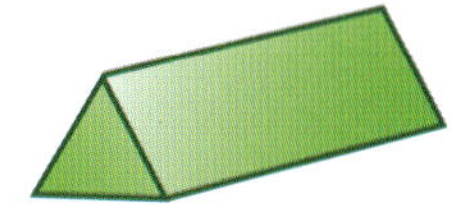
triangular prism

## time words

| morning | day |
|---|---|
| afternoon | night |

| Days | | | |
|---|---|---|---|
| Sunday | Monday | Tuesday | Wednesday |
| Thursday | Friday | Saturday | |

| Months | | | |
|---|---|---|---|
| January | February | March | April |
| May | June | July | August |
| September | October | November | December |

| Seasons | | | |
|---|---|---|---|
| Summer | Autumn | Winter | Spring |

- clocks

analog clock

digital clock

3 o'clock

- o'clock

When the long hand (minute hand) is pointing to 12, the time is an "o'clock" time. The short hand (hour hand) points to the hour (e.g. the hour hand above is pointing to the 3 so it is 3 o'clock).

half past 3

- half past

When the long hand (hour hand) is pointing to the 6, the time is a "half past" time. The short hand (hour hand) above is pointing halfway between the 3 and the 4 so it is half past 3.

## total

The number of items altogether. The result once everything has been added.

## two-dimensional (2D) shapes

Flat shapes are two-dimensional.
They have length and width.

**circle**
1 curved side

**triangle**
3 sides
3 corners

**square**
4 equal sides
4 corners

**rectangle**
2 equal long sides and 2 equal short sides, like a stretched square

**oval**
1 curved side, like a squashed circle

**pentagon**
5 sides
5 corners

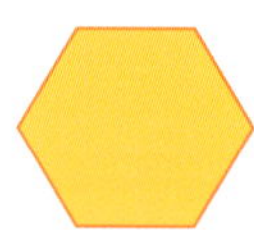

**hexagon**
6 sides
6 corners

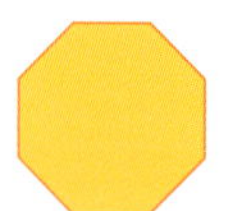

**octagon**
8 sides
8 corners

**quadrilaterals**
4 sides and 4 corners. Squares and rectangles are quadrilaterals.

## vertex (plural is vertices)

A corner of a shape or object.

## volume

Volume is the amount of space an object takes up.

# The mouse and the platypus

1. How many eyes are in this picture?
2. What else can you count in this picture?
3. What are the mouse and the platypus doing?
4. The mouse is going to make a hat for its costume. Why should the mouse's hat have no ears?
5. Would it take longer for the mouse to make its hat or its tail?
6. How many noses can you see in this picture?
7. A snout is the nose and mouth of an animal. Would it take longer for the platypus to make the ears or the snout?
8. How are the mouse and the platypus different?
9. Make up your own question about this picture.
10. Which of these questions do you like best? Why do you like it?

 • *AUSTRALIAN SIGNPOST MATHS 1* • ISBN 9780655708759

# 1A Number revision

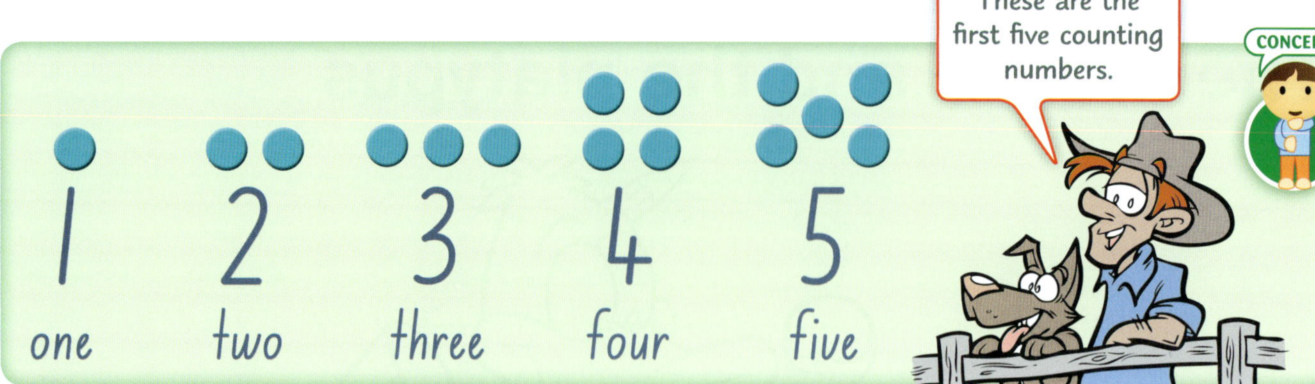


1 Write the numeral and its name. Draw the number of balls.

| | | | | |
|---|---|---|---|---|
| 1 | | | one |  |
| 2 | | | | |
| 3 | | | | |
| 4 | | | | |
| 5 | | | | |

Match each word to a numeral on the number track.

one zero three two five four

This is a number track.

| | | | | | |
|---|---|---|---|---|---|
| | | | | | |
| 0 | 1 | 2 | 3 | 4 | 5 |

 • *AUSTRALIAN SIGNPOST MATHS 1* • ISBN 9780655708759

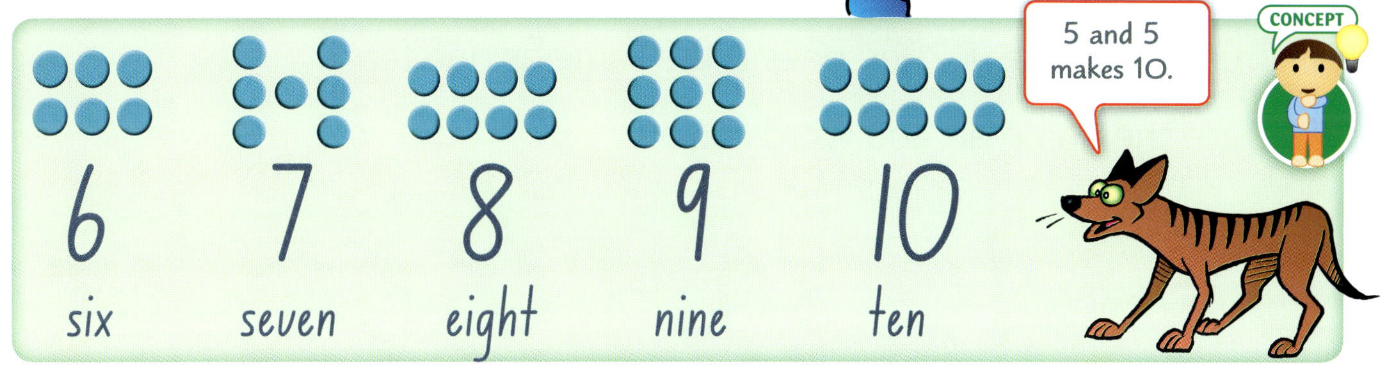


1 Write the numeral and its name. Draw the number of hats.

| 6 | | | six | |
|---|---|---|---|---|
| 7 | | | | |
| 8 | | | | |
| 9 | | | | |
| 10 | | | | |

Match each word to a numeral on the number track.

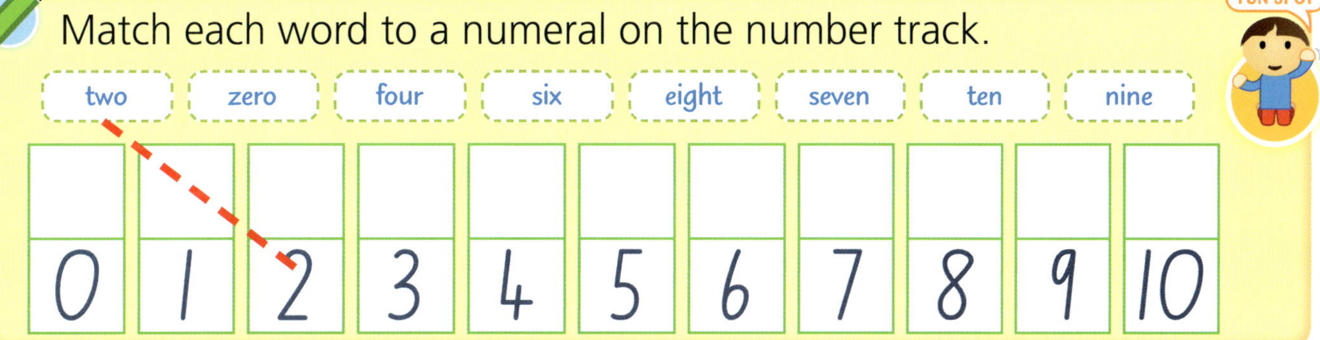


 • *AUSTRALIAN SIGNPOST MATHS 1* • ISBN 9780655708759

# 1C Numbers to 20

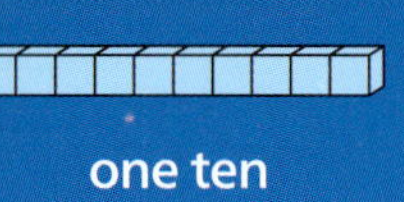

1 True (T) or False (F)? Ten ones is the same as one ten. [ ]

2 Trace the numerals and words below.

3 Count and write the number of objects.

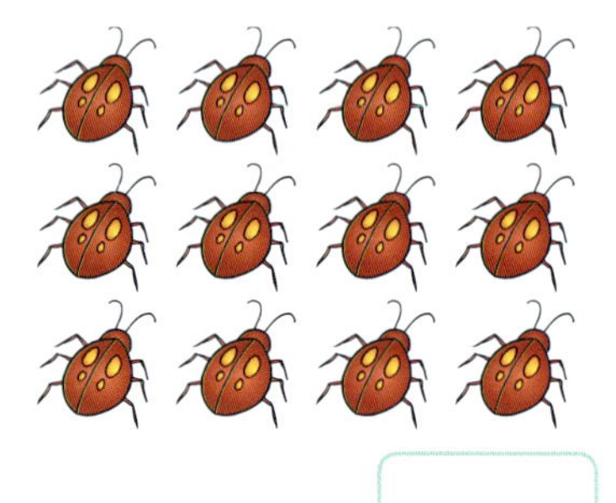

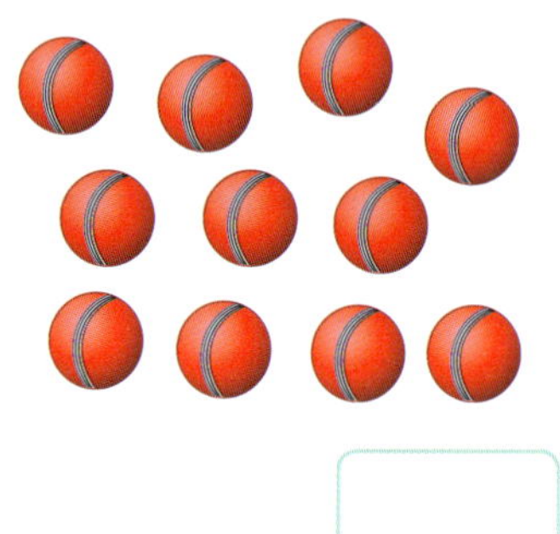

4 Count forwards and backwards. Colour every second number. Discuss.

| 1 | 2 | 3 | 4 | 5 | 6 | 7 | 8 | 9 | 10 |
|---|---|---|---|---|---|---|---|---|---|
| 11 | 12 | 13 | 14 | 15 | 16 | 17 | 18 | 19 | 20 |

5 Trace and write the numerals.

| 9 | 10 | |
|---|---|---|
| 6 | 7 | |
| 7 | | 9 |
| 10 | | 12 |

6 How many blocks?

1 ten and 0 ones

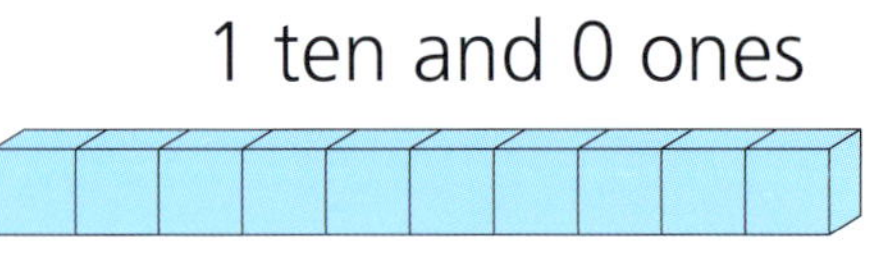

1 ten and 1 one

1 ten and 2 ones

 • *AUSTRALIAN SIGNPOST MATHS 1* • ISBN 9780655708759

# Shapes and patterns

two shape (CT, CT)
three shapes (SCT, SCT)

1 Colour the shapes in the picture:

SCT means "square, circle, triangle".

red

yellow

green

blue

How many circles?

How many squares?

How many triangles?

How many rectangles?

two-shape pattern:
Code: SC, SC, SC ...

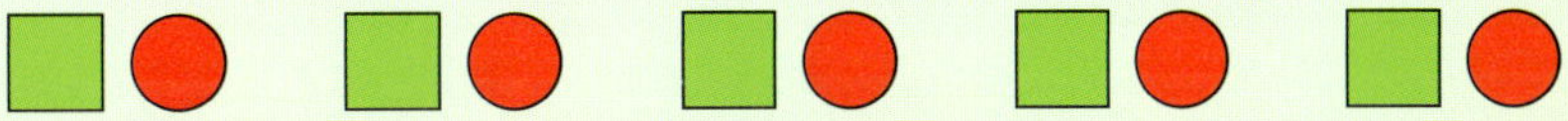

three-shape pattern:
Code: RST, RST ...

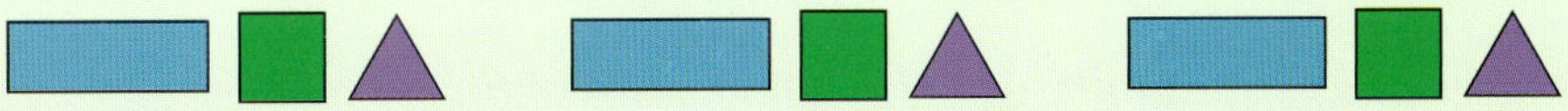

2 Draw a two-shape pattern and a three-shape pattern of your own.

 • *AUSTRALIAN SIGNPOST MATHS 1* • ISBN 9780655708759

# 2A Adding two groups

1 a 4 and ☐ makes ☐.

b ☐ and ☐ makes ☐.

c ☐ and ☐ makes ☐.

d ☐ and ☐ makes ☐.

e ☐ and ☐ makes ☐.

2 Draw your own picture to complete the problem.

5 2

5 balls and 2 balls makes ☐ balls.

3 Write your own number sentence to solve the problem.

How many blocks?

# 2B Addition sentences

1 Complete the number sentences.

a  

b  

c  

d  

Make your own number sentence and number bond.

# 2C Combinations up to 10

1 Numbers can make patterns. Use the faces to find answers. Talk about patterns you can see.

Add each row.

1 and 8 makes ____.

2 and 7 makes ____.

3 and 6 makes ____.

4 and 5 makes ____.

5 and 4 makes ____.

6 and 3 makes ____.

7 and 2 makes ____.

8 and 1 makes ____.

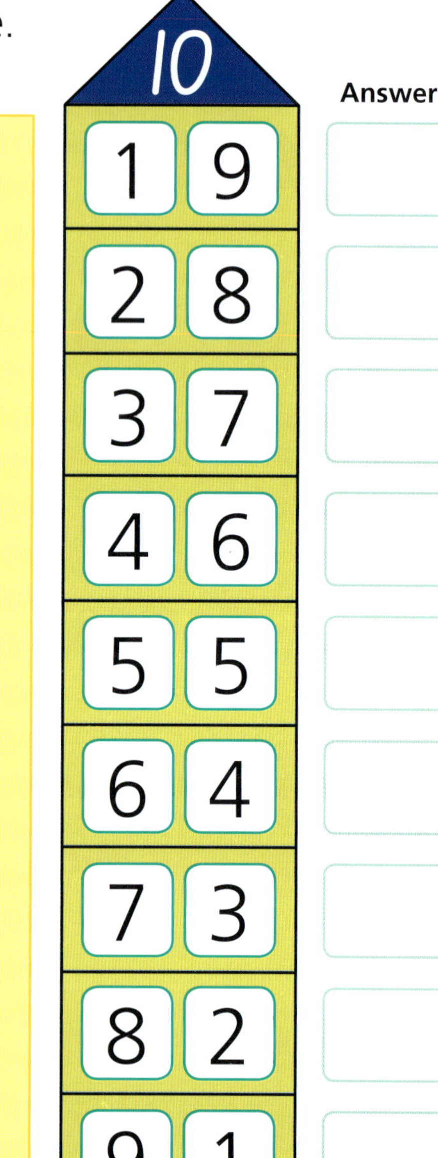


Answer

Use counters to make patterns of your own for 6 and 5.

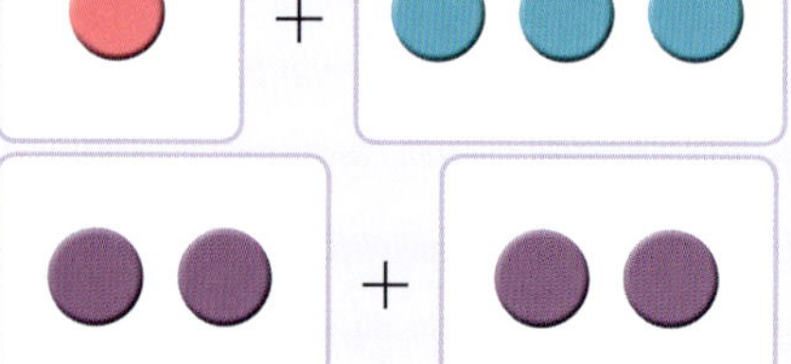

4 = 1 + 3 →

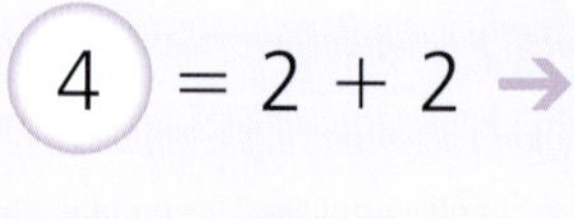

4 = 2 + 2 →

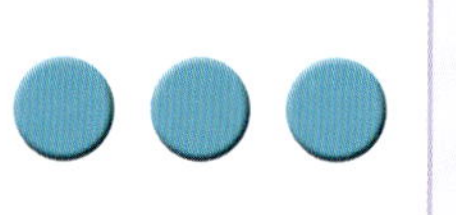

4 = 3 + 1 →

 • *AUSTRALIAN SIGNPOST MATHS 1* • ISBN 9780655708759

# 2D Data displays

1 a How many balls did we win?

b How many bears did we win?

c Which prize did we win most often?

d How many prizes did we win?

Shoes in rooms

Room 1

Room 2

Room 3

2 a Which room had the most shoes?

b Which room had the least shoes?

c How many shoes were in Room 3?

d How many shoes altogether?

Greg's weather chart

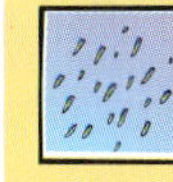

3 a For how many days did Greg draw pictures?

b How many days were sunny?

c How many days were not sunny?

d Write a question of your own.

 • *AUSTRALIAN SIGNPOST MATHS 1* • ISBN 9780655708759

CONCEPT

We can make larger numbers by counting on from 10.

...11, 12, 13, 14

1. Count the objects and complete.

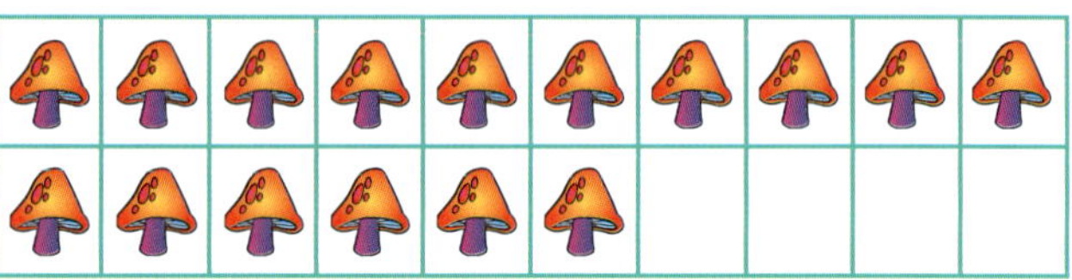

10 and 3 is ☐.

10 and 6 is ☐.

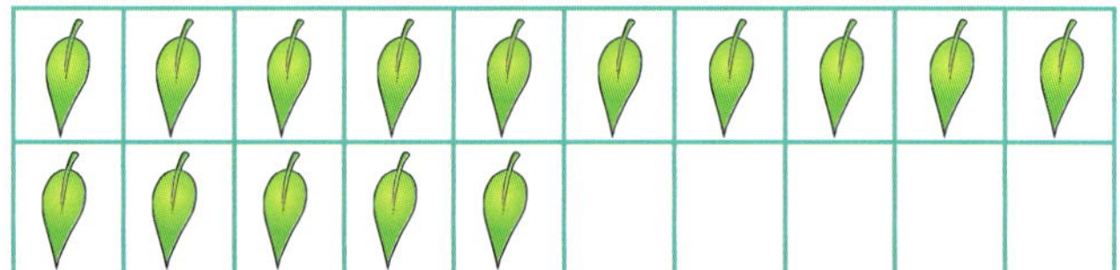

10 and 9 is ☐.

10 and 5 is ☐.

2. 10 and 1 is ☐.

10 and 2 is ☐.

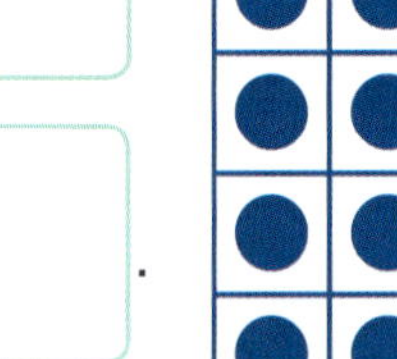

10 and 4 is ☐.

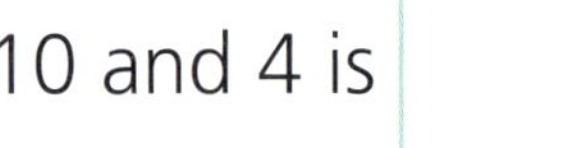

10 and 7 is ☐.

10 and 8 is ☐.

INVESTIGATION

Circle groups of 10.

☐ tens is ☐.



 • *AUSTRALIAN SIGNPOST MATHS 1* • ISBN 9780655708759

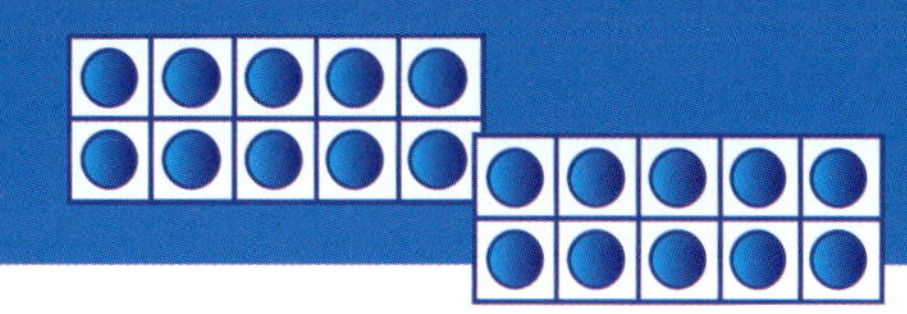

1 Write the missing numbers. Count forwards and backwards to 20.

| 1 | 2 | 3 | | | | 7 | | | |
|---|---|---|---|---|---|---|---|---|---|
| | 12 | | | 15 | | | 18 | | 20 |

2 Use place-value blocks to find:

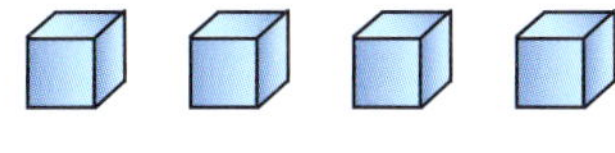

10 and 8 is ☐.
10 and 4 is ☐.
10 and 5 is ☐.
10 and 1 is ☐.
10 and 3 is ☐.
10 and 7 is ☐.
10 and 6 is ☐.
10 and 2 is ☐.

3 Write the numbers before (one less than) and after (one more than).

| | | | | | | | |
|---|---|---|---|---|---|---|---|
| a | | 10 | | b | | 13 | |
| c | | 14 | | d | | 17 | |
| e | | 18 | | f | | 19 | |

Two spiders. How many legs altogether? ☐

 • *AUSTRALIAN SIGNPOST MATHS 1* • ISBN 9780655708759

# 3C Analog time

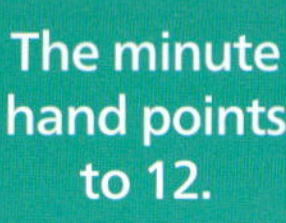

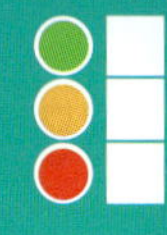

1 Read each time. Complete the labels.

a ☐ o'clock

b ☐ o'clock

c ☐

d ☐

2 Show the time.

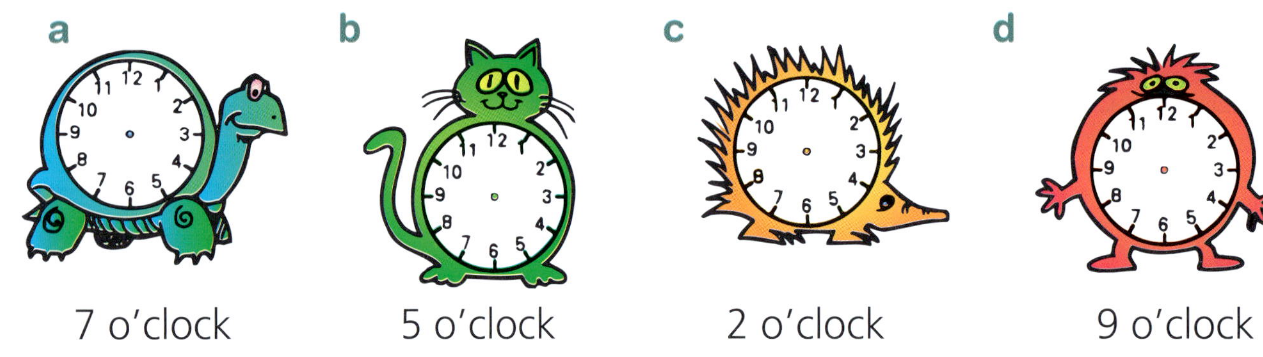

a 7 o'clock

b 5 o'clock

c 2 o'clock

d 9 o'clock

3 Match each picture with the best time.

| morning | | | | | | noon | | afternoon | | | | | night | | | |
|---|---|---|---|---|---|---|---|---|---|---|---|---|---|---|---|---|
| 6 | 7 o'clock | 8 | 9 o'clock | 10 | 11 o'clock | 12 | 1 o'clock | 2 | 3 o'clock | 4 | 5 o'clock | 6 | 7 o'clock | 8 | 9 o'clock | 10 |

 • *AUSTRALIAN SIGNPOST MATHS 1* • ISBN 9780655708759

# 3D Reading the time

Digital o'clock times end in : 00.

1 Write the time shown.

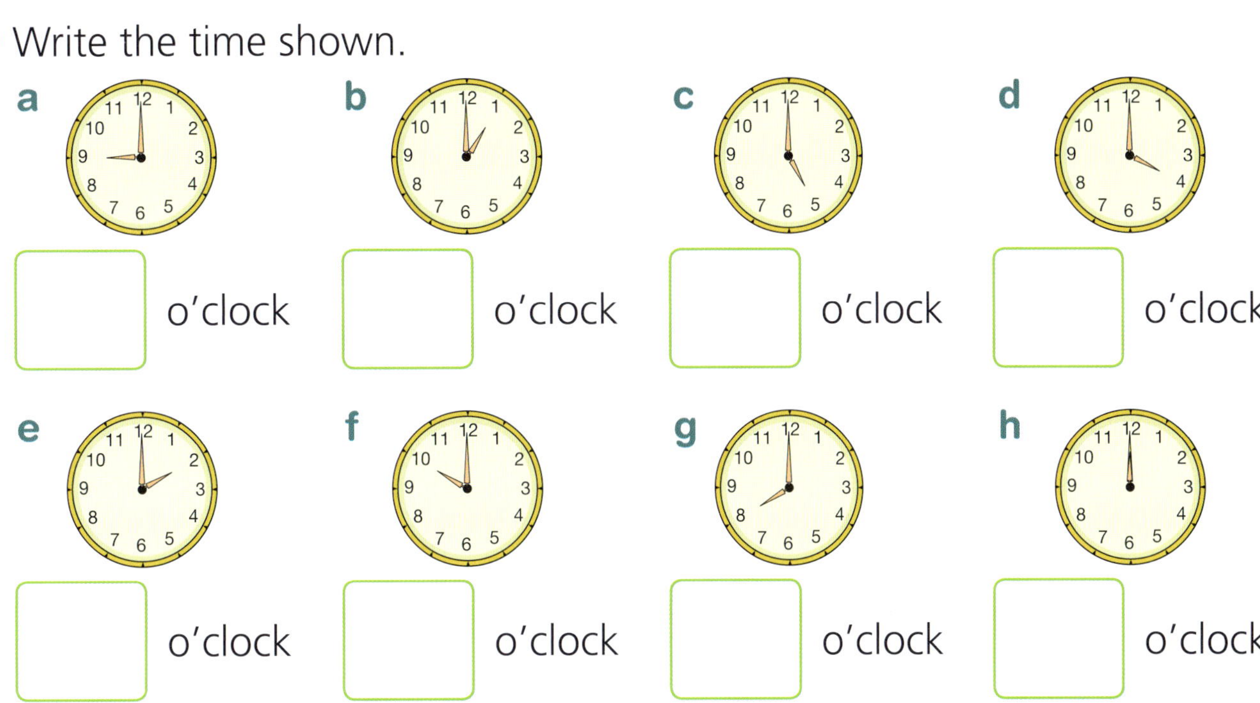


2 Show the analog time.

  ISBN 9780655708759

# 4A Numbers to 20

1 Write the numerals 11 to 19 in order. Match each numeral to its name.

thirteen fourteen seventeen eighteen

| | | | | | | | | | 20 |
|---|---|---|---|---|---|---|---|---|---|

twelve fifteen eleven sixteen nineteen

2 a Trace and order these numbers from smallest to largest.

16 11 19 13

b one more than 16 one less than 20 one less than 18

3 10 and 3 is ___.

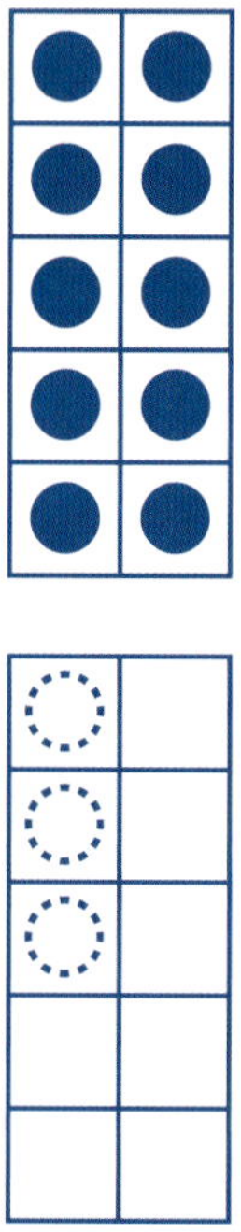

10 and 6 is ___.

10 and 8 is ___.

10 and 9 is ___.

4 Guess how many marbles are in each bag. Circle the largest group.

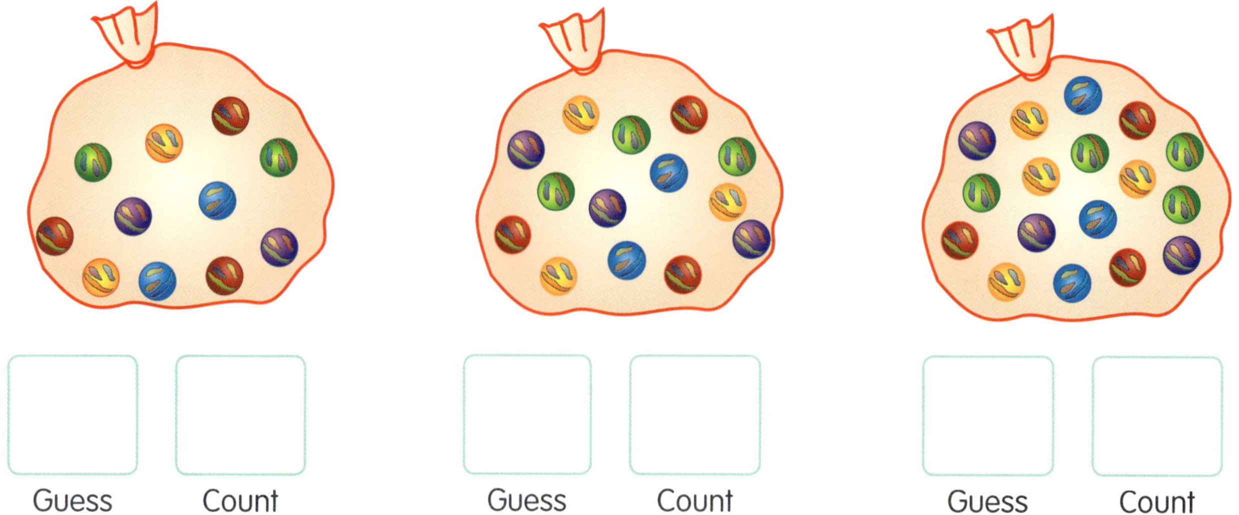

Guess Count Guess Count Guess Count



 • *AUSTRALIAN SIGNPOST MATHS 1* • ISBN 9780655708759

# Friends of 10

1 Add dots so that each has a total of 10.

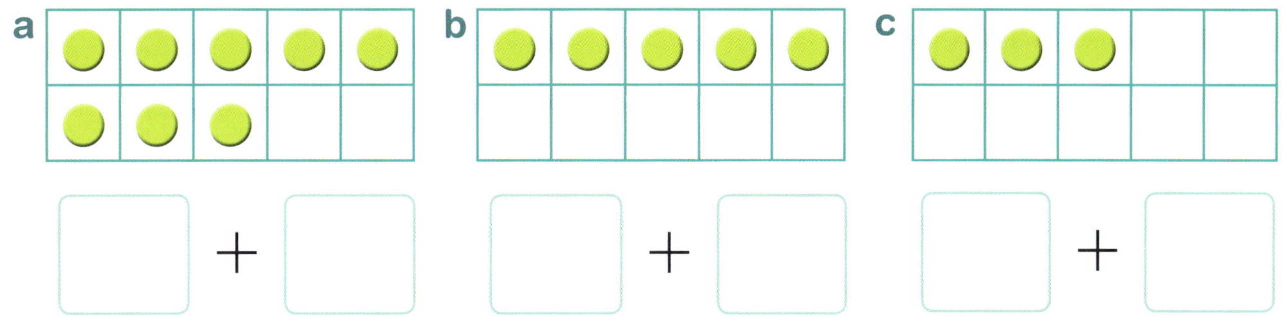


2 Use 10 counters. Find 9 ways we can add the counters to make 10.

3 Write True (T) or False (F).

a $3 + 7 = 9 + 1$ ☐

b $2 + 8 = 8 + 2$ ☐

ACTIVITY

- Match two sets of number cards 0 to 10 to make pairs of numbers that add up to 10. How many matches did you make? ☐

# 4C Position language

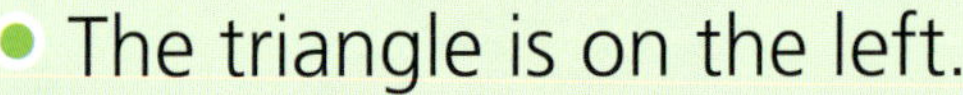

- The triangle is on the left.
- The square is on the right.
- The circle is between the triangle and the square.

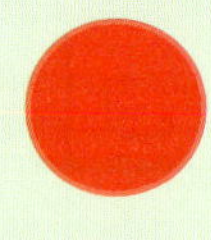

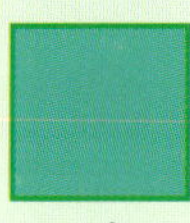

1 Use the picture to answer these questions. Choose the correct position word.

| Position words | |
|---|---|
| next to | towards |
| above | between |
| left | right |
| in front of | |

a The bucket is ______ the sandcastle.

b The cloud is ______ the water.

c The girl is on the ______ of the picture.

d The flag is on the ______ of the picture.

e The girl is walking ______ the flag.

f The sandcastle is ______ the bucket and the flag.

2 Circle the correct answer (from the boy's point of view):

a The ball is on the boy's left / right.

b The bird is on the boy's left / right.

ISBN 9780655708759

# 4D Position language

How could the mouse get into the pram?

1 Look at the picture and circle the correct words in each sentence.

a The caterpillar is crawling along / beneath the stick.

b The mouse is above / below the hawk.

c The house is between / inside the hills.

d The hills are far from / close to the tree.

e The car is in front of / behind the house.

f The ant is under / over the tree.

g The kookaburra is perched on / over the branch.

h The girl is to the right / left of the pram.

i The bat is hanging upside down / right side up.

2 Where would the girl go to take the apples into the house?

→ Talk about this.

3 In this picture, draw:

a a fork on the left of the plate

b a knife on the right of the plate

c a star in the centre of the window

d a book on a corner of the table

e a bottle on the edge of the table

f a picture above the clock

How would you set this table for dinner?

# Addition facts

1 Complete. You can use two dice to practise addition.

a

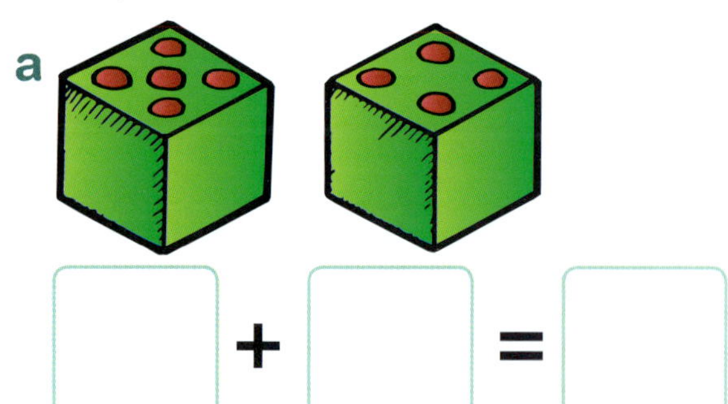

☐ + ☐ = ☐

b

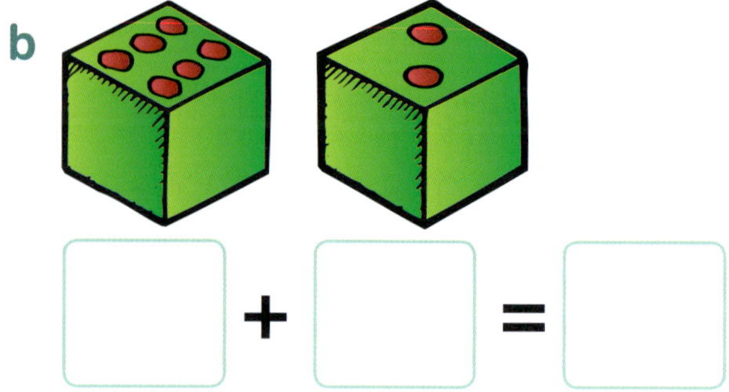

☐ + ☐ = ☐

2

a 6 + 2 = ☐

b 8 + 0 = ☐

c 3 + 7 = ☐

d 0 + 10 = ☐

e 4 + 5 = ☐

f 1 + 6 = ☐

3 Match:

| | | |
|---|---|---|
| 4 + 3 | 5 | 3 + 2 |
| 2 + 3 | 6 | 3 + 4 |
| 5 + 1 | 7 | 1 + 5 |
| 8 + 2 | 8 | 7 + 2 |
| 2 + 7 | 9 | 3 + 5 |
| 5 + 3 | 10 | 2 + 8 |

4 4 dogs, 3 cats, 2 mice. How many animals?

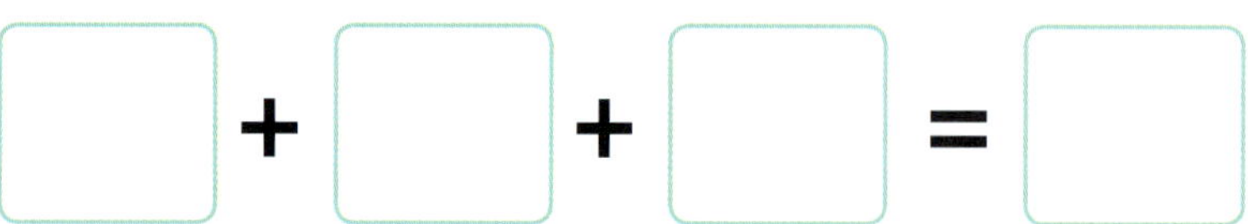

☐ + ☐ + ☐ = ☐

Learn addition facts to 10.



 • *AUSTRALIAN SIGNPOST MATHS 1* • ISBN 9780655708759

| 4 | 2 |
| --- | --- |
| 6 | |

4 + 2 = 6

We can find a different sum by moving the dotted lines.

1

7

☐ + 6 = 7

2 + ☐ = 7

3 + 4 = ☐

4 + ☐ = 7

☐ + 2 = 7

6 + ☐ = 7

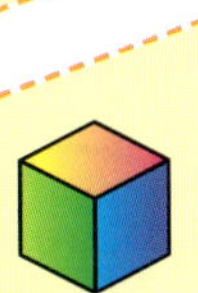

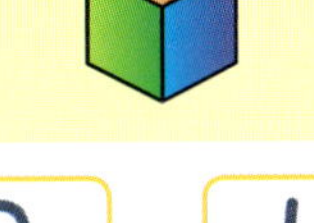

3 + 4

2 The numbers in each row add up to 6.

| 6 | | |
| --- | --- | --- |
| ☐ | 0 | 6 |
| 2 | ☐ | 6 |
| ☐ | 3 | 6 |
| 4 | ☐ | 6 |
| 6 | ☐ | 6 |

- Using counters, make up your own partitioning patterns for 10, 9, 8 and 5.

1 + 2 = 3 →  +  = 

2 + 1 = 3 → 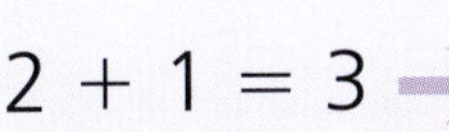 +  = 

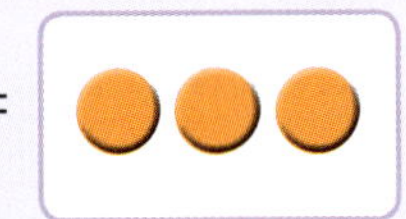

# Identifying objects

**1** Colour the picture, then count all the objects like these.

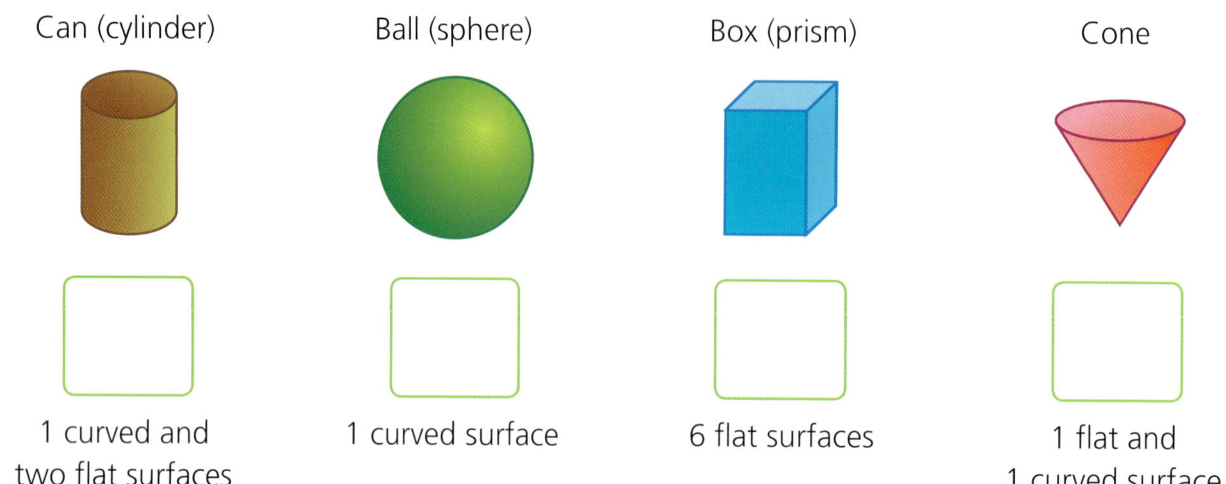

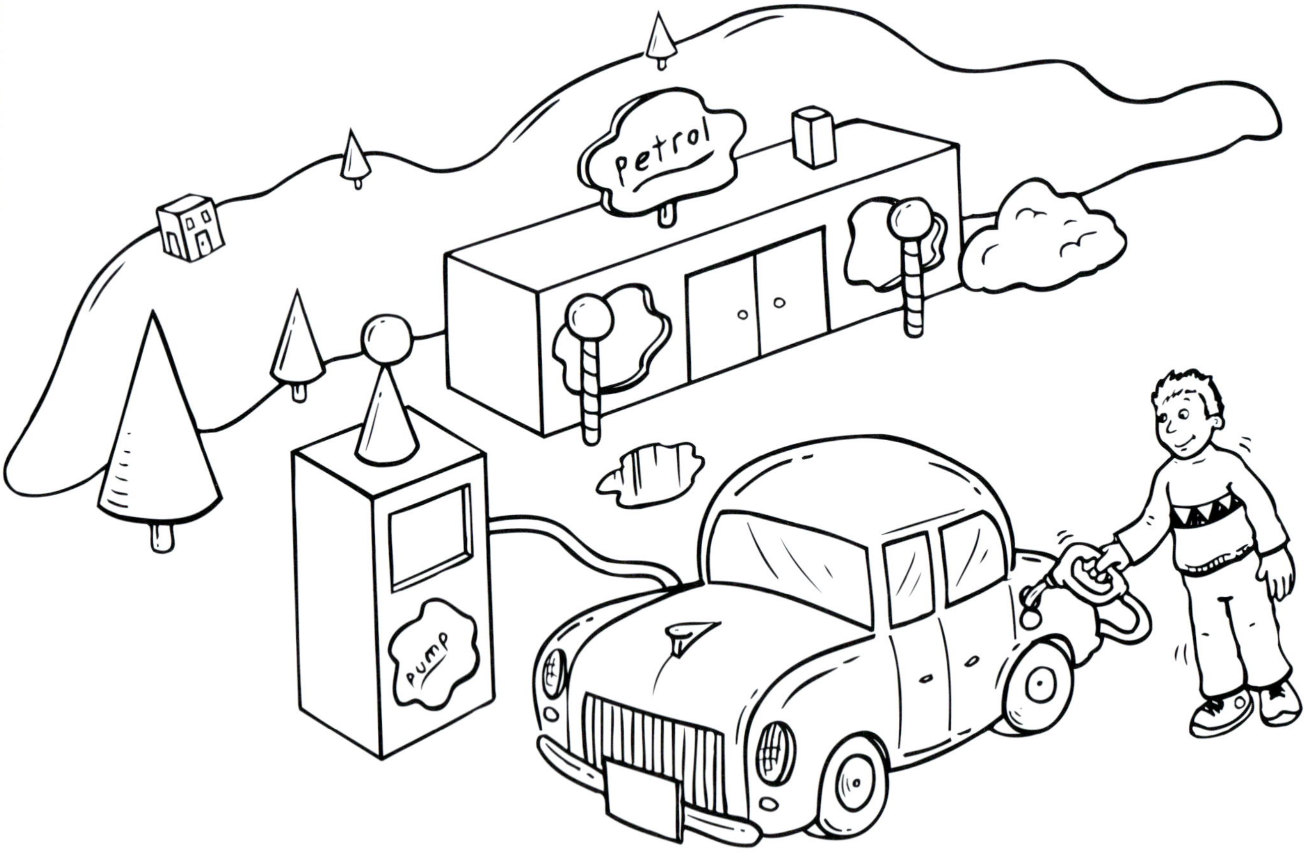

# Objects in our world

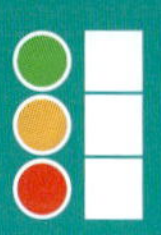

1 Match each photo with one of the objects in the middle.

2 Draw a simple two-dimensional shape (circle or square) that is in each object. Use plasticine or playdough to make these 3D models.

 • *AUSTRALIAN SIGNPOST MATHS 1* • ISBN 9780655708759

# 6A Groups of 10

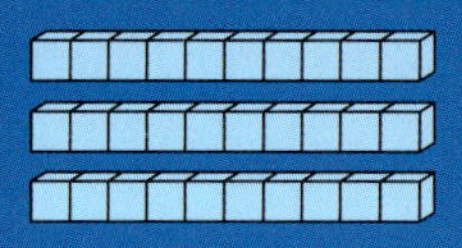

CONCEPT

| 10 | 20 | 30 | 40 | 50 | 60 | 70 | 80 | 90 | 100 |
|---|---|---|---|---|---|---|---|---|---|
| ten | twenty | thirty | forty | fifty | sixty | seventy | eighty | ninety | one hundred |

Practise counting by tens.

This is 8 groups of ten.
There are 80 pencils.

**1** Count the groups of ten.

a 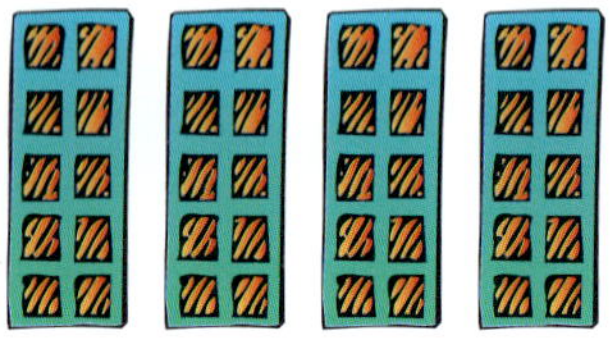 ☐ tens

b 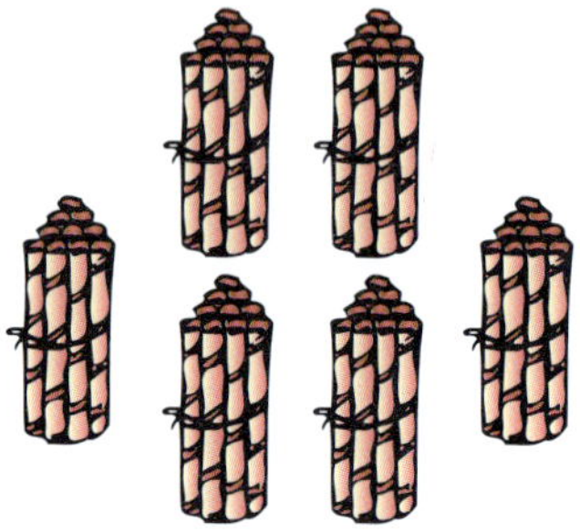 ☐ tens

c  ☐ tens

d  ☐ tens

e 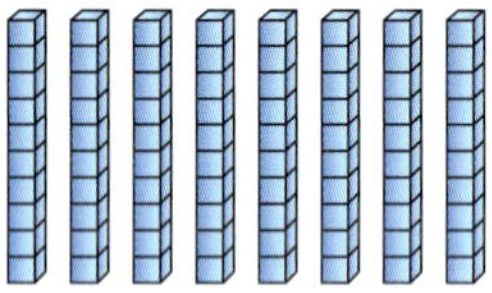 ☐ tens

f 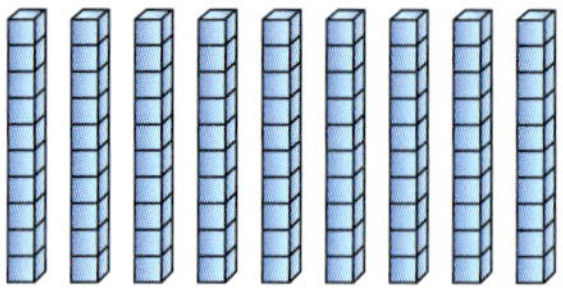 ☐ tens

**2** Circle groups of ten.

☐ tens

Talk about your answer.

**3** Estimate then count.

a  Estimate ☐ tens
Count ☐ tens

b  Estimate ☐ tens
Count ☐ tens

# 6B Counting by tens

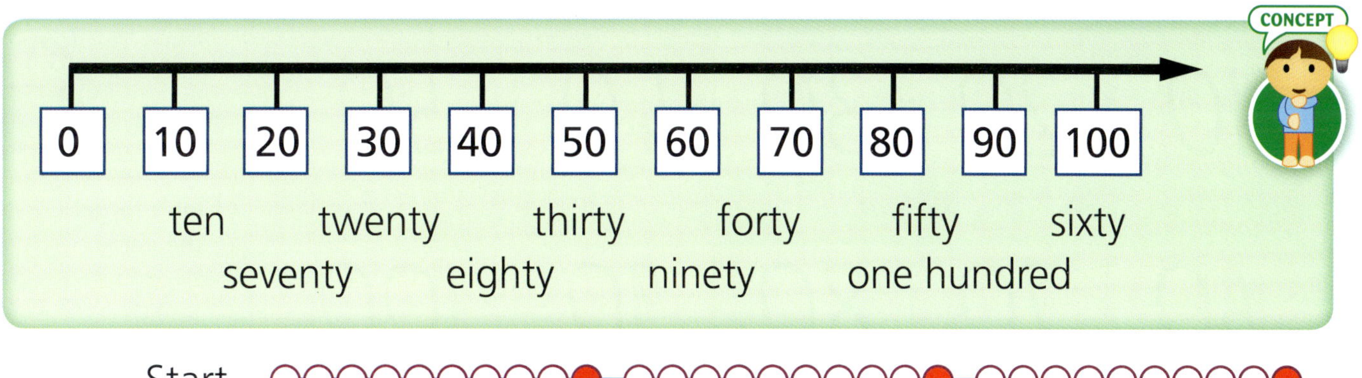


Start

1 Use the beads to count by tens to 100 and then count from 100 to 10.

2 Write the numbers shown.

a 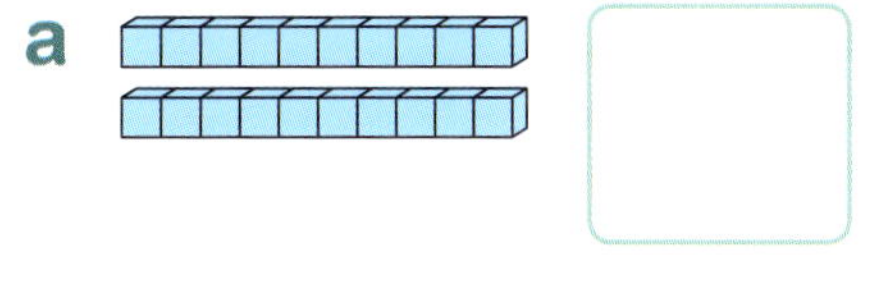

b 

c 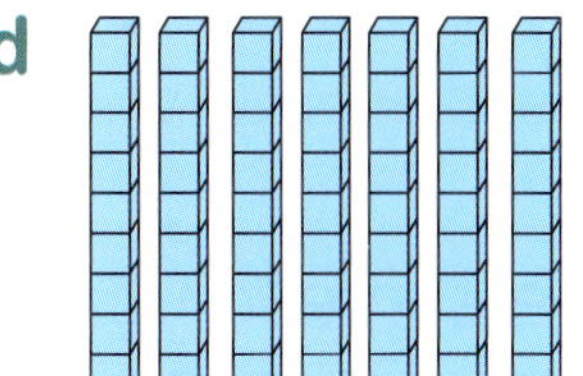

d 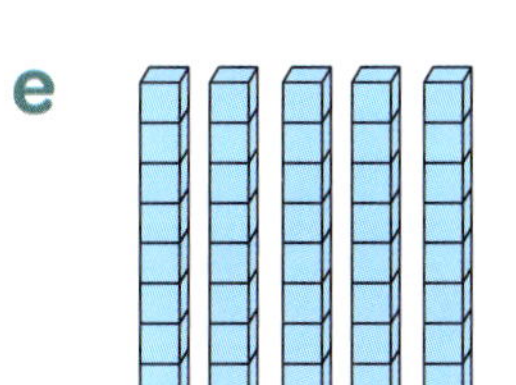

e 

f 

Ninety is 9 tens.

Forty is 4 tens.

Seventy is 7 tens.

3 Write the tens number that comes before and after.

a  20

b  30

c  40

d  50

 • *AUSTRALIAN SIGNPOST MATHS 1* • ISBN 9780655708759

# 6C Counting by tens

CONCEPT

| 10 | 20 | 30 | 40 | 50 |
|---|---|---|---|---|
| ten | twenty | thirty | forty | fifty |
| 60 | 70 | 80 | 90 | 100 |
| sixty | seventy | eighty | ninety | one hundred |

1 a Count forwards by tens to 100.

b Count backwards by tens from 100.

2 Write these numbers as numerals.

a twenty ☐ b eighty ☐ c ninety ☐ d forty ☐

3 Write the next four numbers in each pattern.

a 10, 20, 30, ☐, ☐, ☐, ☐

b 90, 80, 70, ☐, ☐, ☐, ☐

FUN SPOT

- Begin at 10 and join the dots to count forwards by tens.

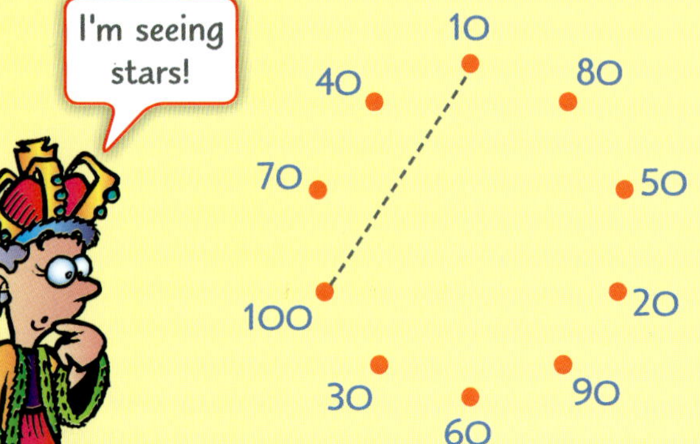


- How much money?

☐ cents

# 6D Units of length

We need a lot more little units.

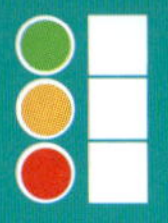

CONCEPT

No gaps. No overlaps.

ACTIVITY

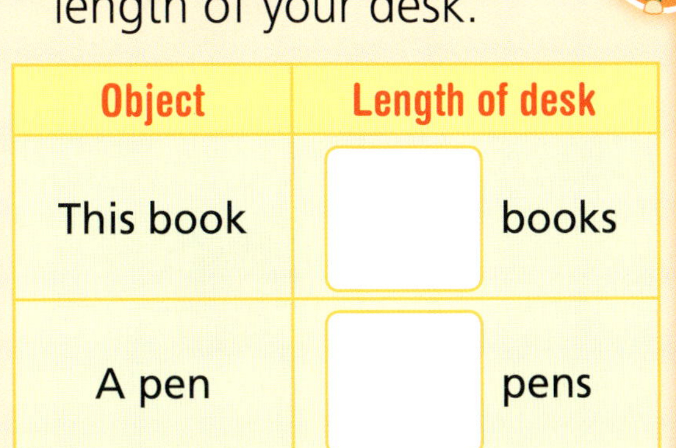

❶ Use objects of the same size to measure the length of your desk.

| Object | Length of desk | |
|---|---|---|
| This book | | books |
| A pen | | pens |
| A tens block | | blocks |

❷ Use a shoe to measure the length of each object.

| | | |
|---|---|---|
| Desk | | shoes |
| Window | | shoes |
| Your arm | | shoes |

- Which is longest?

- Which is shortest?

INVESTIGATION

Count steps to measure distance.

- From your seat to the door: ______ steps
- Along a path: ______ steps
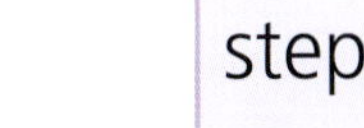

- ______ ______ steps
- Would we use more pencils (P) or steps (S) to measure a distance? ______

# Subtraction

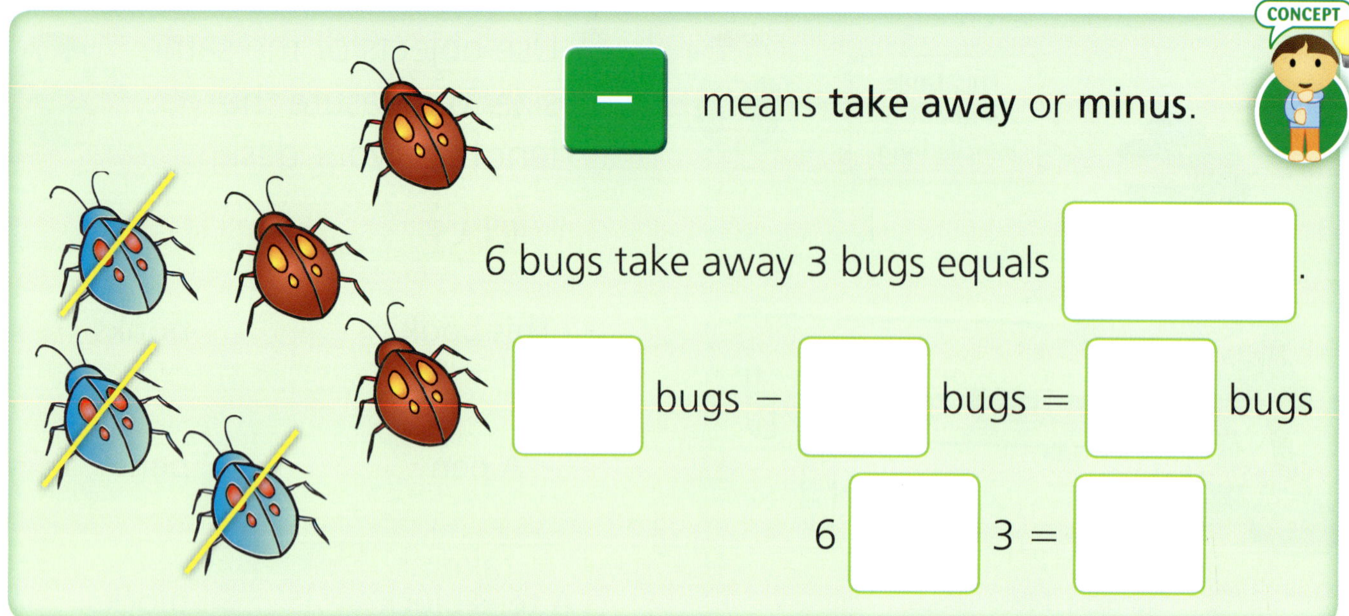


− means **take away** or **minus**.

6 bugs take away 3 bugs equals ☐.

☐ bugs − ☐ bugs = ☐ bugs

6 ☐ 3 = ☐

1

11 − 4 = ☐

2

10 − 5 = ☐

3

15 − 10 = ☐

4

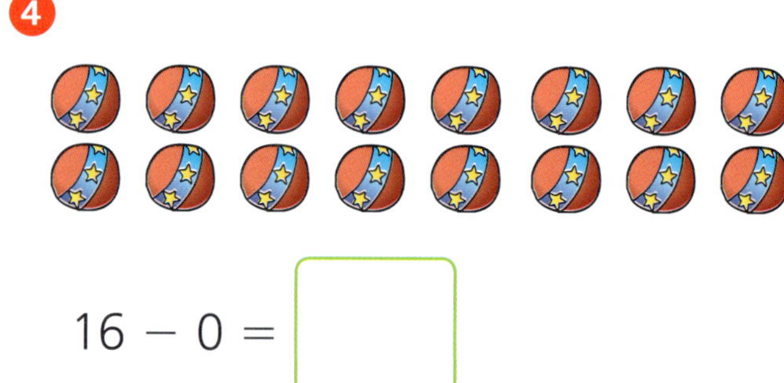

16 − 0 = ☐

5

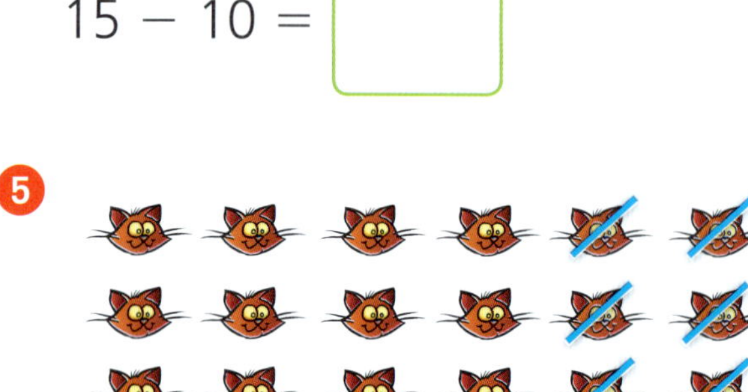

18 − 6 = ☐

6

20 − 10 = ☐



 • *AUSTRALIAN SIGNPOST MATHS 1* • ISBN 9780655708759

# 7B Subtraction

– means take away or minus.
= means equals.

CONCEPT

*Take away* is the same as *subtraction* or *minus*.

8 – 2

Cross out 2 dogs and complete the story.

8 take away 2 equals .

1  4 take away 1 equals .

2 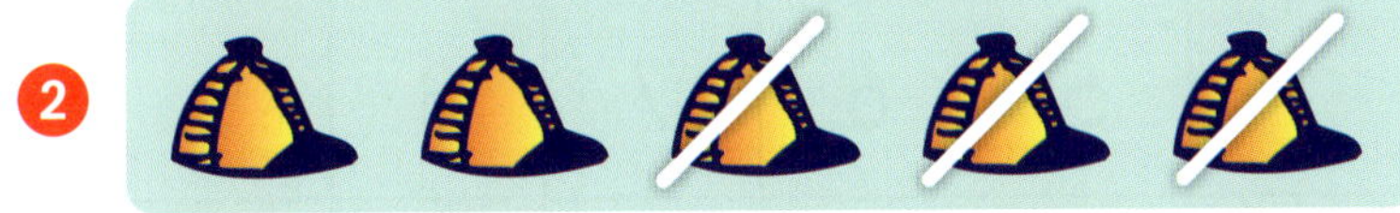 5 take away 3 equals .

3  6 take away 4 equals .

4 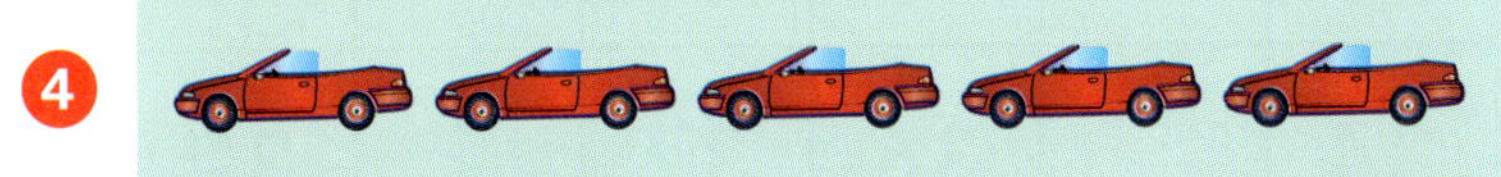 5 take away 5 equals .

5 8 – 6 = 

6  9 – 3 =

7  10 – 5 =

ACTIVITY

Cross out some balls and record your number sentence.

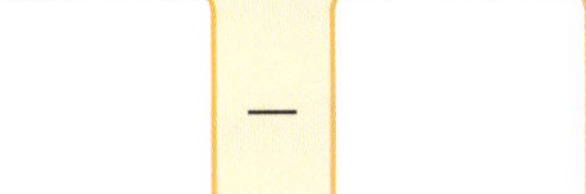

 –  =

 • *AUSTRALIAN SIGNPOST MATHS 1* • ISBN 9780655708759

# 7C Numbers to 100

1. Write the numbers that you will see when the flaps with arrows are lifted.

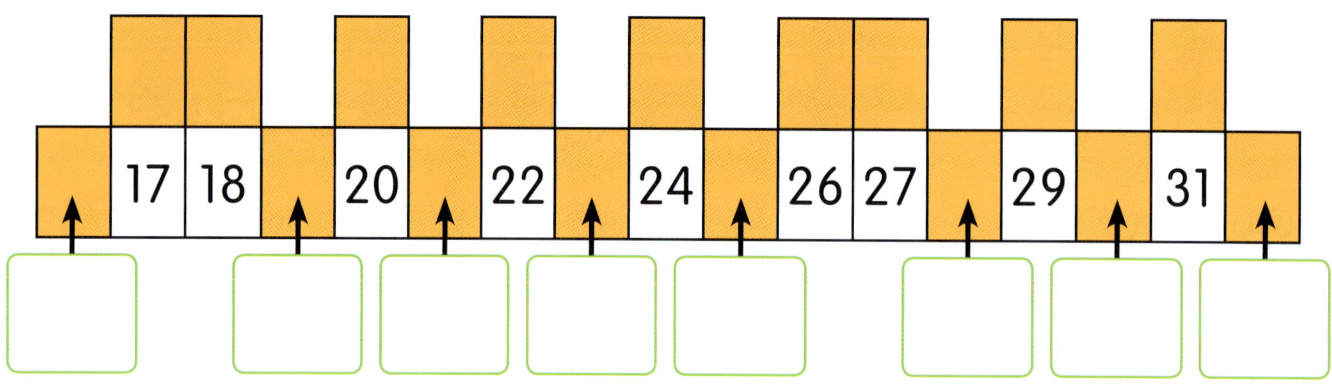


2. Practise counting to 100. Fill in the missing numbers. Discuss the pattern.

| | | | | | | | | | |
|---|---|---|---|---|---|---|---|---|---|
| 0 | 1 | 2 | 3 | | 5 | 6 | 7 | 8 | 9 |
| 10 | | 12 | 13 | 14 | | 16 | | 18 | 19 |
| | 21 | 22 | 23 | 24 | 25 | | 27 | 28 | |
| 30 | | 32 | 33 | 34 | | 36 | 37 | | 39 |
| 40 | 41 | | 43 | | 45 | 46 | | 48 | 49 |
| | 51 | 52 | 53 | 54 | 55 | | 57 | 58 | |
| 60 | | 62 | 63 | 64 | 65 | | 67 | 68 | |
| 70 | 71 | | 73 | | 75 | 76 | | 78 | 79 |
| | 81 | 82 | 83 | 84 | | 86 | 87 | | 89 |
| 90 | 91 | | | | 95 | 96 | 97 | | 99 |

# 7D Informal units of length

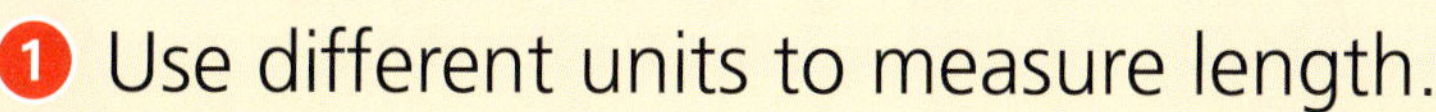

1 Use different units to measure length.

| Length | Tally | Measurement unit | |
|---|---|---|---|
| Length of pencil | \|\|\|\| | 4 | toothpicks |
| Height of desk | | | hand spans |
| Width of book | | | paperclips |
| Width of door | | | straws |
| Length of room | | | books |

What do we do with the bit left over?

- over 4
- less than 5
- 4 and a bit

2 Estimate (guess) and then measure these lengths using craft sticks.

a 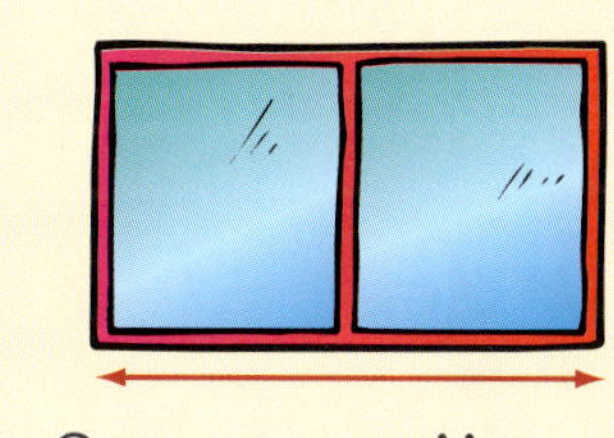

Guess | Measure

b 

Guess | Measure

c 

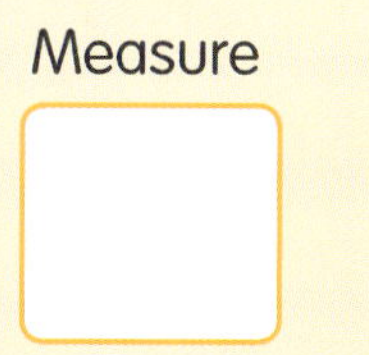

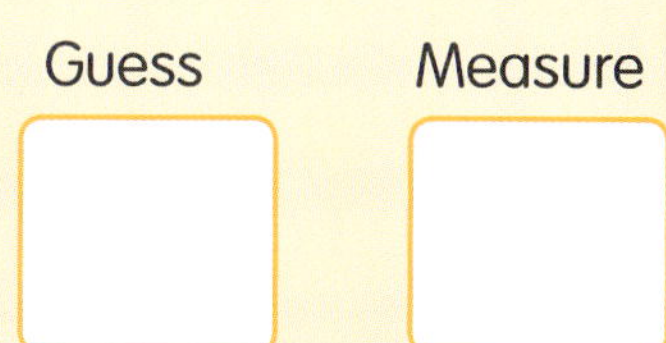

Guess | Measure

d 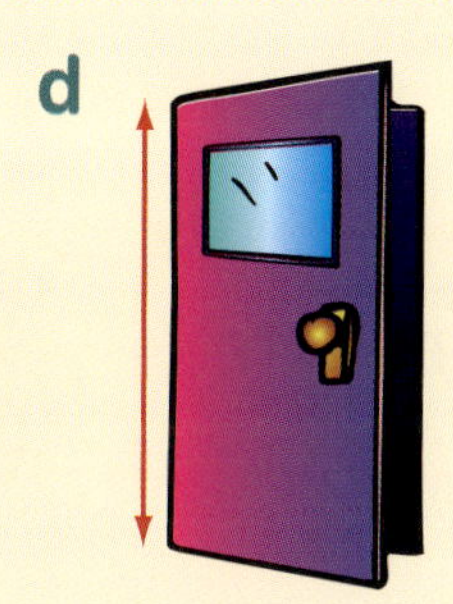

Guess

Measure

e 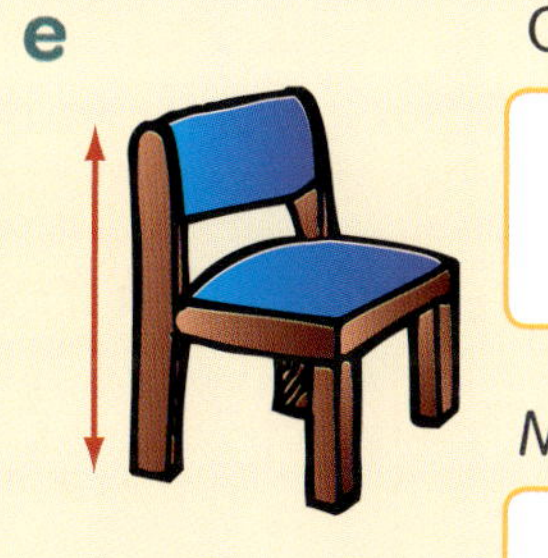

Guess

Measure

f 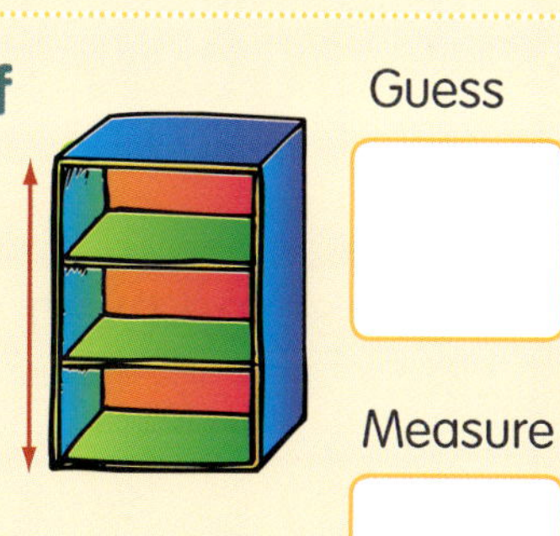

Guess

Measure

 • *AUSTRALIAN SIGNPOST MATHS 1* • ISBN 9780655708759

# 8A Odd and even numbers

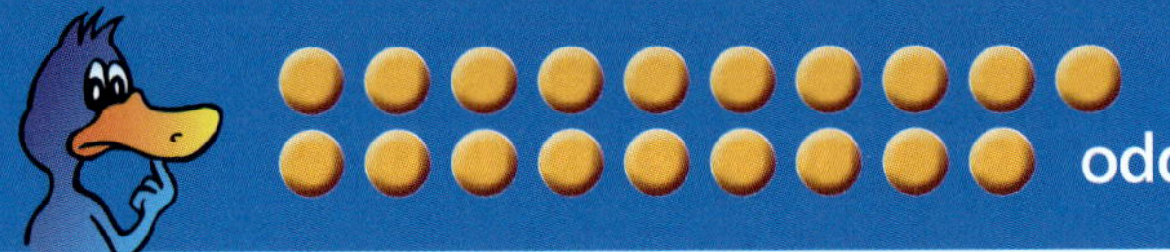


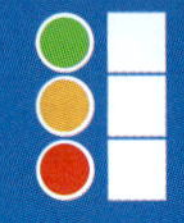

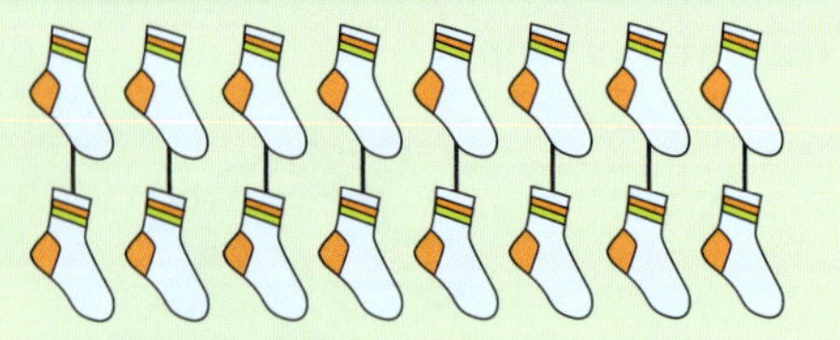

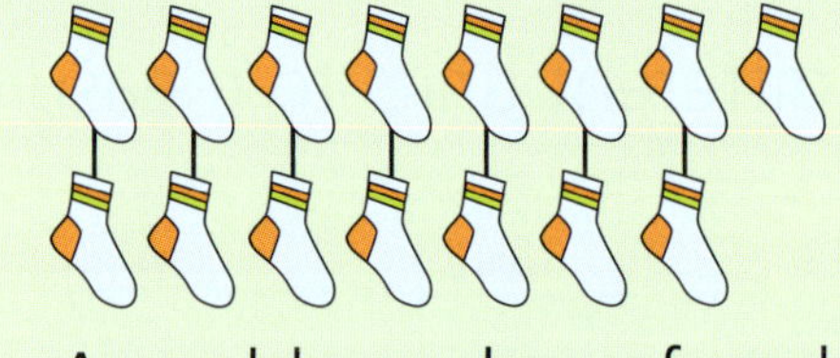

An even number of socks can be drawn in pairs.

Even numbers end in 0, 2, 4, 6 or 8.
16 is an even number.

24

37

An odd number of socks cannot be drawn in pairs. There is always one left over.

Odd numbers end in 1, 3, 5, 7 or 9.
15 is an odd number.

1 Under each group, write **odd** or **even** and then write the number.

a

b

c

d

e

f

| Write some even numbers here. | Write some odd numbers here. |
|---|---|
| | |



 • *AUSTRALIAN SIGNPOST MATHS 1* • ISBN 9780655708759

# 8B Addition to 20

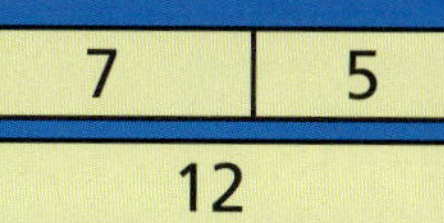

 means **add**, **and** or **plus**.

 means **makes** or **equals**.

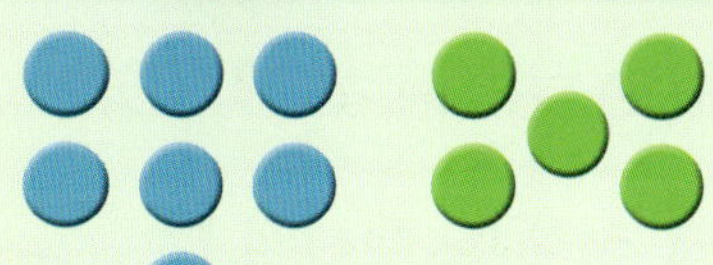

7 + 5 = ☐

1 Complete the number sentences.

Adding zero does not change the number.

a
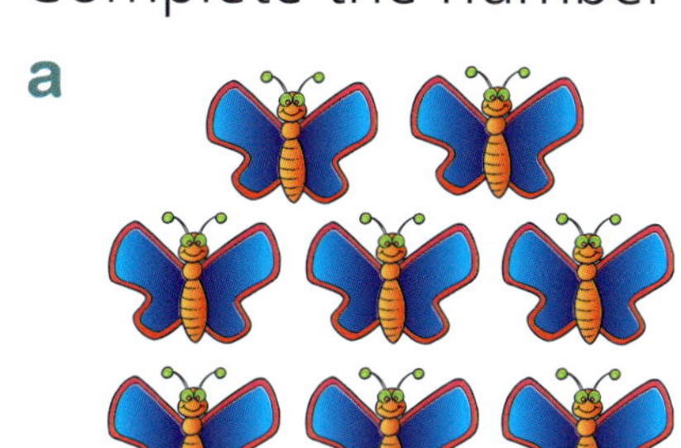 and 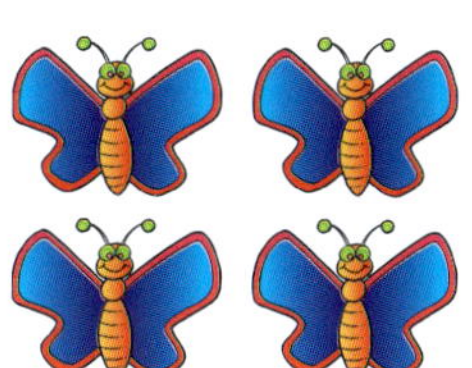

8 + 4 = ☐

b
 and 

9 + 7 = ☐

c
 and 

10 + 10 = ☐

Draw pictures to make up your own number stories. Write a number sentence to match.

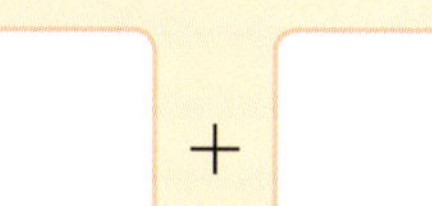

☐ + ☐ = ☐

Draw pictures above and below the dotted line.

# Half past

The minute hand is halfway around the clock face.

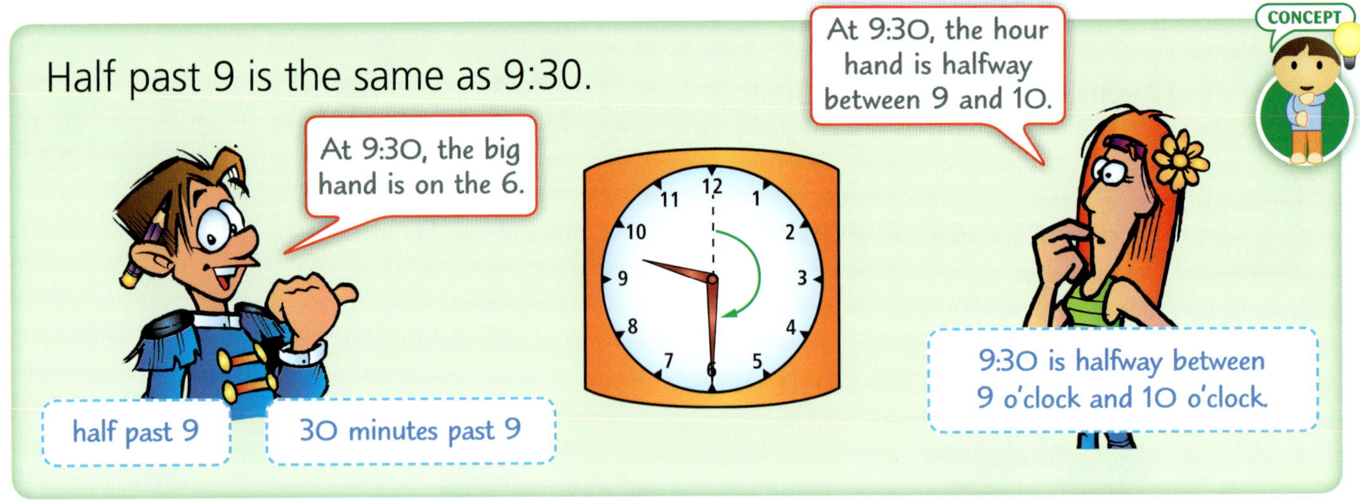


**1** Write the times shown.

**a**  half past ☐

**b**  half past ☐

**c**  half past ☐

**d**   half past ☐

**e**  half past ☐

**f**  half past ☐

**2** Show these times.

**a** half past 3

**b** 10 thirty

**c** 30 minutes past 1

 • *AUSTRALIAN SIGNPOST MATHS 1* • ISBN 9780655708759

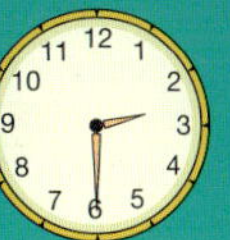

CONCEPT

What would you be doing at half past 7:
- in the morning?
- at night?

half past 7

seven thirty

30 minutes past 7

The hour hand is halfway between the 7 and the 8.

1 Read and write each time.

a

half past   thirty

minutes past

b

half past   thirty

minutes past

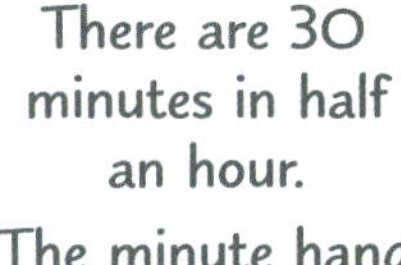

There are 30 minutes in half an hour.
The minute hand is halfway around the clock.

2 Draw the time on each clock.

a half past 2

b half past 4

c five thirty

d half past 9

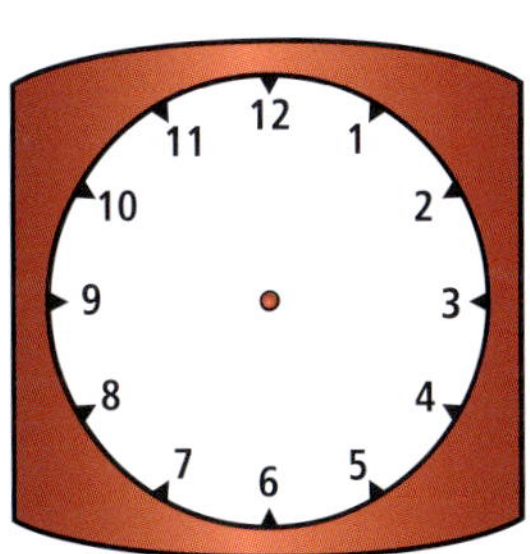

e half past 11

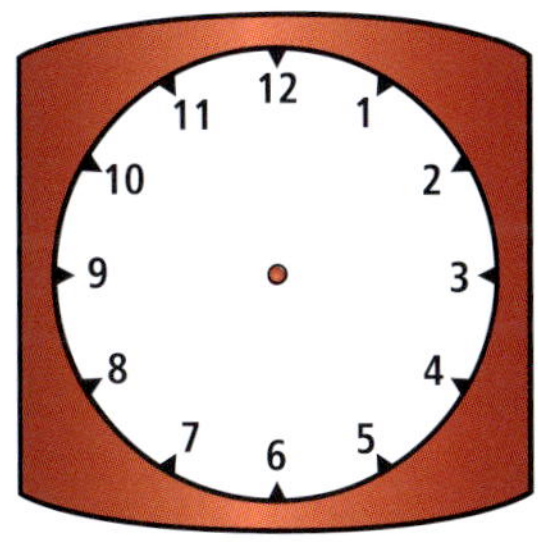

f thirty minutes past 10

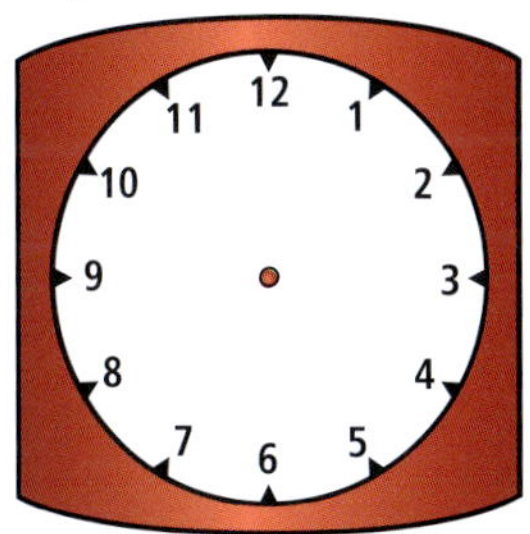

# 9A Counting on

1 Count on to find how many altogether.

a
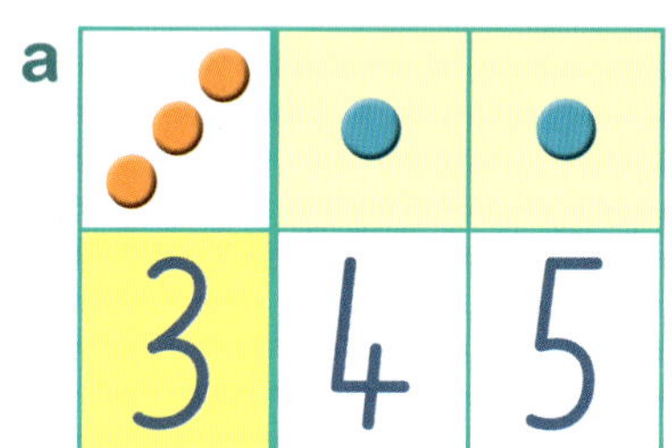


3 and 2 more = ☐

b
6 7 8

6 and 2 more = ☐

c
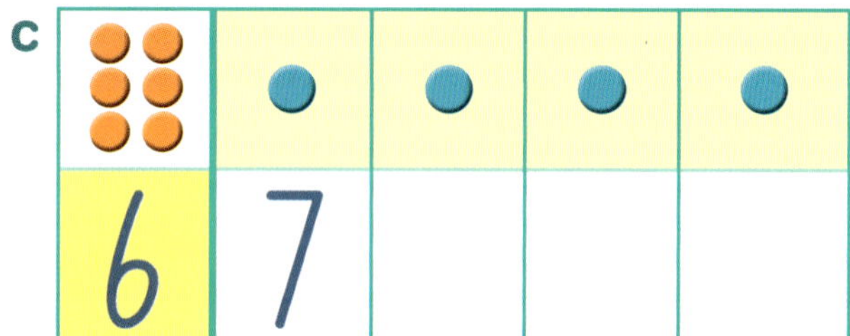


6 and 4 more = ☐

d
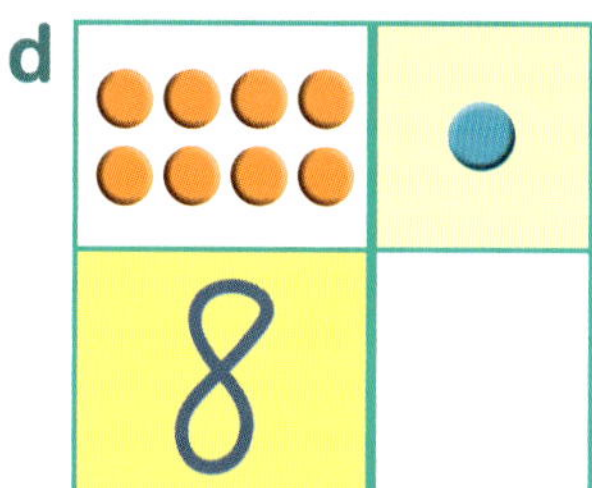


8 and 1 more = ☐

e
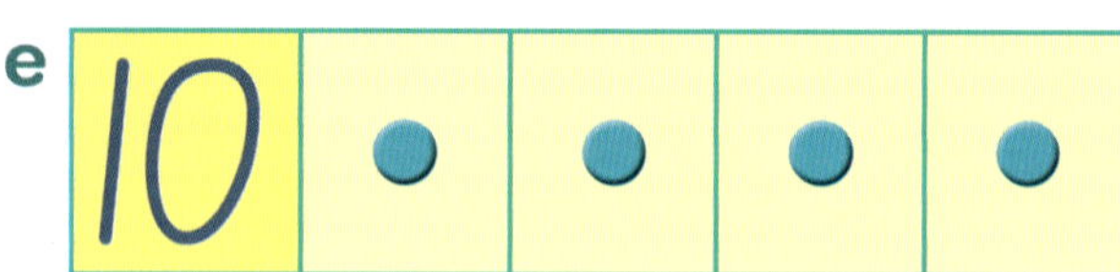


10 and 4 more = ☐

f
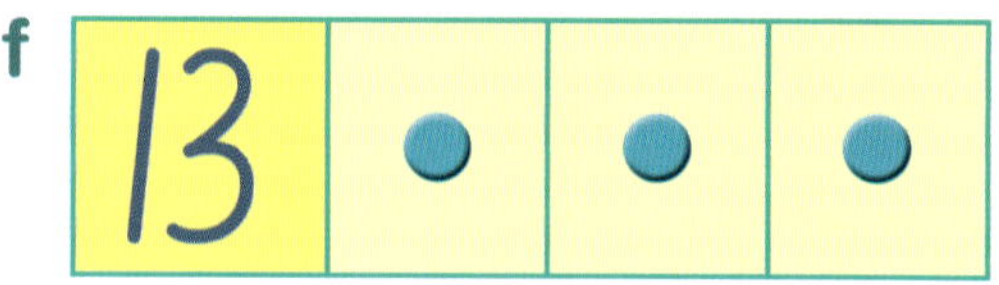


13 and 3 more = ☐

Use counters to count on from a chosen number.
Discuss and record your number sentences.



 • *AUSTRALIAN SIGNPOST MATHS 1* • ISBN 9780655708759

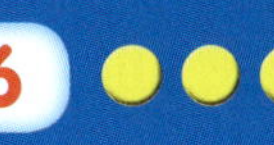
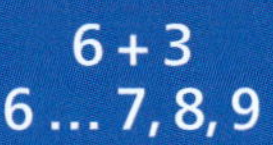

CONCEPT

**6 + 3 = 9**

You can start with 6 and then use your fingers to count on 3 more.

1 Use fingers to count on.

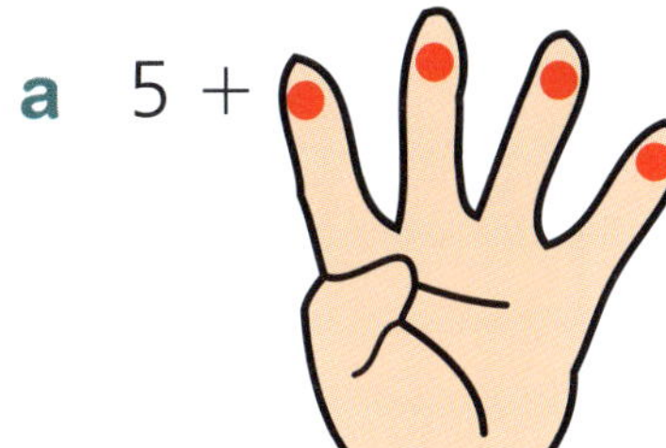
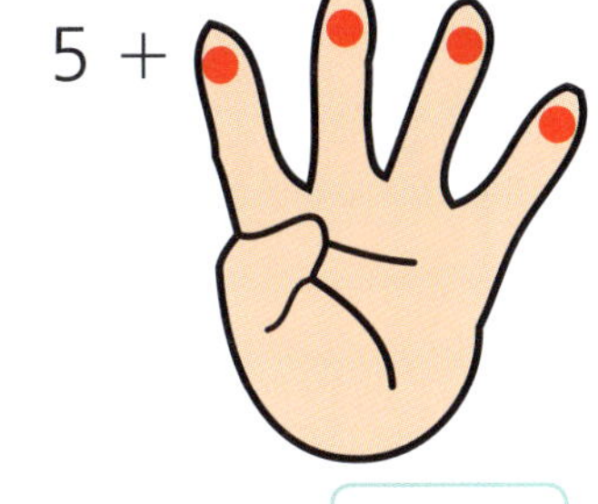

a 5 + 

5 + 4 = ☐

b 8 + 

8 + 3 = ☐

c 9 + 

9 + 3 = ☐

d 9 + 

9 + 2 = ☐

e 13 + 

13 + 5 = ☐

f 11 + 

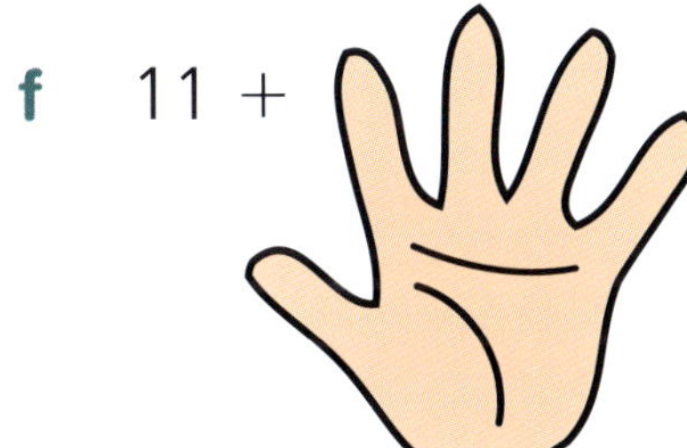

11 + 5 = ☐

ACTIVITY

Use your own fingers to count on.

a 7 + 4 = ☐

b 14 + 4 = ☐

c 9 + 3 = ☐

d 17 + 2 = ☐

e 16 + 4 = ☐

Make up more questions of your own.

 • *AUSTRALIAN SIGNPOST MATHS 1* • ISBN 9780655708759

# 9C Analog time

quarter past 2
2 fifteen
fifteen past 2

quarter to 3
2 forty- five
forty-five past 2

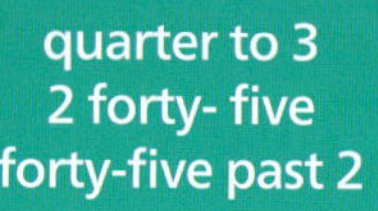

- At **a quarter past**, the minute hand points to 3.

a quarter past 7

- At **a quarter to**, the minute hand points to 9.

a quarter to 8

**1** Write the time shown on each face using **quarter to** or **quarter past**.

a 

b 

c 

d 

e 

f 

**2** On each face show the time given.

a 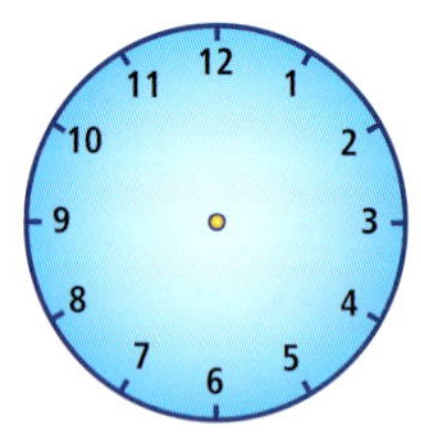
a quarter past 2

b 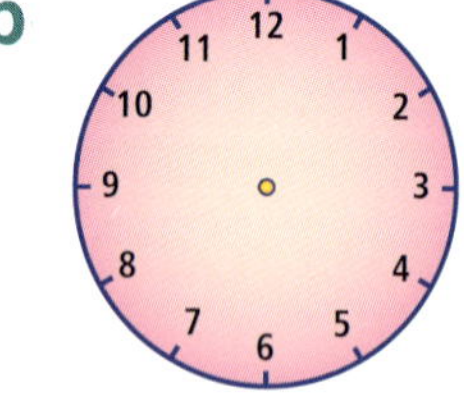
a quarter to 4

c 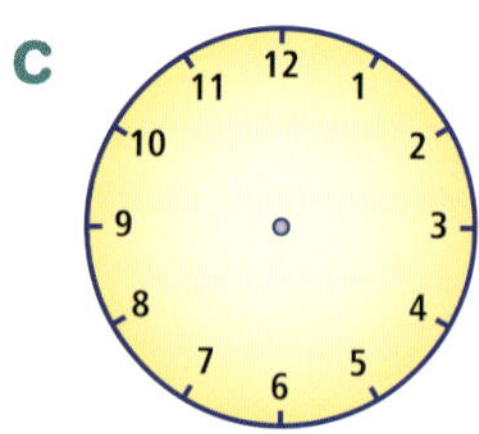
a quarter to 10

**3** At a quarter past ten:

a the hour hand is just past the .

b the minute hand is pointing to the .

15 past 10, ten fifteen



 • *AUSTRALIAN SIGNPOST MATHS 1* • ISBN 9780655708759

# 9D Analog time

CONCEPT

**1** Write the time shown on each face.

a 

b 

c 

d 

e 

f 

**2** On each face show the time given.

a 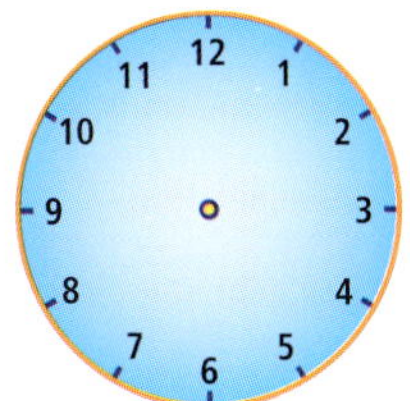
a quarter past 10

b 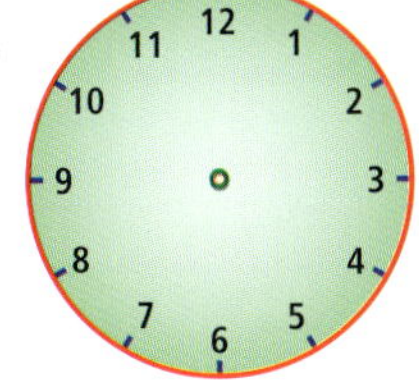
a quarter to 8

c 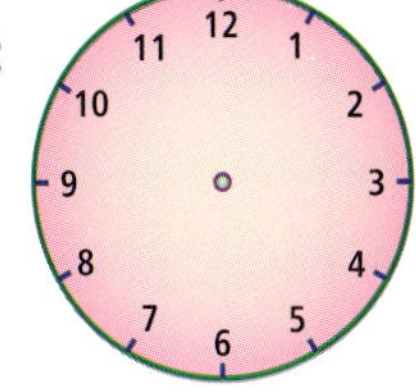
a quarter to 4

d 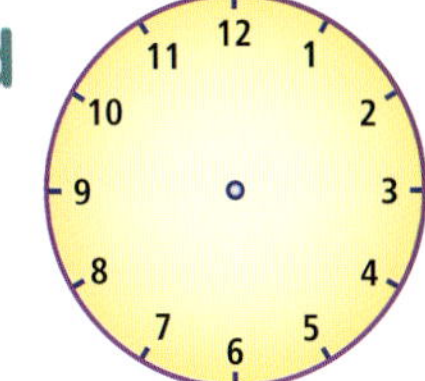
half past 7

e 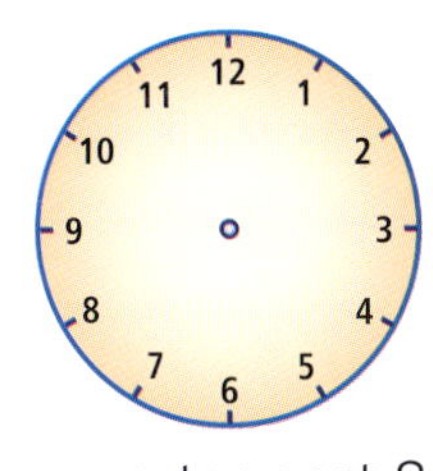
a quarter past 8

f 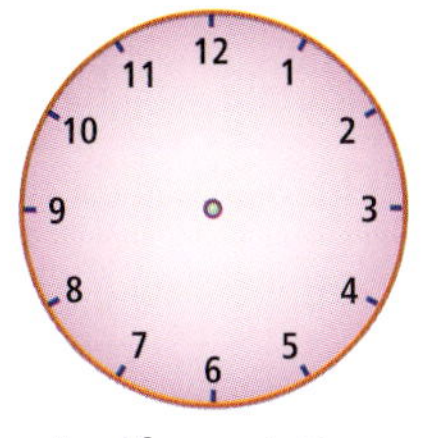
half past 2

g 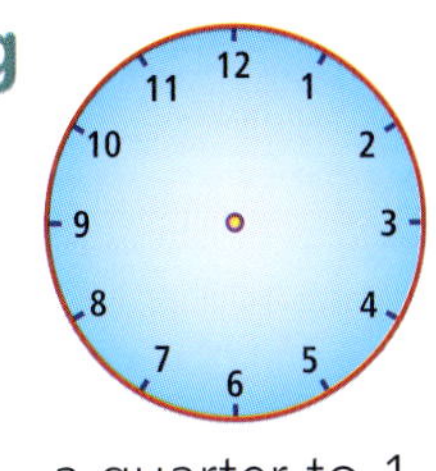
a quarter to 1

h 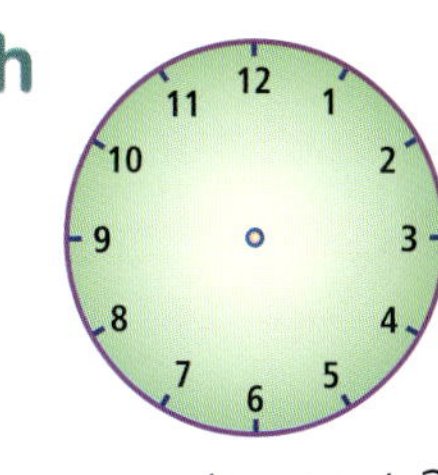
a quarter past 2

 • *AUSTRALIAN SIGNPOST MATHS 1* • ISBN 9780655708759

Number

# 10A Addition to 20

Write the first number then count on.

INVESTIGATION

**1** Write number sentences about the picture.

| | + | | = | |
|---|---|---|---|---|

| | + | | = | |
|---|---|---|---|---|

 • *AUSTRALIAN SIGNPOST MATHS 1* • ISBN 9780655708759

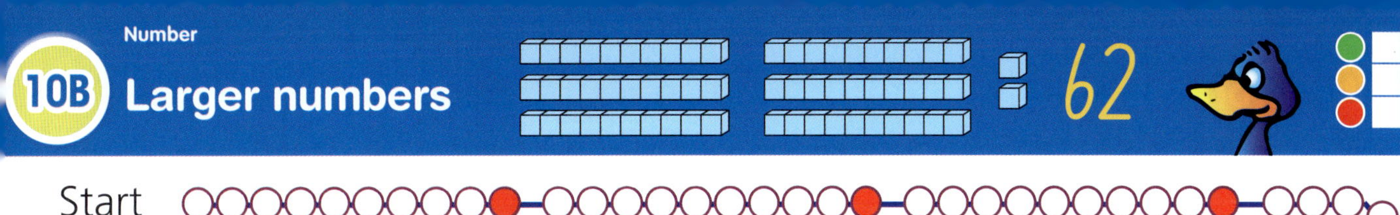


Start 10 20 30 40 50 60 70 80 90 100

CONCEPT

Numbers can be written in groups of **tens** and **ones**.

2 tens 4 ones

24

4 tens 2 ones

42

1 Write the number modelled.

a

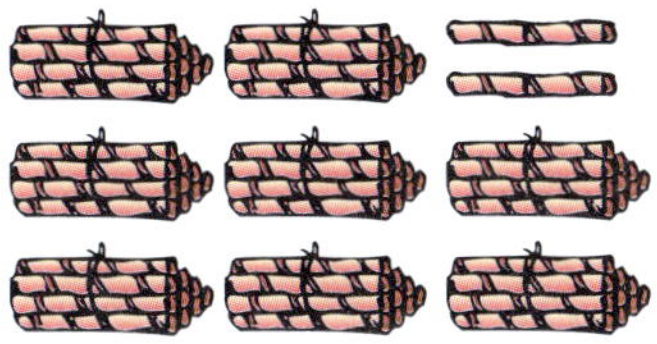

tens ones

b

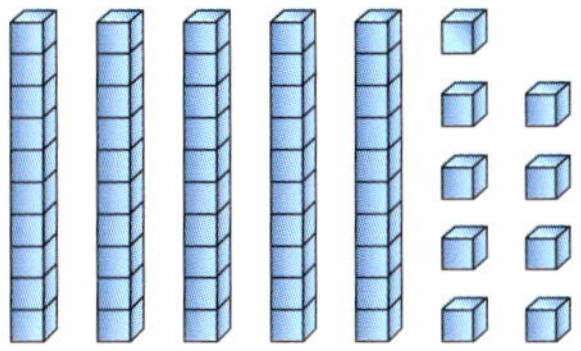

tens ones

c

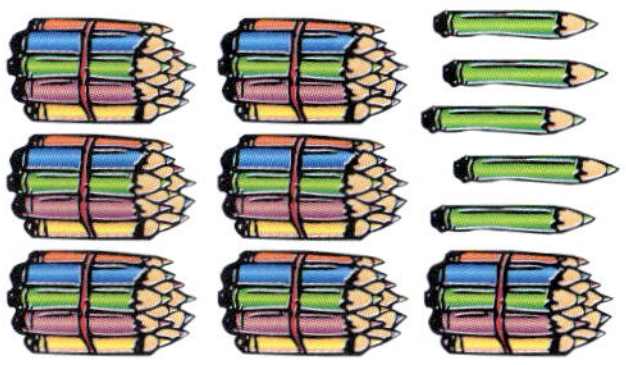

tens ones

2 From Question 1, write the number that is:

a the smallest

b the largest

ACTIVITY

Starting from the top, every 10th bead around this page is coloured. Circle the beads at these numbers:

a 13 b 29 c 45 d 67 e 80 f 98 g 120

For each number say how many tens and how many ones.

# 10C Informal units of length

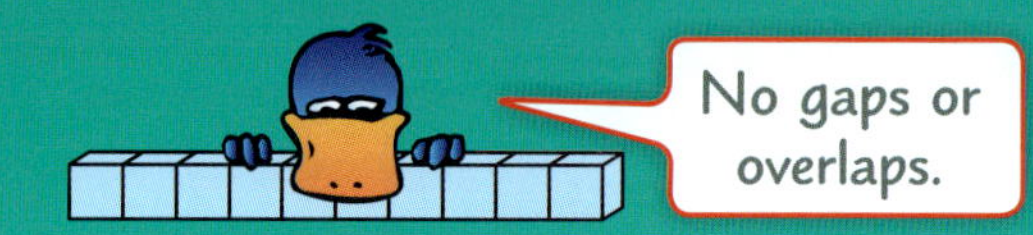


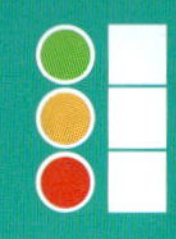

1. Use pencils  to measure the length. Circle the longest length.

a ☐ pencils

b ☐ pencils

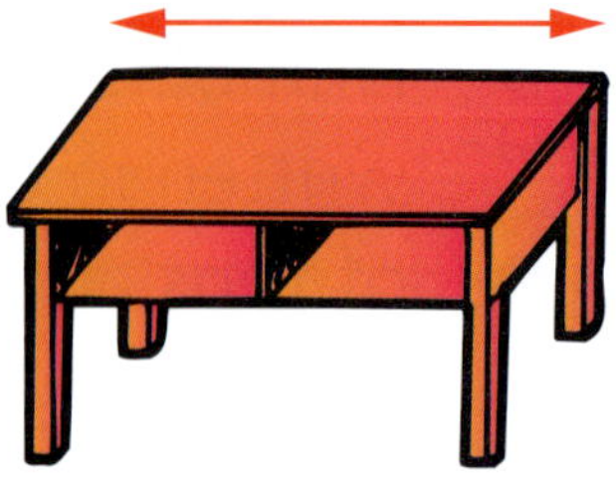

2. a ☐ pencils (guess)
☐ pencils

b ☐ pencils (guess)
☐ pencils

3.

| Unit of length | Length of desk | | Width of desk | |
|---|---|---|---|---|
| | Guess | Check | Guess | Check |
|  peg | | | | |
|  brush | | | | |

Why do we need more pegs than brushes?

INVESTIGATION

- How would you record this length of string?
Tick two ways. Discuss your answers.

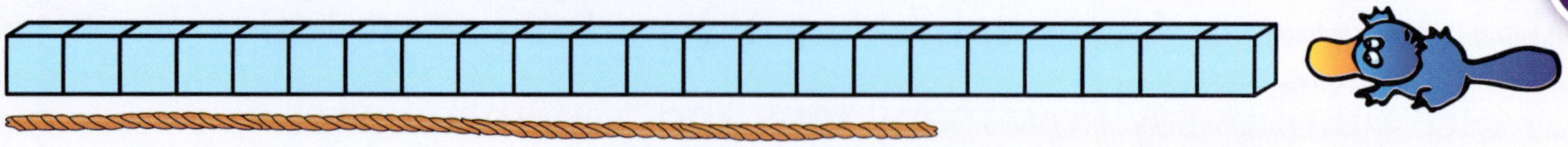

more than 16 blocks ☐ sixteen and a half blocks ☐ less than 17 blocks ☐



 • *AUSTRALIAN SIGNPOST MATHS 1* • ISBN 9780655708759

# Measuring length

Does a length change if we bend it?

1 Estimate the longer line in each pair.
Use a piece of string to check. Circle the longer line.

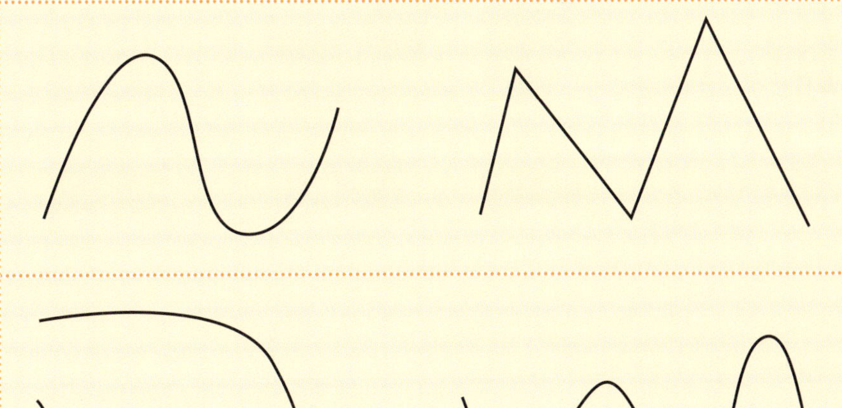

2 Measure and record the lengths of these objects. Place the objects side-by-side and end-to-end to check your answers. Tick the longer object for each pair.

a

| Book | | blocks | ✓ |
|---|---|---|---|
| Paper | | blocks | ✓ |

b

| Pencil | | finger widths | ✓ |
|---|---|---|---|
| Your hand | | finger widths | ✓ |

c

| Scissors | | blocks | ✓ |
|---|---|---|---|
| Felt pen | | blocks | ✓ |

d

| Ruler | | hand spans | ✓ |
|---|---|---|---|
| Book | | hand spans | ✓ |

3 Discuss different ways of comparing lengths: using string, placing objects side-by-side and using concrete materials.

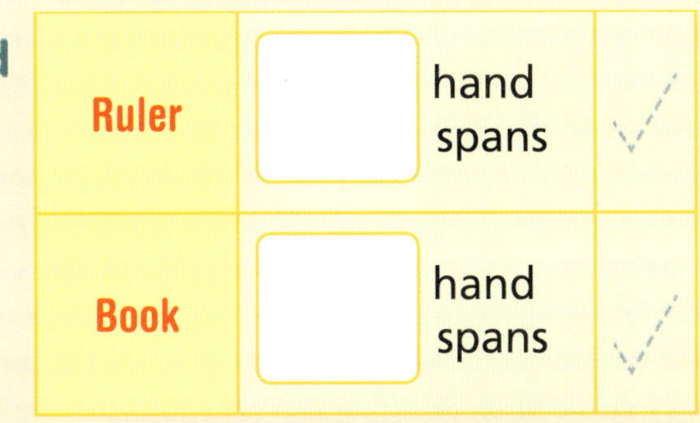

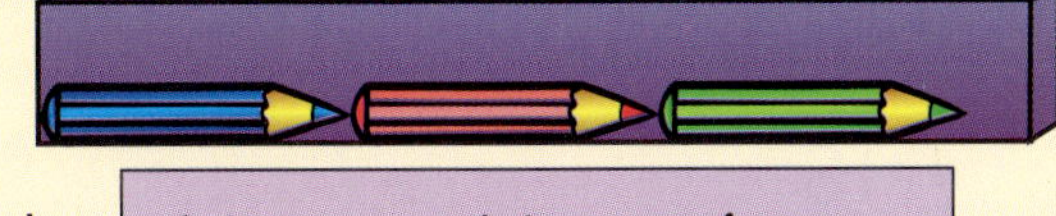

# 11A Numbers to 100

1 Complete each numeral expander and label.

a
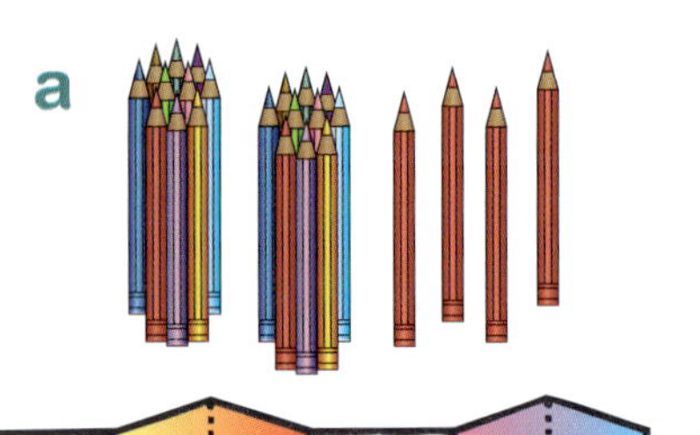

b

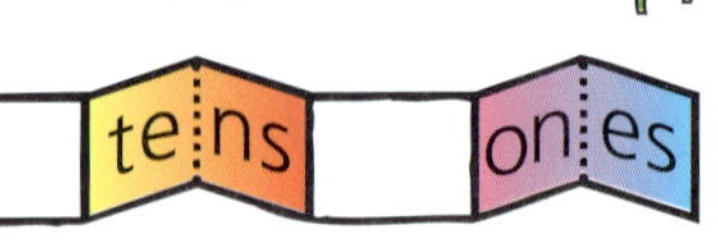


c
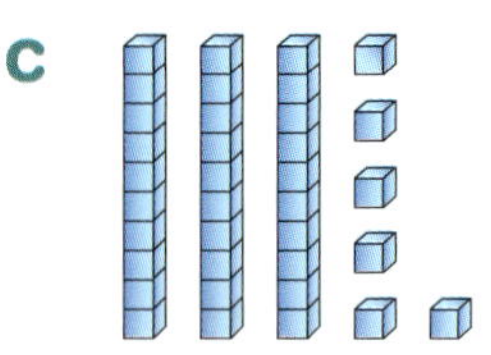

d
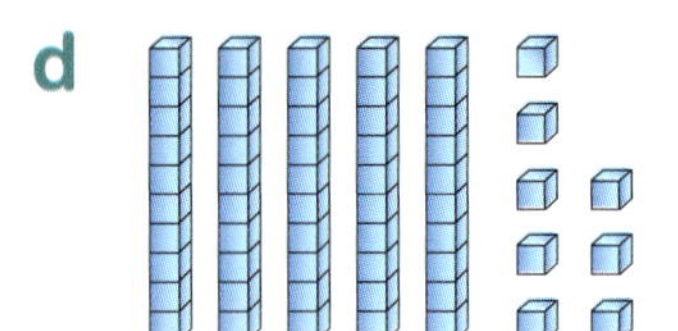

e
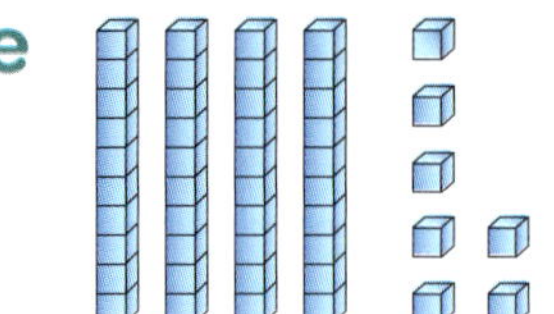

f
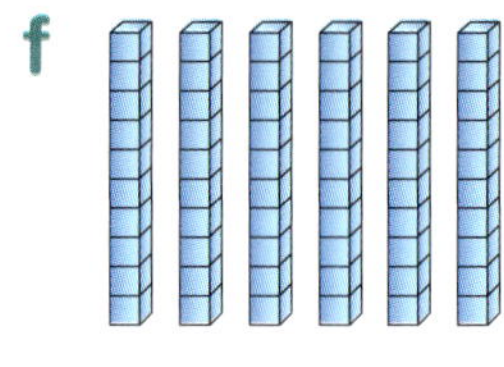

g
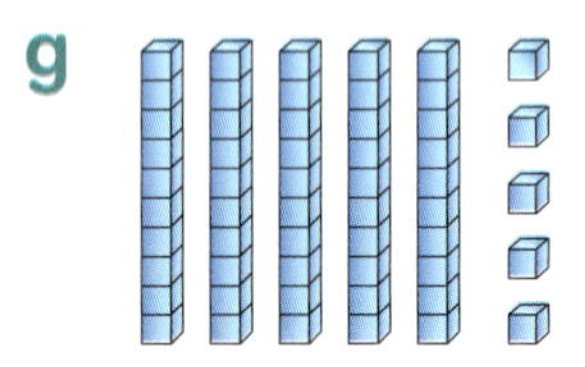

h
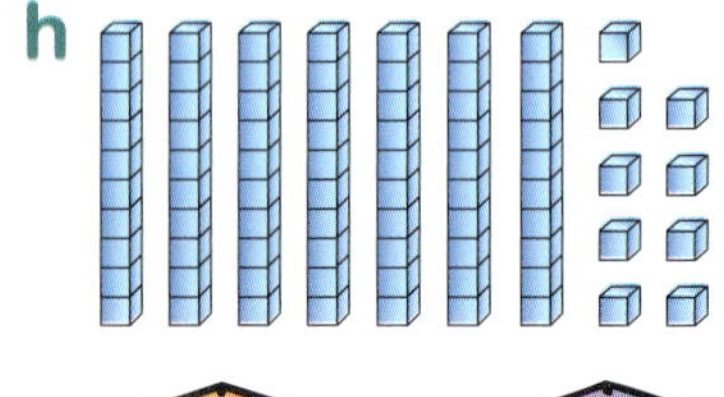

i
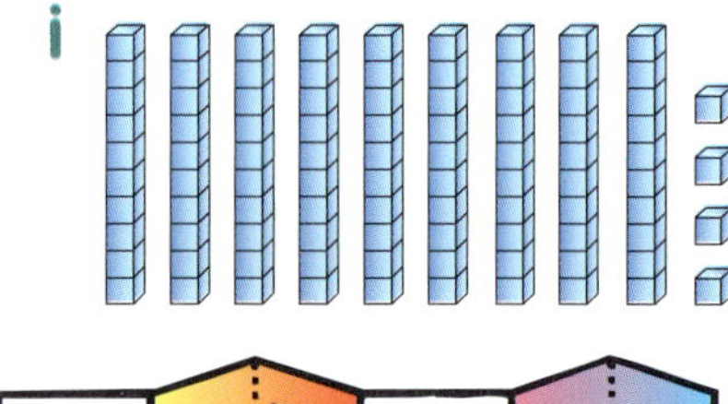

ACTIVITY

With a partner, use place-value blocks to model these numbers. Talk about your answers.

- 18
- 27
- 40
- 31
- 64
- 83
- 50
- 79
- 99
- 90

 • *AUSTRALIAN SIGNPOST MATHS 1* • ISBN 9780655708759

# 11B Subtraction to 20

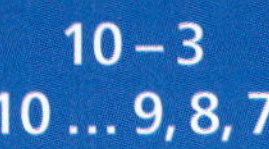

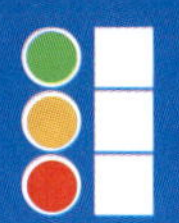

 Count back to complete each number sentence.

a

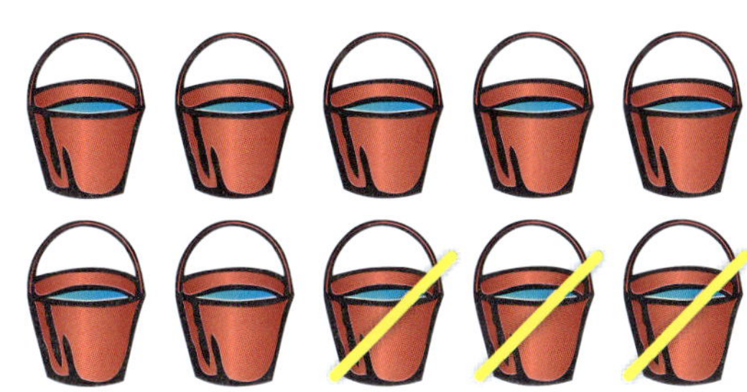

10 − 3 = ☐

b

11 − 6 = ☐

c

16 − 4 = ☐

d

15 − 9 = ☐

e

19 − 8 = ☐

f

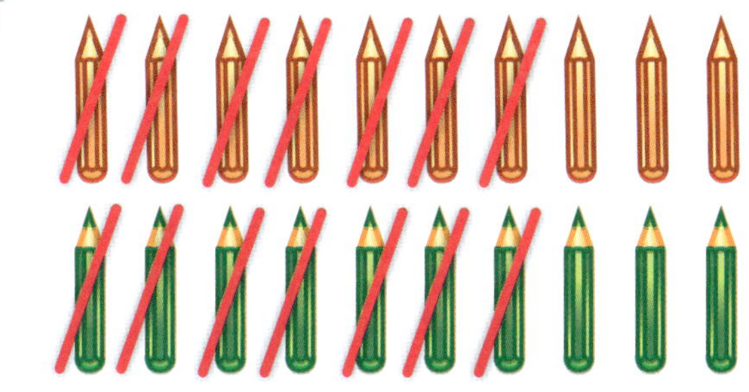

20 − 14 = ☐

2 a Count back 2.

11, ☐, ☐

14, ☐, ☐

b Count back 4.

17, ☐, ☐, ☐, ☐

20, ☐, ☐, ☐, ☐

 •  • ISBN 9780655708759

# 11C Comparing capacities

To find which holds more, pour the contents of one into the other.

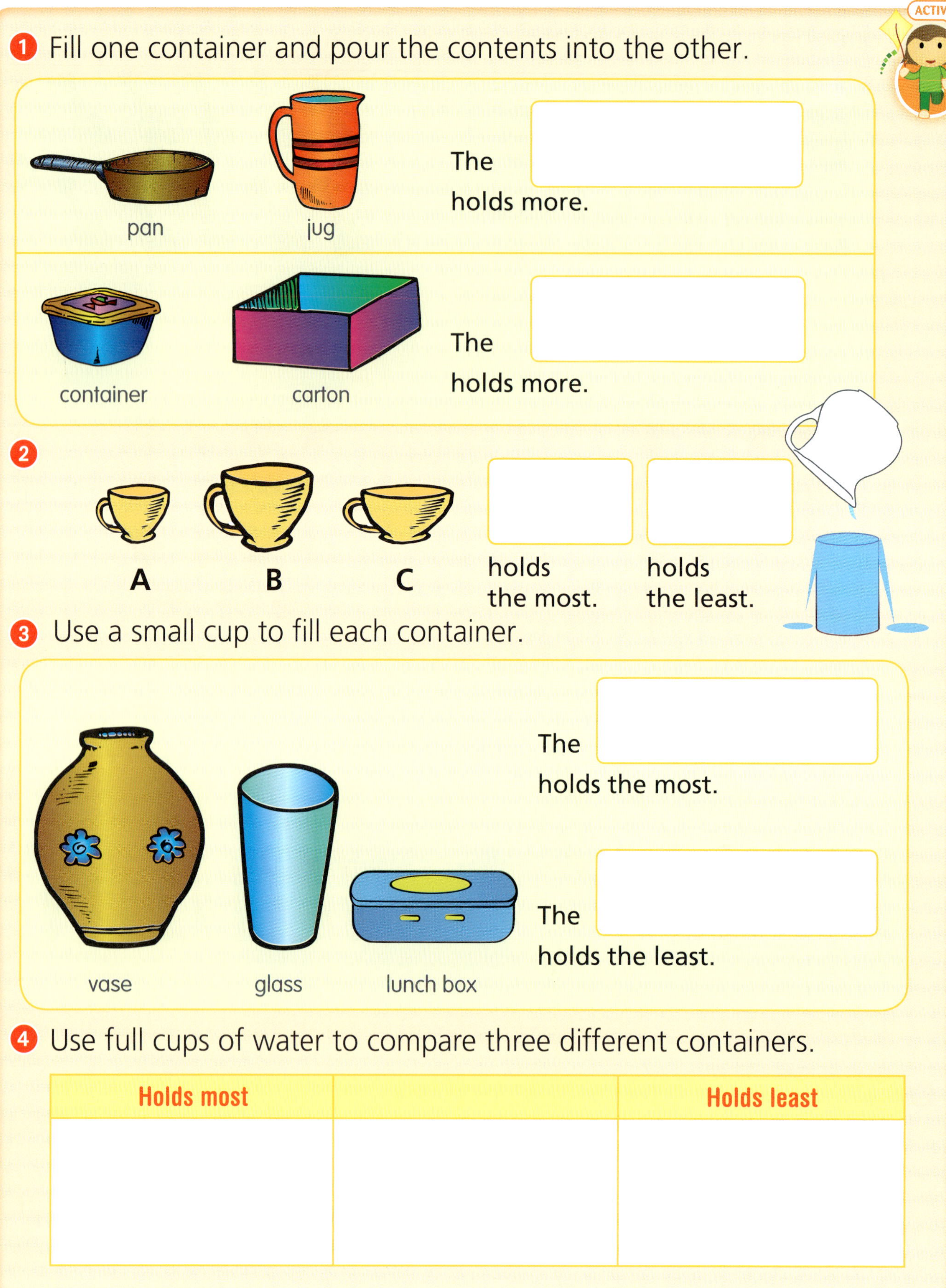


1 Fill one container and pour the contents into the other.

The ______ holds more.

The ______ holds more.

2 ______ holds the most. ______ holds the least.

3 Use a small cup to fill each container.

The ______ holds the most.

The ______ holds the least.

4 Use full cups of water to compare three different containers.

| Holds most | | Holds least |
|---|---|---|
| | | |

# 11D Informal units of capacity

Which holds more?

INVESTIGATION

1 Estimate then measure how many units fill the containers.

| | Cups of water | | Bottles of water | |
|---|---|---|---|---|
| pan  | Guess | Check | Guess | Check |
| ice-cream container  | Guess | Check | Guess | Check |
| jug  | Guess | Check | Guess | Check |
| bucket 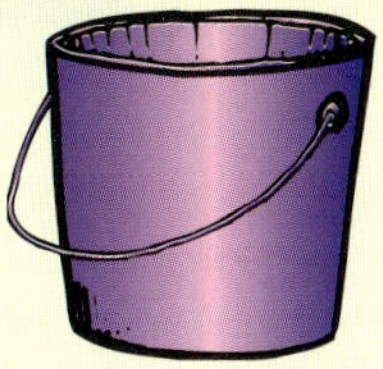 | Guess | Check | Guess | Check |

2 Which holds more?

**a** the pan or the bucket?

**b** the jug or the pan?

3 Which unit was better to use in each case, cups or bottles?

**a** pan cups bottles

**b** ice-cream container cups bottles

**c** jug cups bottles

**d** bucket cups bottles

Discuss your answers.

4 Why are more cups than bottles needed to fill each container?

 • *AUSTRALIAN SIGNPOST MATHS 1* • ISBN 9780655708759

# 12A Addition sentences

+ means and, add or plus.
= means makes or is equal to.

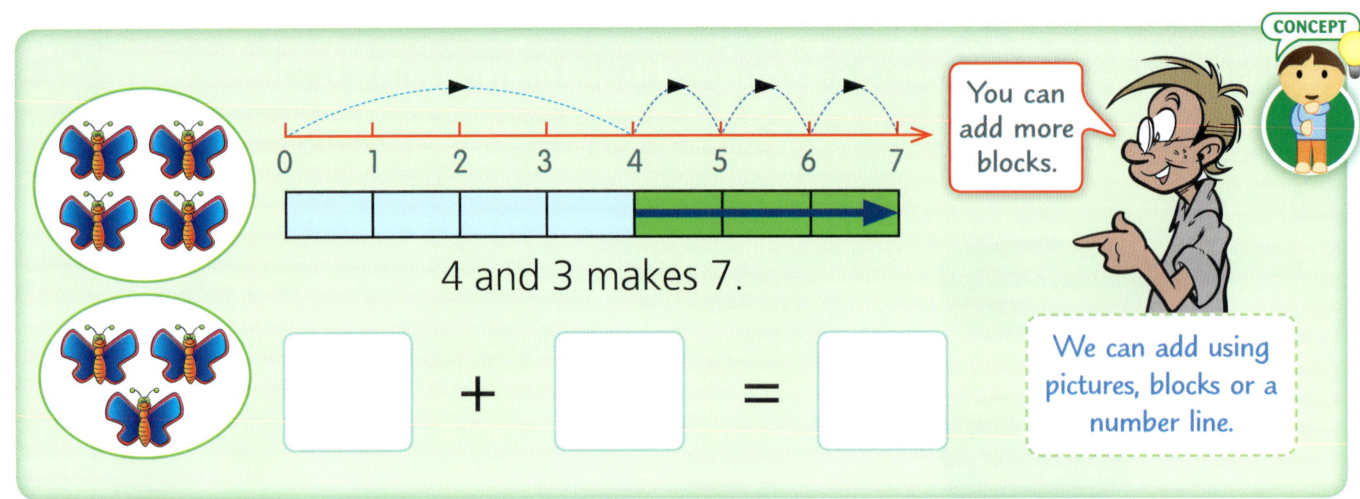


4 and 3 makes 7.

□ + □ = □

We can add using pictures, blocks or a number line.

1. 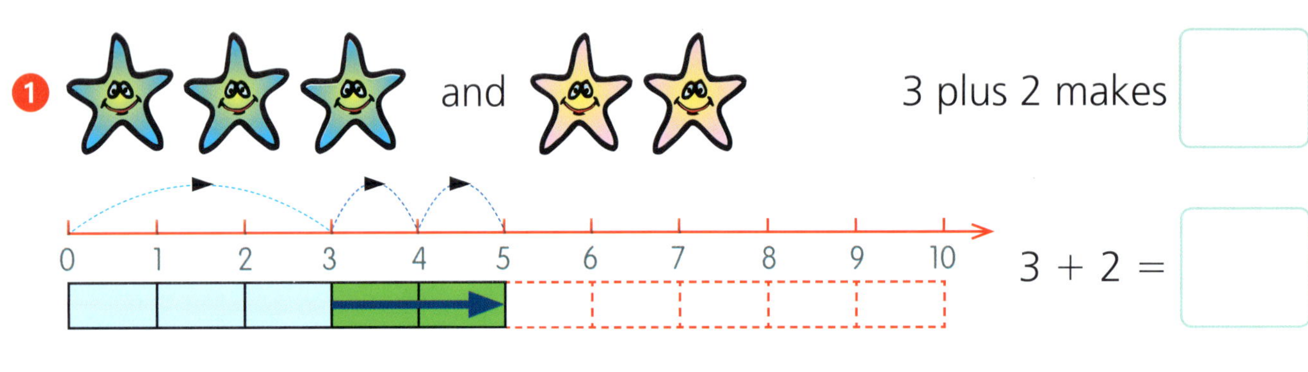


3 plus 2 makes □.

$3 + 2 =$ □

2. 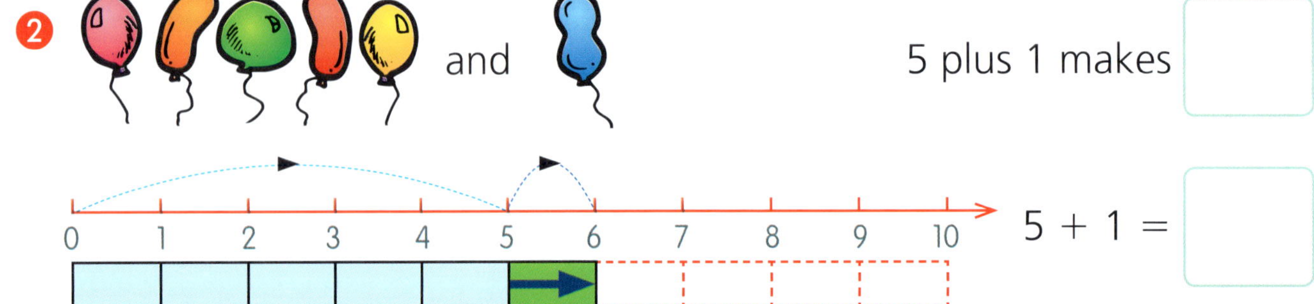


5 plus 1 makes □.

$5 + 1 =$ □

ACTIVITY

Find the answers by placing blocks below the number line.
Trace the jumps with your finger.
Make up some questions of your own.

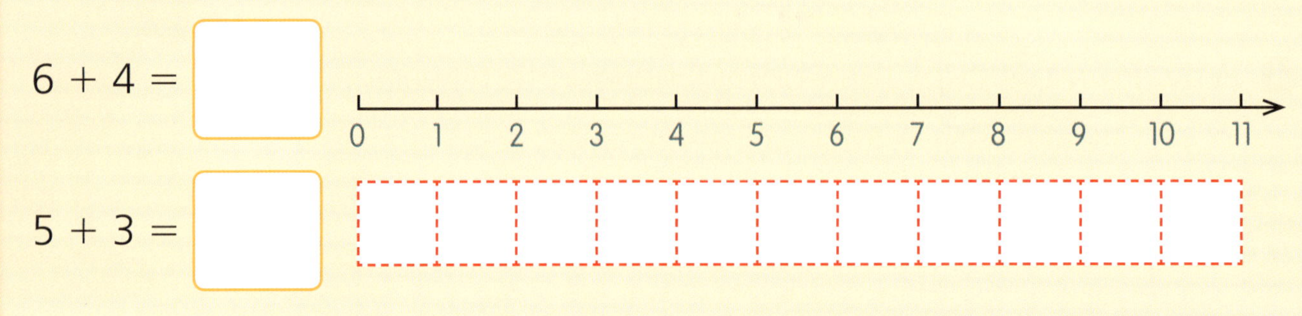


$6 + 4 =$ □

$5 + 3 =$ □


 • *AUSTRALIAN SIGNPOST MATHS 1* • ISBN 9780655708759

# 12B Addition

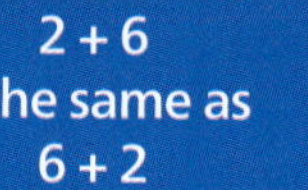


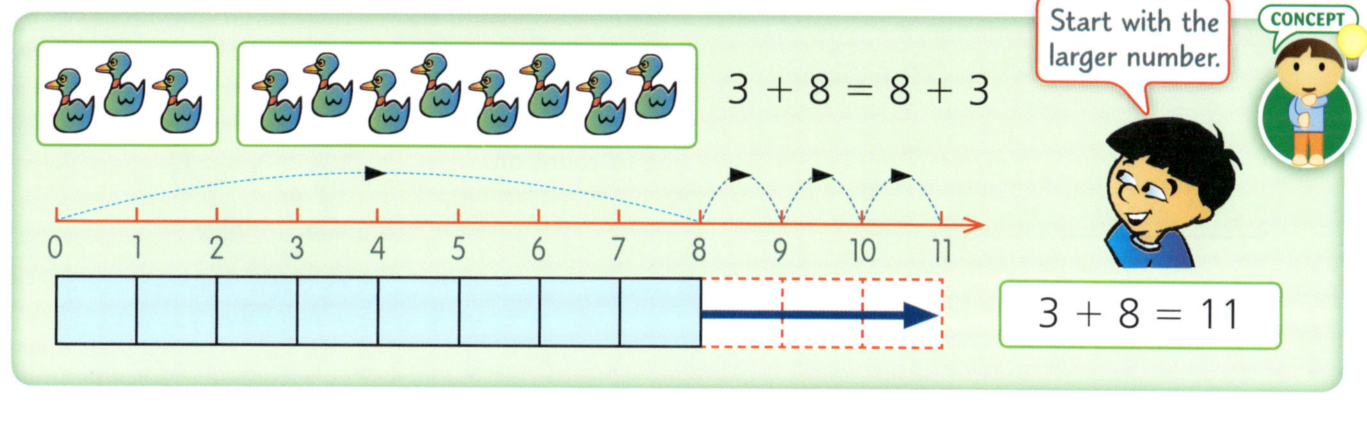

**1** Use the number line above to answer these questions.

**a** 2 and 5 makes ☐.  **b** 5 and 4 makes ☐.

**c** $9 + 3 =$ ☐  **d** $6 + 5 =$ ☐  **e** $7 + 3 =$ ☐

**f** $8 + 3 =$ ☐  **g** $5 + 5 =$ ☐  **h** $6 + 6 =$ ☐

**i** $7 + 4 =$ ☐  **j** $8 + 7 =$ ☐  **k** $5 + 4 =$ ☐

**l** $6 + 3 =$ ☐  **m** $2 + 7 =$ ☐  **n** $1 + 8 =$ ☐

**o** $5 + 6 =$ ☐  **p** $4 + 6 =$ ☐  **q** $8 + 9 =$ ☐

**r** $9 + 7 =$ ☐  **s** $6 + 9 =$ ☐  **t** $7 + 7 =$ ☐

# 12C Addition by counting on

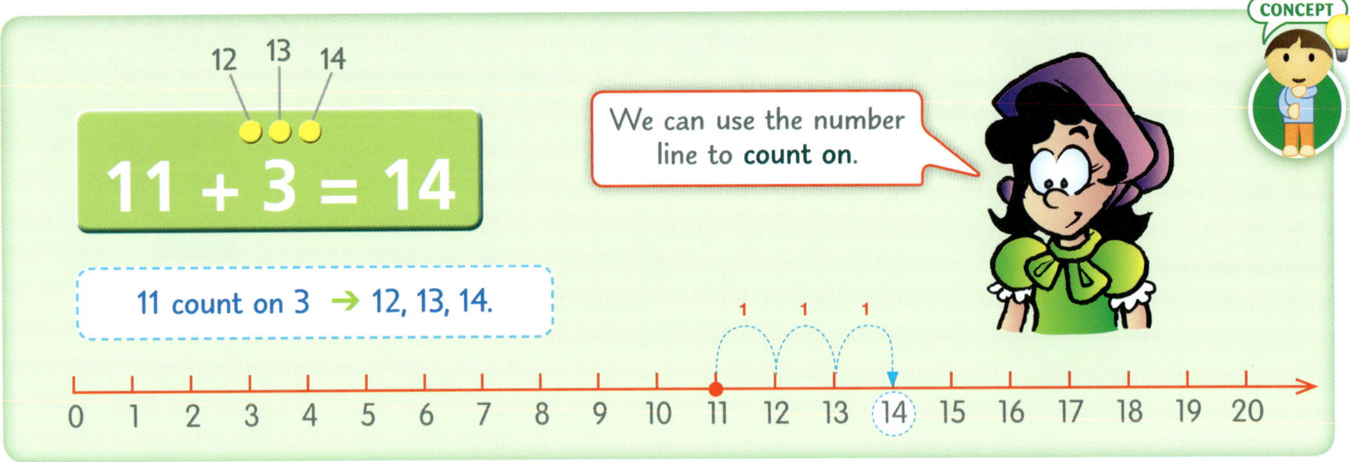


**1** Use the dots to count on.

a $8 + 1 =$ ☐

b $9 + 2 =$ ☐

c $17 + 1 =$ ☐

d $12 + 2 =$ ☐

e $18 + 1 =$ ☐

f $15 + 2 =$ ☐

g $9 + 3 =$ ☐

h $8 + 2 =$ ☐

i $11 + 4 =$ ☐

j $14 + 2 =$ ☐

k $17 + 3 =$ ☐

l $19 + 1 =$ ☐

**2** Use the number line to find the answers.

0 1 2 3 4 5 6 7 8 9 10 11 12 13 14 15 16 17 18 19 20 21

a $8 + 4 =$ ☐

b $9 + 5 =$ ☐

c $16 + 3 =$ ☐

d $7 + 6 =$ ☐

e $12 + 4 =$ ☐

f $17 + 4 =$ ☐

 • *AUSTRALIAN SIGNPOST MATHS 1* • ISBN 9780655708759

# Comparing capacities

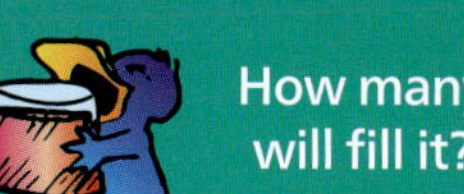

How many will fill it?

INVESTIGATION

1 How many times can one jug fill each container?

jug

| | A bottle | B glass | C lunch box |
|---|---|---|---|
| Guess | | | |
| Measure | | | |

Which container (A, B or C):

a holds the most? ☐

b holds the least? ☐

2 How many cups fill each container?

| | | |
|---|---|---|
|  teapot | ☐ cups | The ☐ holds more. |
|  container | ☐ cups | The ☐ holds less. |

 • *AUSTRALIAN SIGNPOST MATHS 1* • ISBN 9780655708759

# 13A Numbers to 120

| one hundred and seven | 107 |
|---|---|
| one hundred and nineteen | 119 |
| one hundred and ten | 110 |

1 Write the numeral.

a sixty-one

b twenty-two

c eighty-four

d seventy-nine

| twenty | two |
|---|---|
| thirty | three |
| forty | four |
| fifty | five |
| sixty | six |
| seventy | seven |
| eighty | eight |
| ninety | nine |
| one hundred | |

2 Write the number in words. Remember to use a hyphen.

a 65

b 43

c 80

d 27

e 96

3 Write the number that is 1 more than:

a 33

b 59

c 110

ACTIVITY

Practise counting to 120 from any number on this grid.

| 91 | 92 | 93 | 94 | 95 | 96 | 97 | 98 | 99 | 100 |
|---|---|---|---|---|---|---|---|---|---|
| 101 | 102 | 103 | 104 | 105 | 106 | 107 | 108 | 109 | 110 |
| 111 | 112 | 113 | 114 | 115 | 116 | 117 | 118 | 119 | 120 |

Practise counting backwards from 120 to 91.

# Numbers to 120

| one hundred and nine | 109 |
| --- | --- |
| one hundred and nineteen | 119 |
| one hundred and twenty | 120 |

**1** Use numerals to write these numbers.

**a** sixteen 

**b** one hundred and sixteen 

**c** sixty-six 

**d** one hundred and seven 

**e** one hundred

**f** one hundred and seventeen 

**2** Write the numbers in words.

**a** 21 

**b** 101

**c** 116

Don't forget to use a hyphen for twenty-one.

**3**

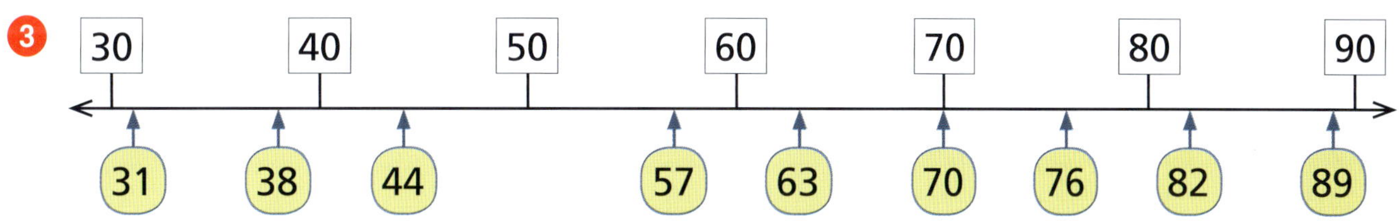


Look at the number line and write the nearest ten to:

**a** 63 

**b** 31 

**c** 82

**d** 38 

**e** 70 

**f** 89 

**g** 44 

**h** 57 

**i** 76 

 • *AUSTRALIAN SIGNPOST MATHS 1* • ISBN 9780655708759

# The hexagon

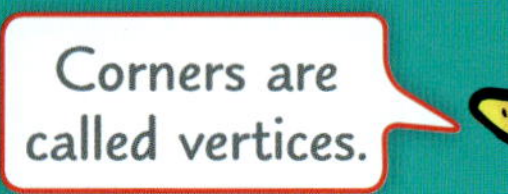

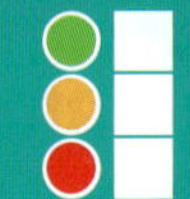

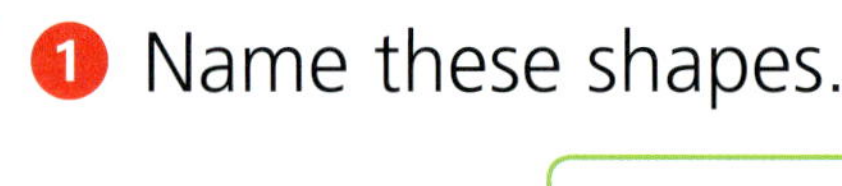

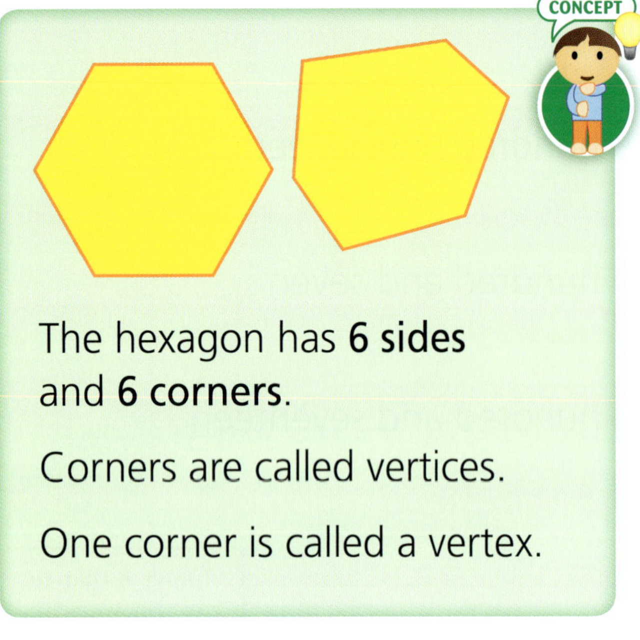


The hexagon has **6 sides** and **6 corners**.

Corners are called vertices.

One corner is called a vertex.

1 Name these shapes.

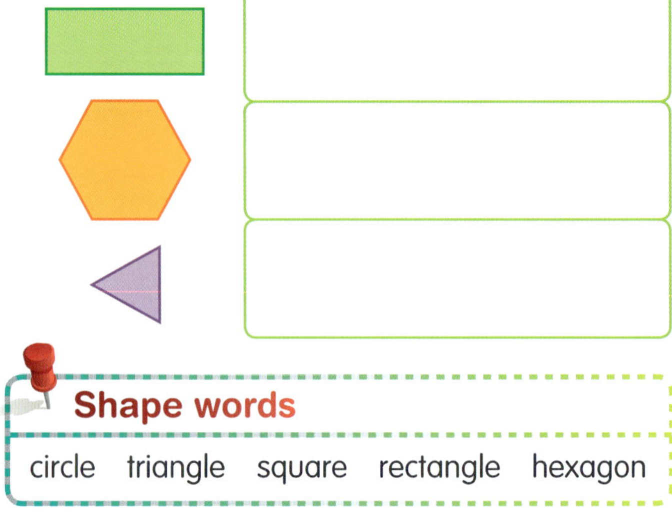

**Shape words**

circle triangle square rectangle hexagon

2 Trace each shape. Write its name.

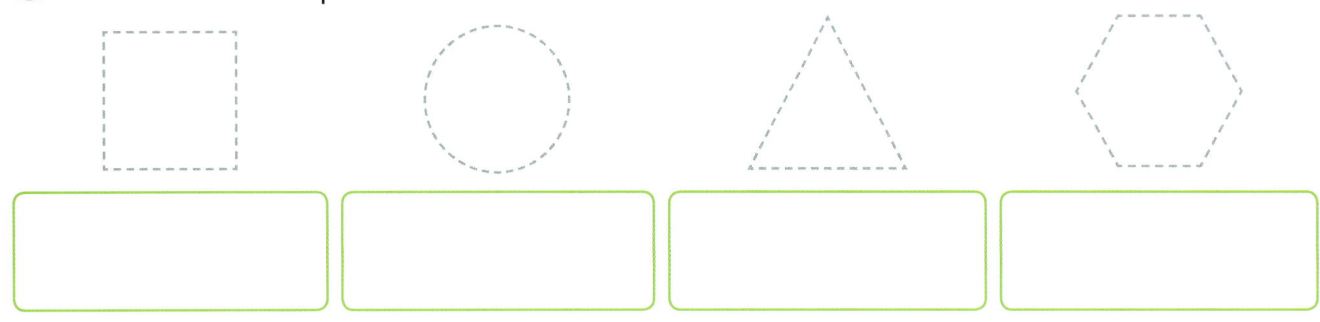

3 Colour the hexagons red.

4 Draw a hexagon.

All of these are hexagons.

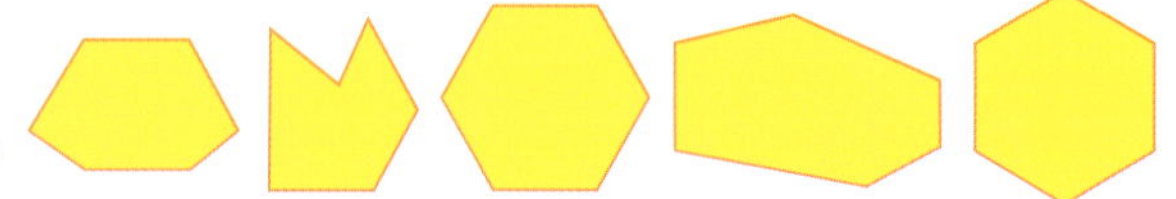

5 A hexagon has ☐ sides and ☐ vertices.



 • *AUSTRALIAN SIGNPOST MATHS 1* • ISBN 9780655708759

# 13D Picture graphs

1

## Straight or curly hair

Straight hair

Curly hair

a How many people had straight hair?

b How many people had curly hair?

c How many people are shown altogether?

d How many more people had straight hair than curly hair?

2

## Favourite school day for Class 1M

Monday

Tuesday

Wednesday

Thursday

Friday

a Which day was chosen least?

b How many of the class chose Monday?

c How many people chose a day?

d What is your favourite day?

 • *AUSTRALIAN SIGNPOST MATHS 1* • ISBN 9780655708759

# 14A Subtraction

– means take away or minus.
= means leaves or is equal to.

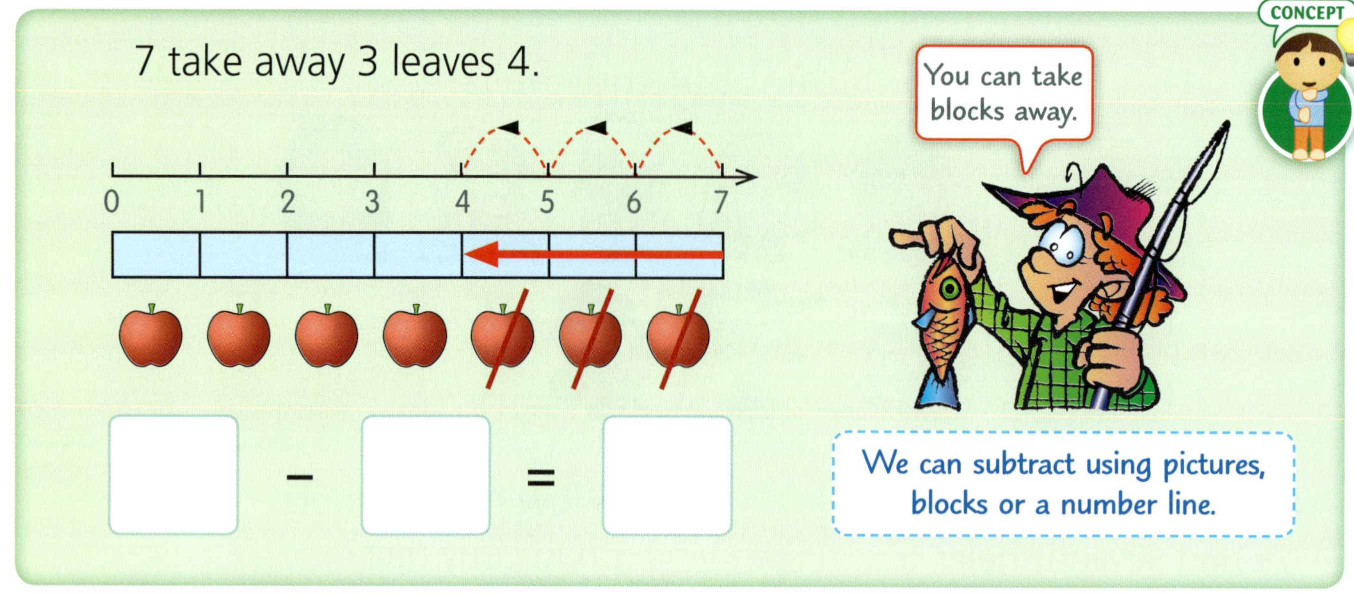


□ – □ = □

1 6 minus 2 equals □.

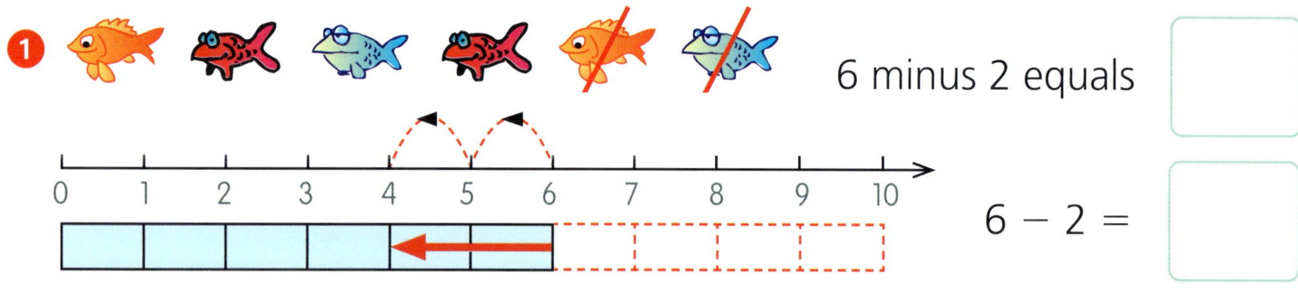


6 – 2 = □

2 8 minus 4 equals □.

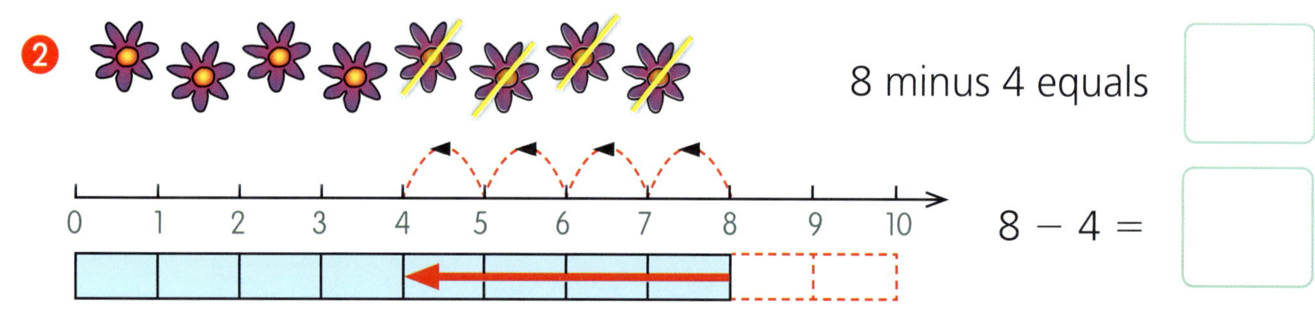


8 – 4 = □

ACTIVITY

Find the answers by taking away blocks placed below the number line. Trace the jumps with your finger. Make up some questions of your own.

9 – 7 = □

10 – 4 = □

0 1 2 3 4 5 6 7 8 9 10 11

# 14B Subtraction

CONCEPT

9 take away 4 leaves 5. 9 – 4 = 5. 9 minus 4 is equal to 5.

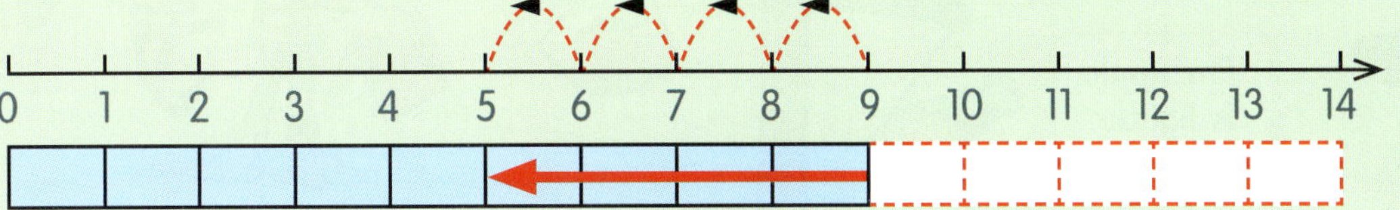


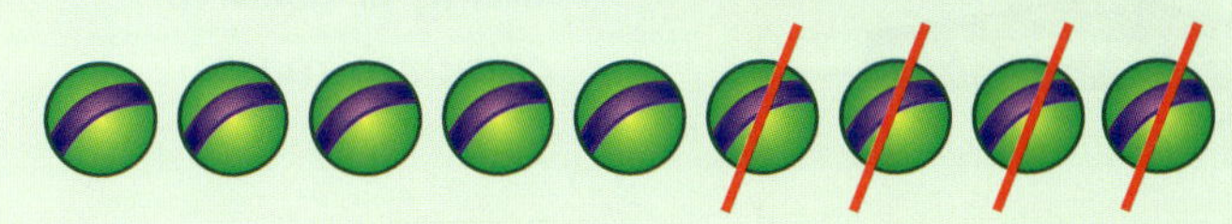

Count back four.

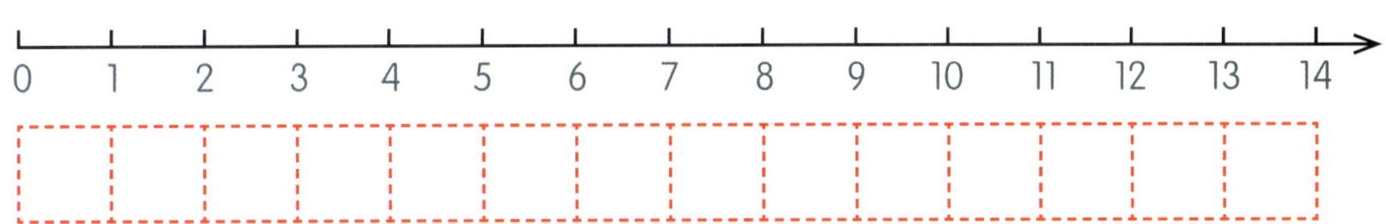


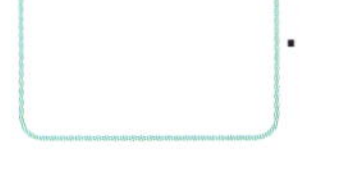

**1** Use the number line above to answer these questions.

**a** 7 minus 4 equals ☐.  **b** 6 minus 3 equals ☐.

**c** 8 – 1 = ☐  **d** 6 – 5 = ☐  **e** 7 – 2 = ☐

**f** 9 – 5 = ☐  **g** 5 – 5 = ☐  **h** 8 – 5 = ☐

**i** 9 – 6 = ☐  **j** 8 – 3 = ☐  **k** 9 – 3 = ☐

**l** 10 – 3 = ☐  **m** 11 – 4 = ☐  **n** 7 – 5 = ☐

**o** 12 – 4 = ☐  **p** 13 – 6 = ☐  **q** 9 – 7 = ☐

# 14C Comparing the mass of objects

CONCEPT

The heavier one goes down.

1 Circle the lighter object. Colour the heavier object. Trace the words.

ACTIVITY

Predict the heavier object by hefting. Use a balance scale to check. Circle the heavier object. Explain how you used the balance scales.

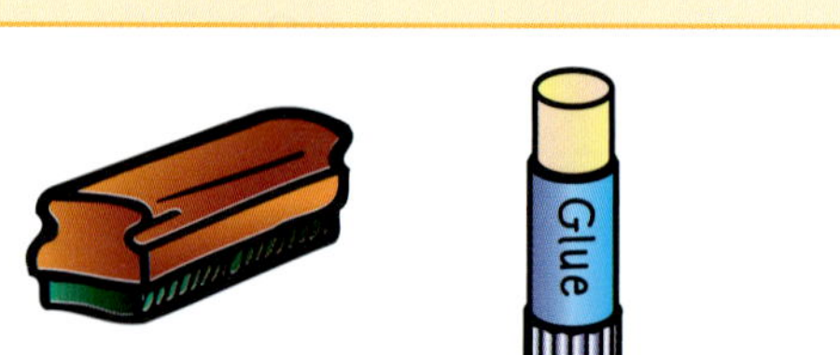

# Mass

CONCEPT

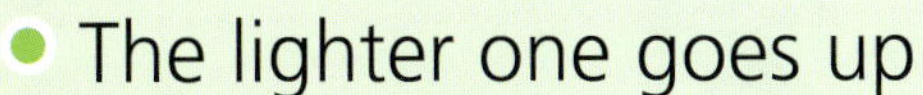

- The lighter one goes up.

The bottle is heavier.

- The scales are balanced.

The apple and orange have the same mass.

1. Cross out the heavier object. Circle objects that are balanced.

a 

b 

c 

d 

e 

f 

g 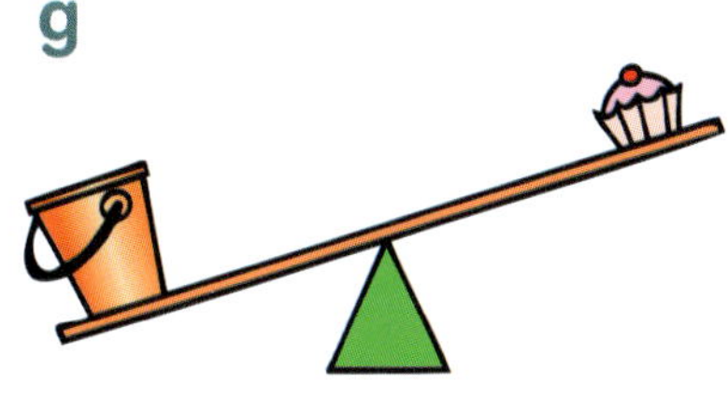

h 

i 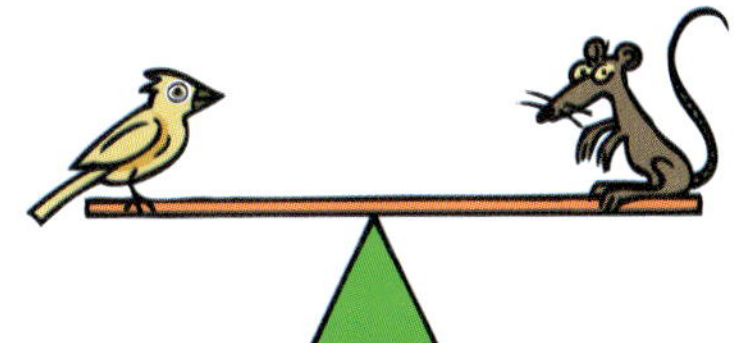

ACTIVITY

Use balance scales to compare these objects.
Circle the heavier object.

| | | | |
|---|---|---|---|
|  |   |  |  |
| 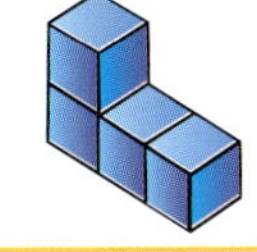 | 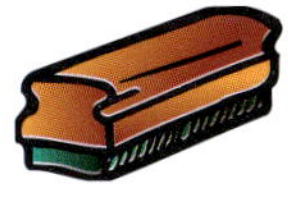 |   | 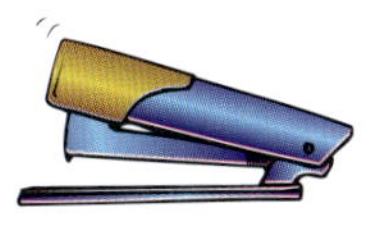 |

Which is heavier?

 • *AUSTRALIAN SIGNPOST MATHS 1* • ISBN 9780655708759

# 15A Counting back

We can use part of the line.

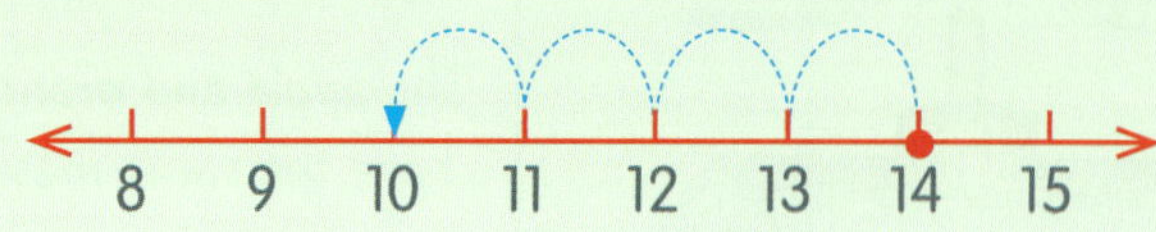

14 – 4 = 10

Start at 14.
Jump back 4.

1 Use these number lines to count back.

**a**

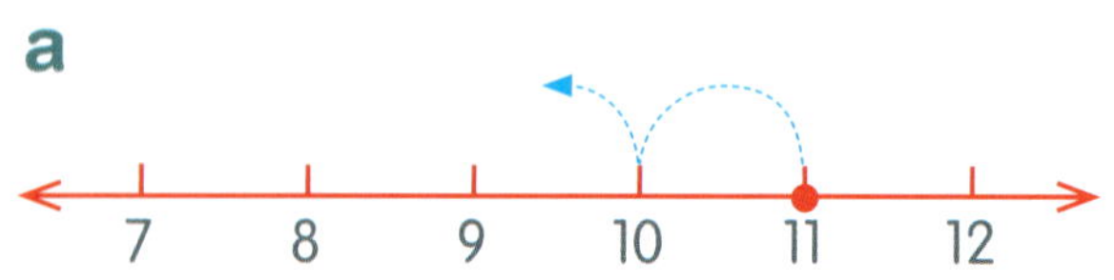

11 – 4 = ☐

**b**

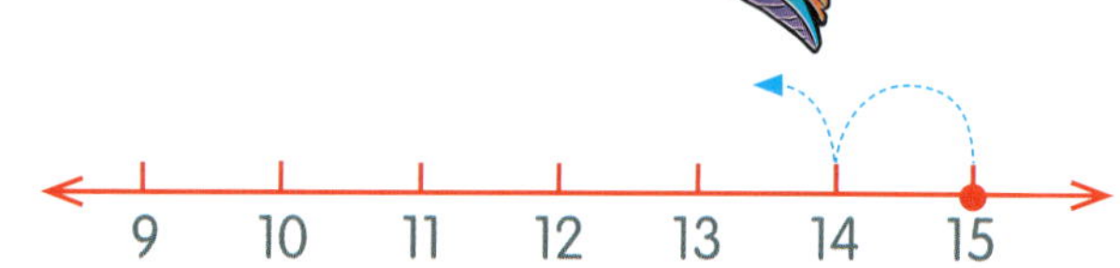

15 – 5 = ☐

**c**

12 – 3 = ☐

**d**

16 – 6 = ☐

**e**

17 – 2 = ☐

**f**

19 – 4 = ☐

ACTIVITY

Use this number line to create your own subtraction sentences.

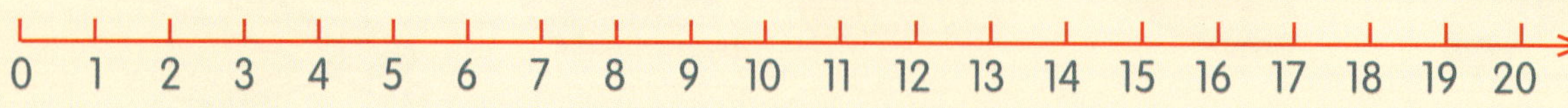



 *AUSTRALIAN SIGNPOST MATHS 1* • ISBN 9780655708759

Number

# 15B Subtraction

11 – 6 ... 10, 9, 8, 7, 6, 5

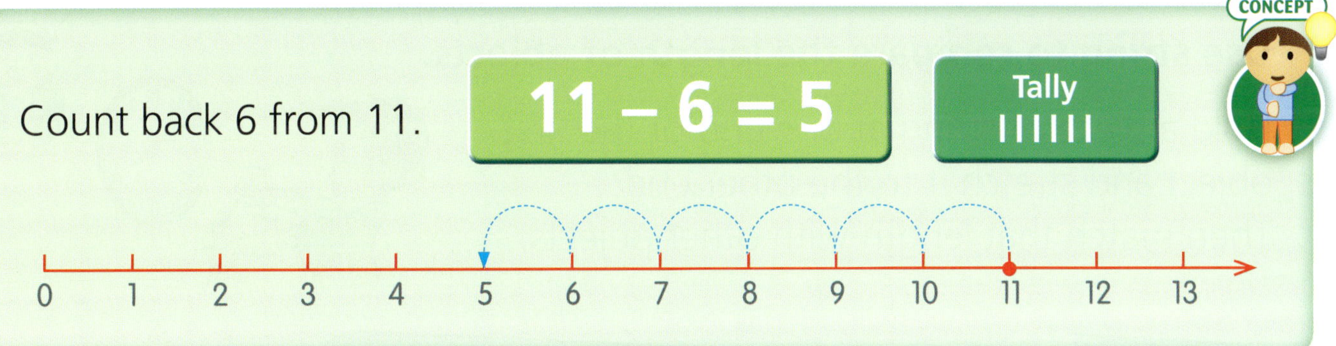


1. Use the number line to complete each number sentence.

**a** $6 - 3 =$ ☐ **b** $13 - 6 =$ ☐ **c** $9 - 5 =$ ☐

**d** $14 - 9 =$ ☐ **e** $16 - 8 =$ ☐ **f** $15 - 9 =$ ☐

**g** $17 - 0 =$ ☐ **h** $20 - 5 =$ ☐ **i** $19 - 7 =$ ☐

2. **a** Ruby had $15.
She spent $4.
How much does she have left?

| 15 | |
|---|---|
| | 4 |

___ – ___ = ___

$ ☐

**b** Matt had 18 worms.
10 worms wriggled away.
How many worms are left?

___ – ___ = ___

3. Colour the words that mean .

| add | plus | difference between | |
|---|---|---|---|
| take away | less than | subtract | minus |

 • *AUSTRALIAN SIGNPOST MATHS 1* • ISBN 9780655708759

# 15C Indirect comparison of length

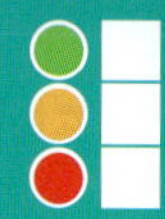

CONCEPT

**Use string to compare the length of objects.**

Hold a piece of string at one end of the first object and stretch it to the other end. Then match that length with other objects.

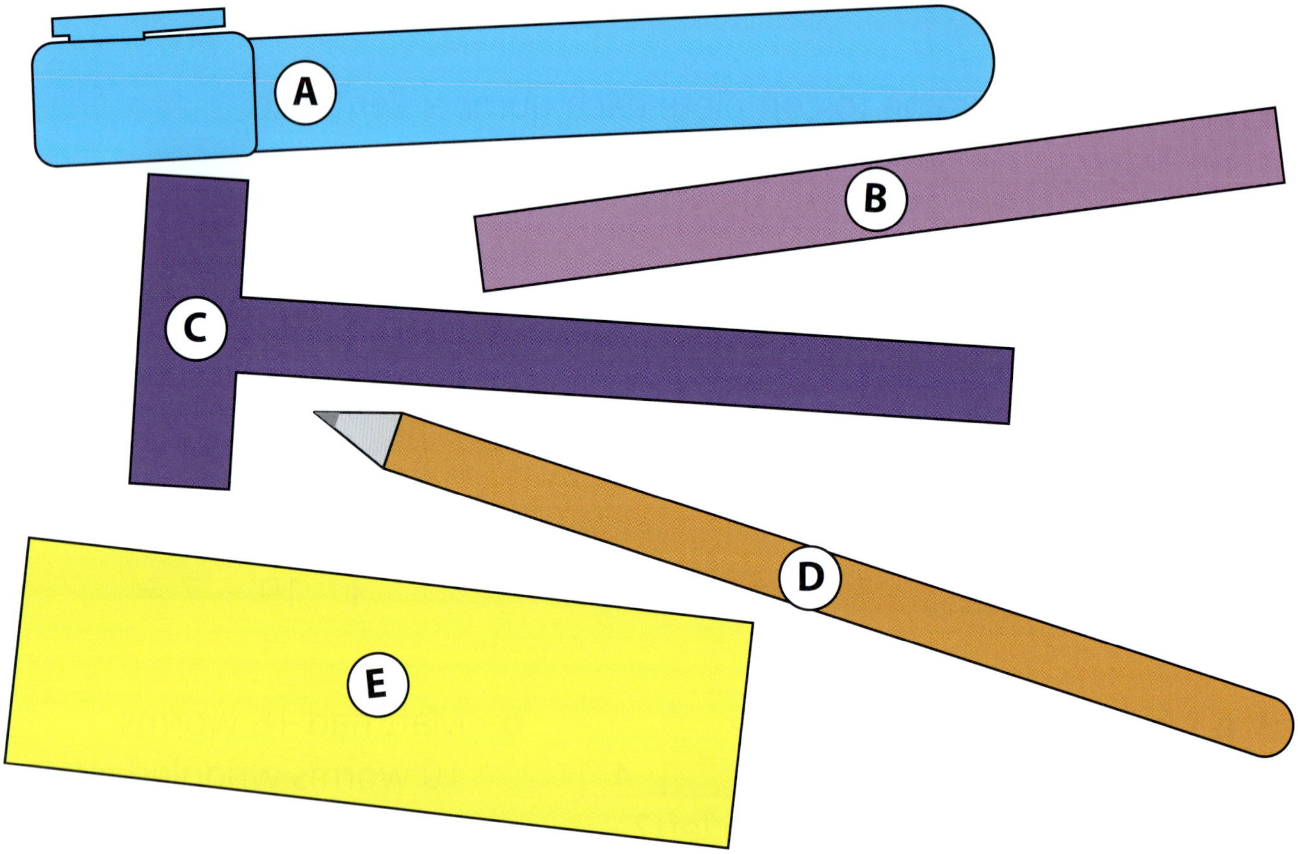

A

B

C

D

E

❶ Use a piece of string to find which is longer:

a B or D ☐ b B or C ☐ c A or D ☐ d B or E ☐

e Write the lengths of A, B, C, D and E in order from shortest to longest. ☐

ACTIVITY

Choose 3 objects of about the same length. What is the longest object you chose? ☐

 • *AUSTRALIAN SIGNPOST MATHS 1* • ISBN 9780655708759

## Pet day

Everybody brought their pets to school.

1 Look at the picture and complete this table.

| Pets brought to school | | | |
|---|---|---|---|
| Birds | Cats | Dogs | Rabbits |
| | | | |

2 Draw a data display of the pets.

| Pets brought to school | | | | | |
|---|---|---|---|---|---|
| Birds | | | | | |
| Cats | | | | | |
| Dogs | | | | | |
| Rabbits | | | | | |

3 Write about this data display.

INVESTIGATION

What pets do people in your class have? Find out and fill in this graph.

| | | | | | | | | | |
|---|---|---|---|---|---|---|---|---|---|
| Birds | | | | | | | | | |
| Cats | | | | | | | | | |
| Dogs | | | | | | | | | |
| Fish | | | | | | | | | |
| Rabbits | | | | | | | | | |
| Other | | | | | | | | | |

# Doubles

CONCEPT

When we add two numbers or groups that are the same, they are called **doubles**.

- Some doubles are: 1 + 1 2 + 2 3 + 3
- We say "Double 1", "Double 2", "Double 3".

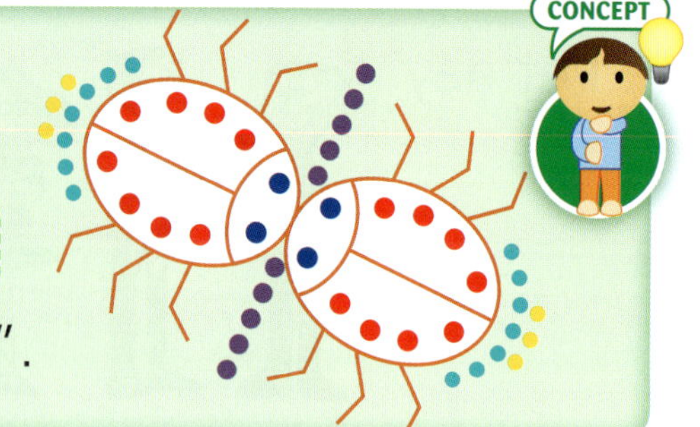

1 Use these pictures to complete the doubles.

a

| 2 | 2 |
|---|---|
| ? | |

2 horns and 2 horns

2 + ☐ = ☐

Double ☐ = ☐

b

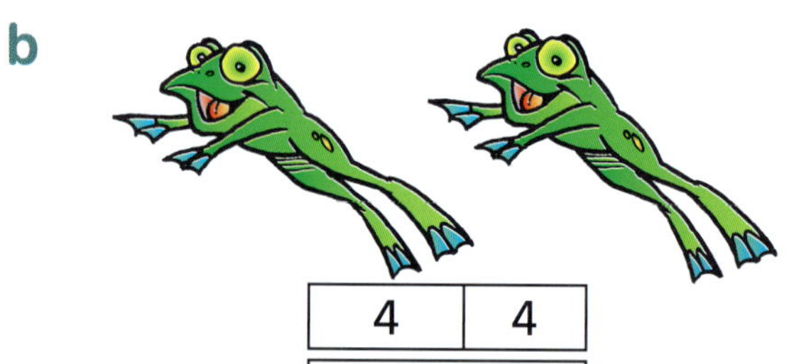

| 4 | 4 |
|---|---|
| ? | |

4 legs and 4 legs

4 + ☐ = ☐

Double ☐ = ☐

c

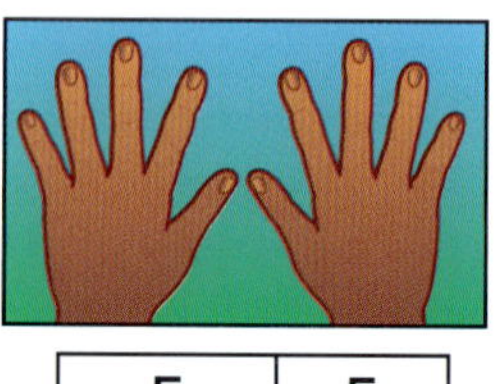

| 5 | 5 |
|---|---|
| ? | |

5 fingers and 5 fingers

☐ + ☐ = ☐

Double ☐ = ☐

INVESTIGATION

Circle all the doubles you can find on the bugs at the top.

Write four doubles.

☐ + ☐ = ☐ ☐ + ☐ = ☐

☐ + ☐ = ☐ ☐ + ☐ = ☐

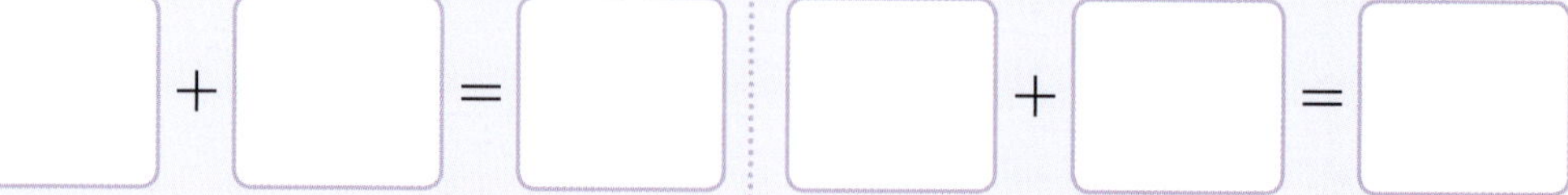

1 + 1 = 2 2 + 2 = 4 3 + 3 = 6 4 + 4 = 8 5 + 5 = 10

6 + 6 = 12 7 + 7 = 14 8 + 8 = 16 9 + 9 = 18 10 + 10 = 20



 • *AUSTRALIAN SIGNPOST MATHS 1* • ISBN 9780655708759

# 16B Doubling and near doubling

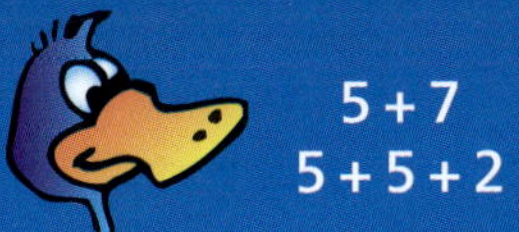

When you **double** a number, the answer will be **even**.

1 Complete each number sentence.

a double 3 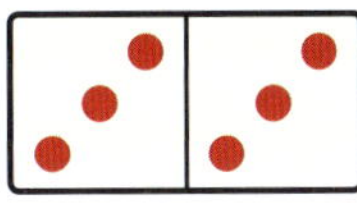

☐ + ☐ = ☐

b double 4 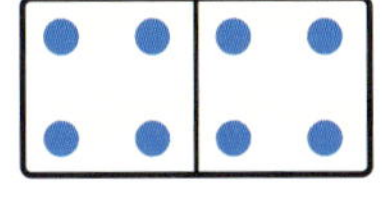

☐ + ☐ = ☐

c double 7 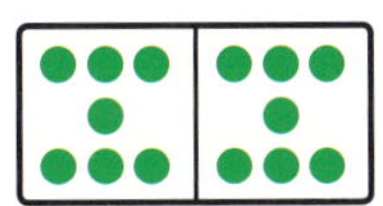

☐ + ☐ = ☐

d double 9 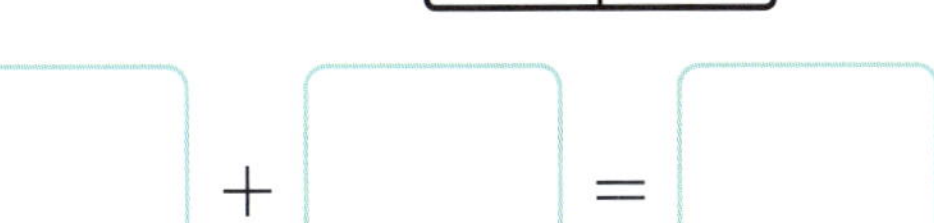

☐ + ☐ = ☐

2 a 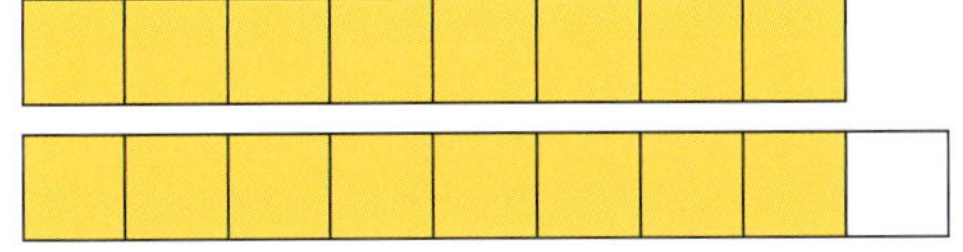

8 + 9 is double 8 plus 1.

8 + 8 + 1 = ☐

b 

6 + 7 is double 6 plus 1.

6 + 6 + 1 = ☐

c 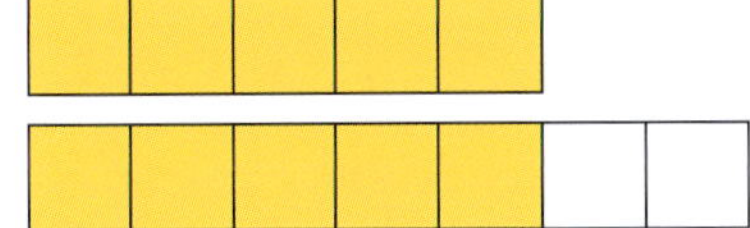

5 + 7 is double ☐ plus ☐.

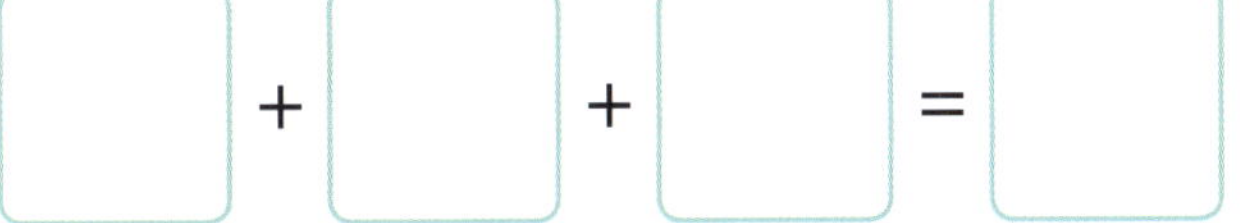

☐ + ☐ + ☐ = ☐

d

7 + 9 is double ☐ plus ☐.

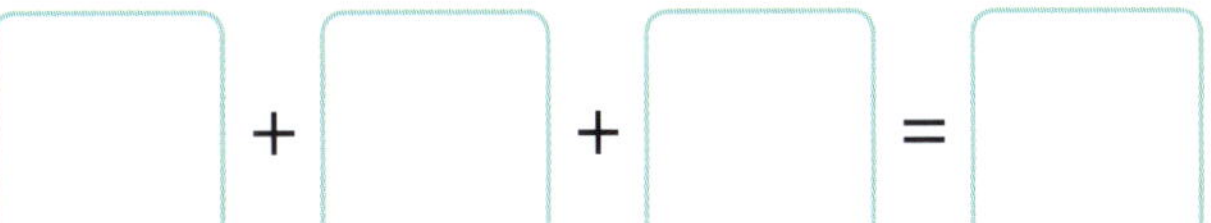

☐ + ☐ + ☐ = ☐

 • *AUSTRALIAN SIGNPOST MATHS 1* • ISBN 9780655708759

# 16C Months of the year

The months of the year repeat in this order:

January, February, March, April, May, June, July, August, September, October, November, December

1 Which month comes after:

a February?

b August?

c October?

d December?

2 How many months are between January and:

a May?

b October?

c August?

d July?

e March?

f June?

g April?

h December?

i September?

3 Which month comes before:

a January?

b June?

c September?

d March?

Use the internet to find the months in which these events occur.

a Chinese New Year

b Valentine's Day

c Mother's Day

d Father's Day

# 16D Months and seasons

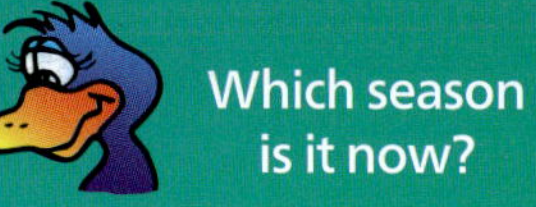

CONCEPT

There are four seasons in one year. Describe each season.

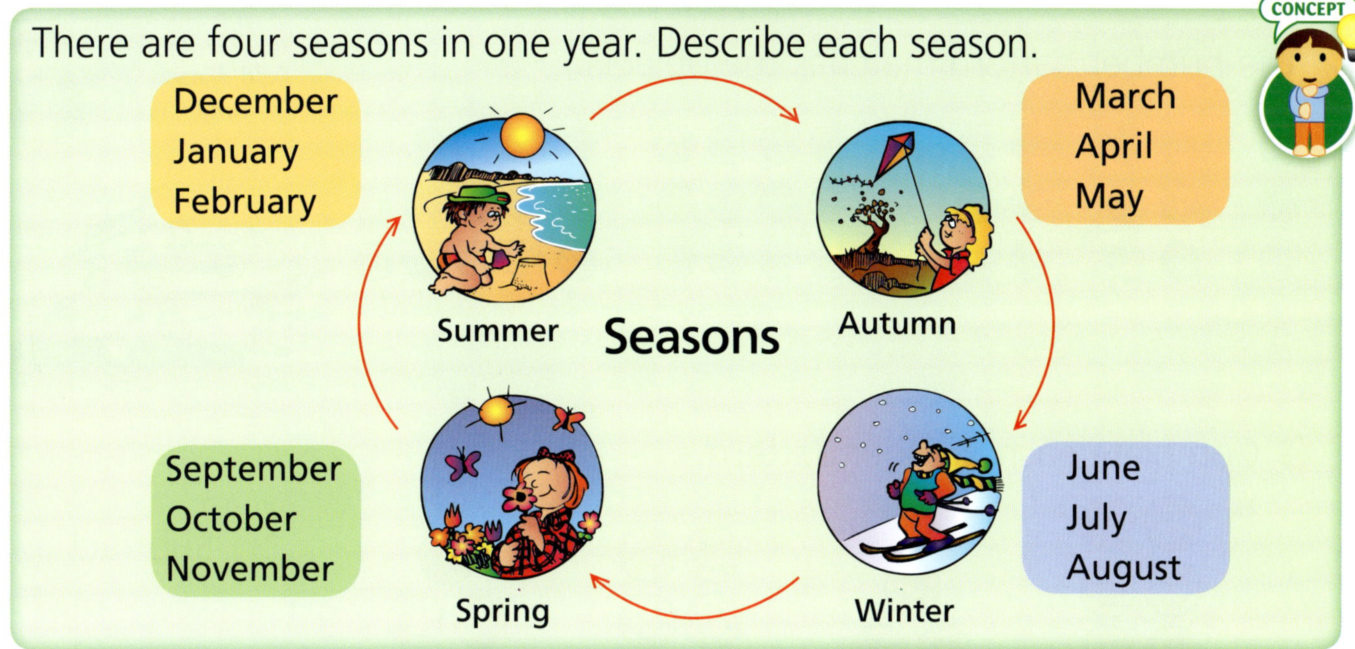


1. Write the months in their correct order within a calendar year.

| March | July | November | January |
|---|---|---|---|
| August | June | December | February |
| May | September | April | October |

| | | | |
|---|---|---|---|
| 1 | | 2 | |
| 3 | | 4 | |
| 5 | | 6 | |
| 7 | | 8 | |
| 9 | | 10 | |
| 11 | | 12 | |

Colour the summer months yellow. Colour the winter months blue.

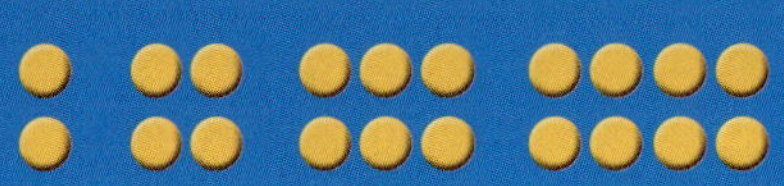

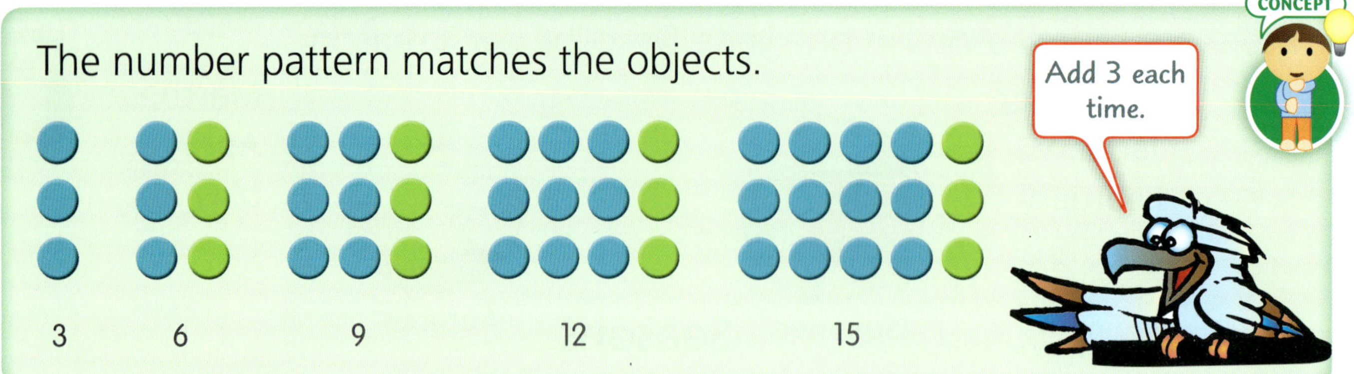


1 Complete each number pattern.

a

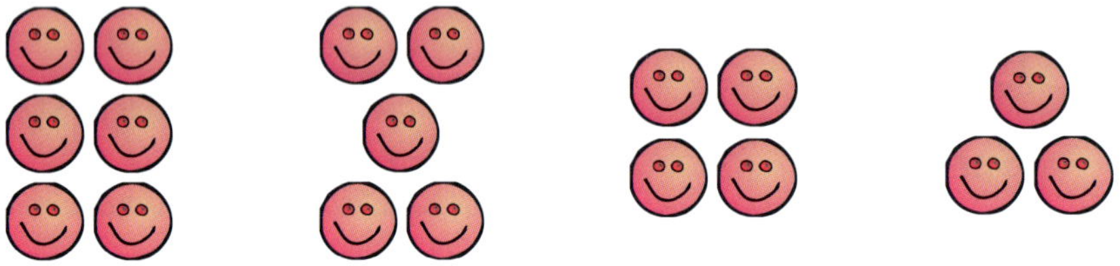

☐, ☐, ☐, ☐,

Subtract ☐ is the rule.

b

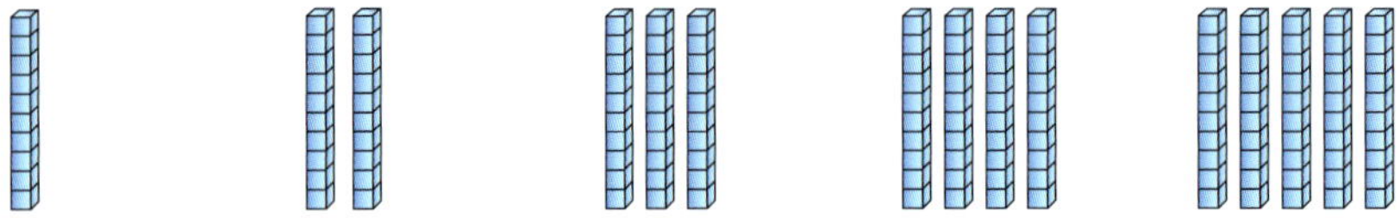

☐, ☐, ☐, ☐, ☐

Add ☐ is the rule.

c

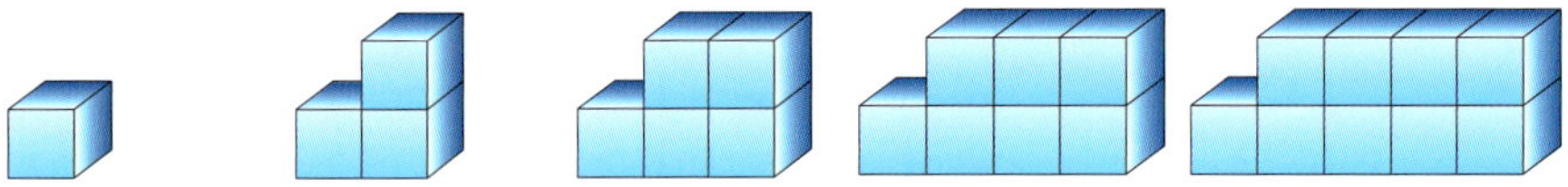

☐, ☐, ☐, ☐, ☐

Add ☐ is the rule.

ACTIVITY

Use blocks to make your own number patterns. Write one here.

☐, ☐, ☐, ☐, ☐, ☐, ☐


 • *AUSTRALIAN SIGNPOST MATHS 1* • ISBN 9780655708759

# 17B Combinations for numbers

There are many ways to name the number nine.

one less than 10
three groups of 3
double 4 and one more

one more than 8
5 combined with 4
4 groups of 2 plus 1

1 Write the number 10 in different ways.

2 The numbers at the bottom add to give 9.

a

b

c

number bonds

3 Complete the number bond houses.

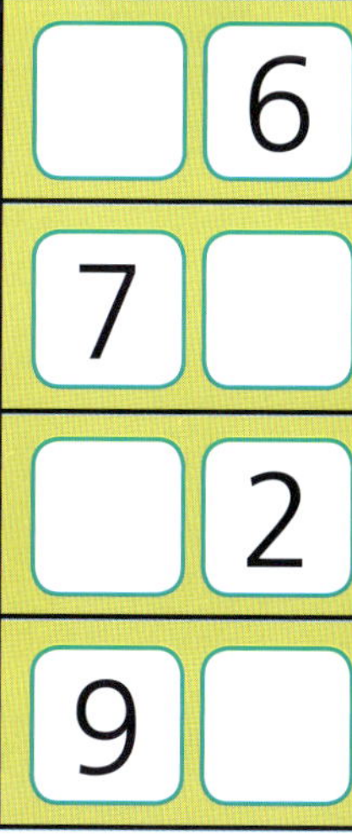


4 Circle true or false.

a $1 + 8 = 2 + 7$

true false

b $3 + 6 = 4 + 5$

true false

c $6 + 3 = 3 + 6$

true false

 • *AUSTRALIAN SIGNPOST MATHS 1* • ISBN 9780655708759

# 17C Object hunt

1 Draw an everyday object to match each 3D object below.

sphere

It is a ball-shaped object that has 1 curved surface. It can roll. It does not stack.

cube

It is a box-shaped object that has 6 flat, square surfaces. It can slide and it stacks easily.

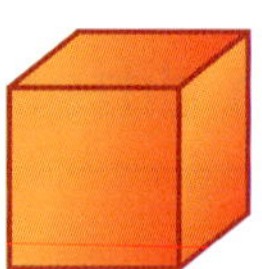

cylinder

It is a can-shaped object that has 2 flat circular surfaces and 1 curved surface. It can roll and it can slide. It stacks easily.

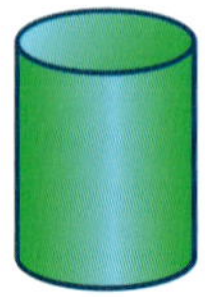

cone

It is a cone-shaped object that has 1 flat circular surface and 1 curved surface. It can roll and it can slide. It does not stack.

ACTIVITY

Use plasticine to make a model of each object.

prism

sphere

cylinder

cone

# Recognising 3D objects

1 Match each picture with a 3D object in the centre.

2 a Name two shapes that are the faces of each 3D object.

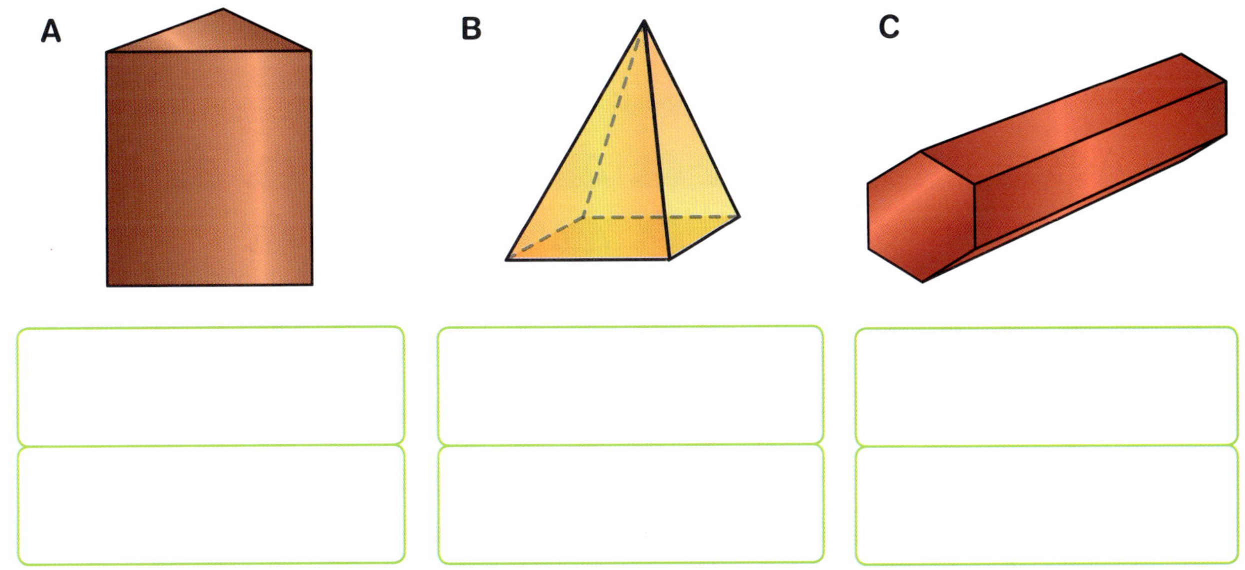


b How many faces? (A face is a flat surface with straight edges.)

A

B

C

 • *AUSTRALIAN SIGNPOST MATHS 1* • ISBN 9780655708759

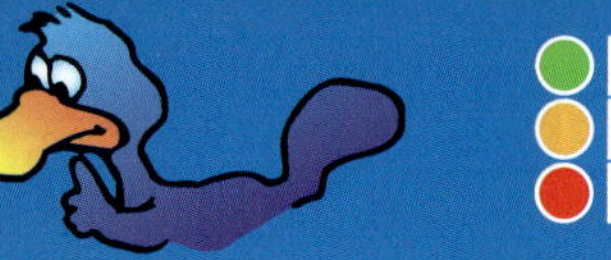

can mean the **difference between**.

You can find the difference by counting on.
There are 4 more green counters.

1 Jane has ☐ ducks.  

Alex has ☐ ducks.  

☐ has ☐ more ducks than ☐.

2 

☐ – ☐ = ☐

There are ☐ more 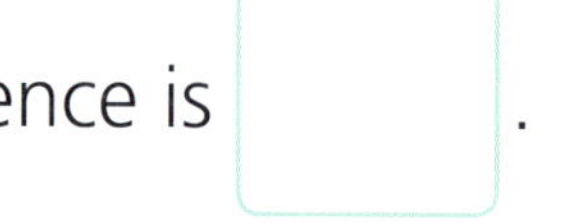 than . The difference is ☐.

3 How many more caps has Aki than Ella?

- Aki's caps: 
- Ella's caps: 

☐ – ☐ = ☐ Aki has ☐ more caps.

4 How many more 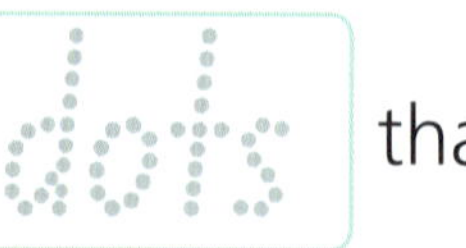 dots than crosses ?

Dots: 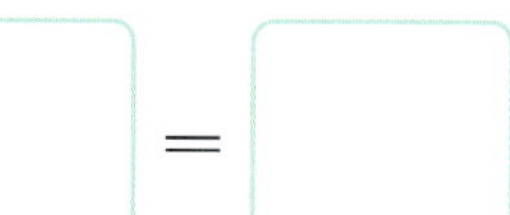

Crosses: X X X X X X X X X X X X X X

☐ – ☐ = ☐

Use ones blocks to make examples of your own.



 • *AUSTRALIAN SIGNPOST MATHS 1* • ISBN 9780655708759

# 18B Difference between groups

– also means the **difference between**.
Find the difference by counting on.
There are 3 more green counters.

1 There are ☐ more  than . ☐ – ☐ = ☐ The difference is ☐.

2 There are ☐ more  than . ☐ – ☐ = ☐ The difference is ☐.

3 There are ☐ more  than ☐. ☐ – ☐ = ☐ The difference is ☐.

4 There are ☐ more  than . ☐ – ☐ = ☐ The difference is ☐.

Make 2 lines of counters that have a difference of 4.

Write a number sentence to match. 4 = ☐ – ☐

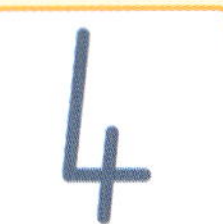

 • *AUSTRALIAN SIGNPOST MATHS 1* • ISBN 9780655708759

# 18C The pentagon and octagon

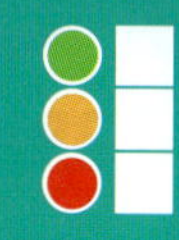

CONCEPT

A pentagon has 5 sides and 5 vertices (corners).

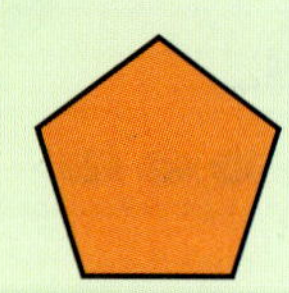

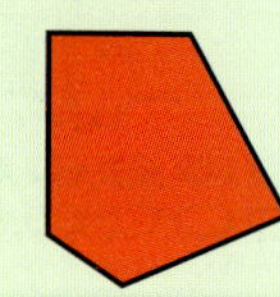

An octagon has 8 sides and 8 vertices (corners).

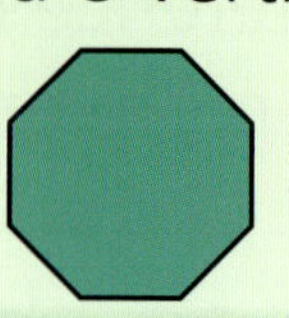

1 Trace around each shape. Write its name.

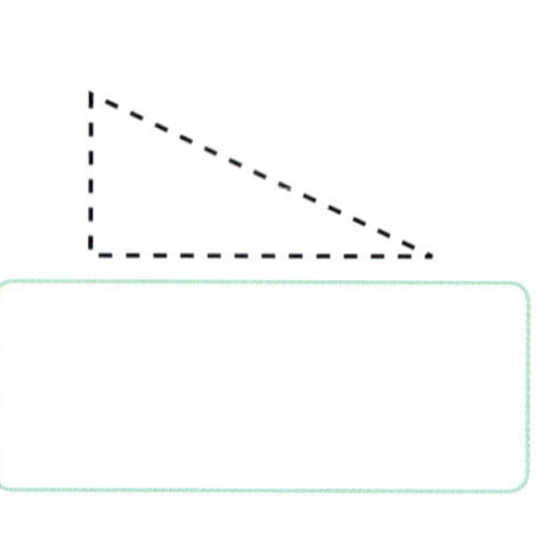

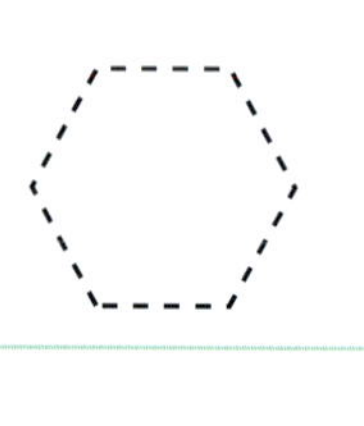

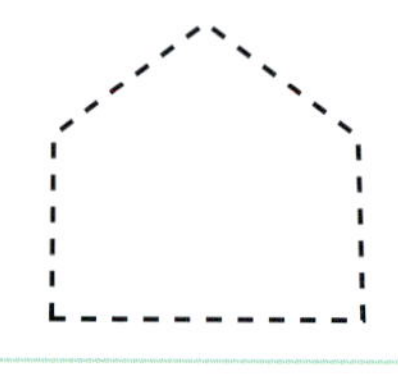

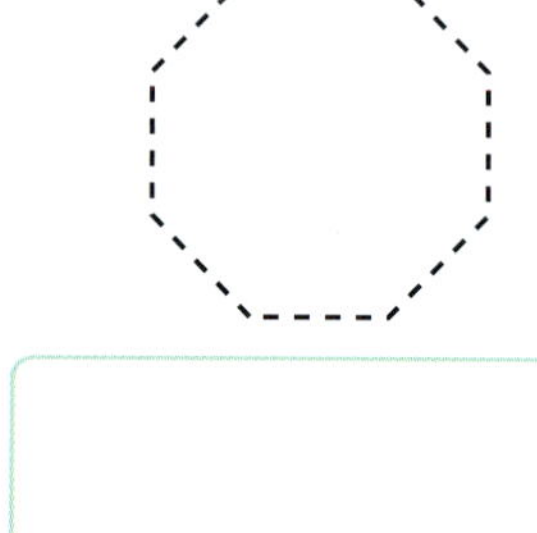

2 Colour the pentagons red and the octagons blue.

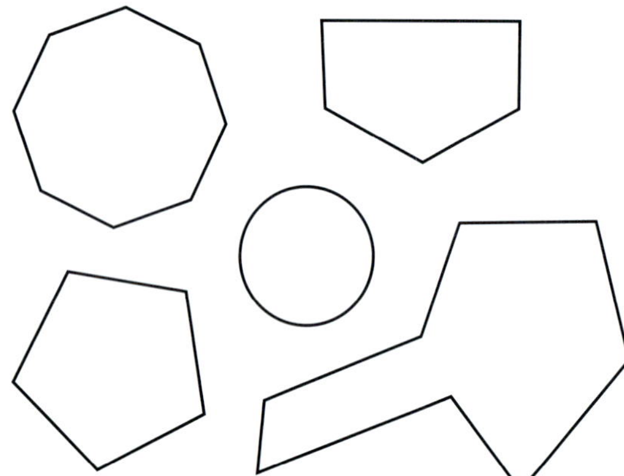

3 What am I?

a I have 5 sides and 5 vertices.

b I have 8 sides and 8 vertices.

c How many sides does a hexagon have?

4 Draw a pentagon.

5 Draw an octagon.

# 18D Analog time

quarter past 8 | half past 8 | quarter to 9

8 fifteen | 8 thirty | 8 forty-five

CONCEPT

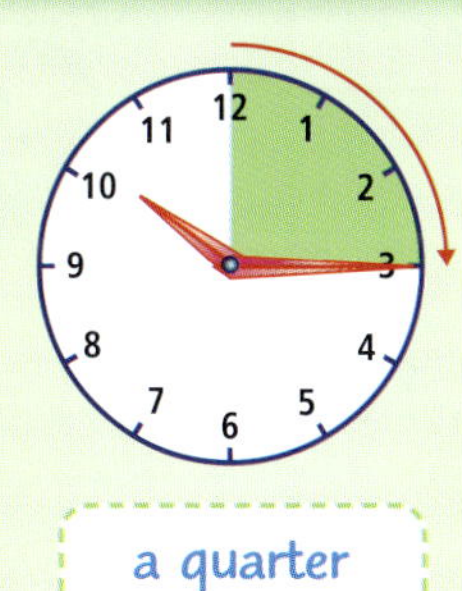


The minute hand has moved a quarter of the way around the clock.

a quarter past 10

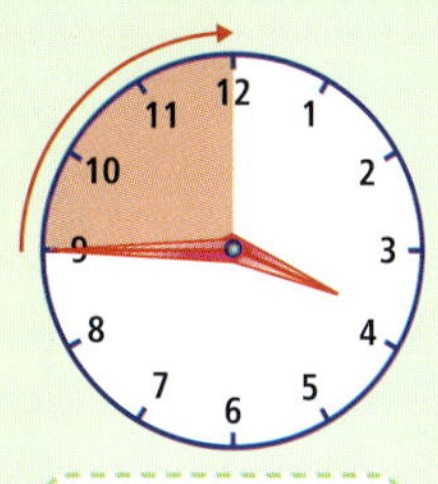


The minute hand has a quarter of the clock to go before it is 4 o'clock.

a quarter to 4

**1** Write the time shown.

a 

b 

c 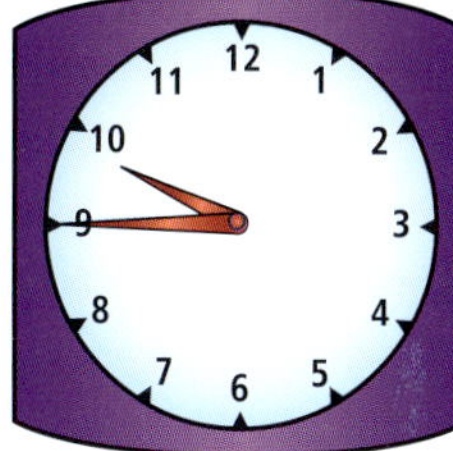

d 

e 

f 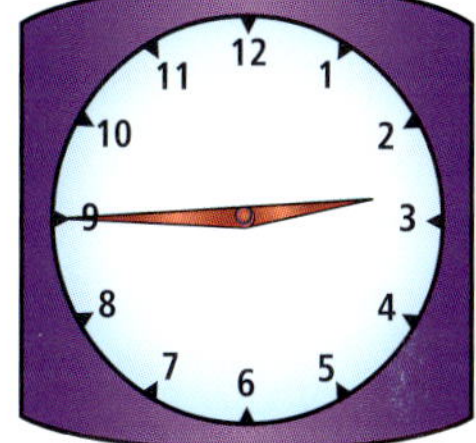

**2** Show the time.

a 
a quarter to 1

b 
a quarter past 7

c 
a quarter to 5

**3** Which number does the minute hand point to when it is:

a half past 3? 

b a quarter to 3? 

c 3 o'clock?

 • *AUSTRALIAN SIGNPOST MATHS 1* • ISBN 9780655708759

# 19A Place value

70 + 9

**1** Write the number shown by each numeral expander.

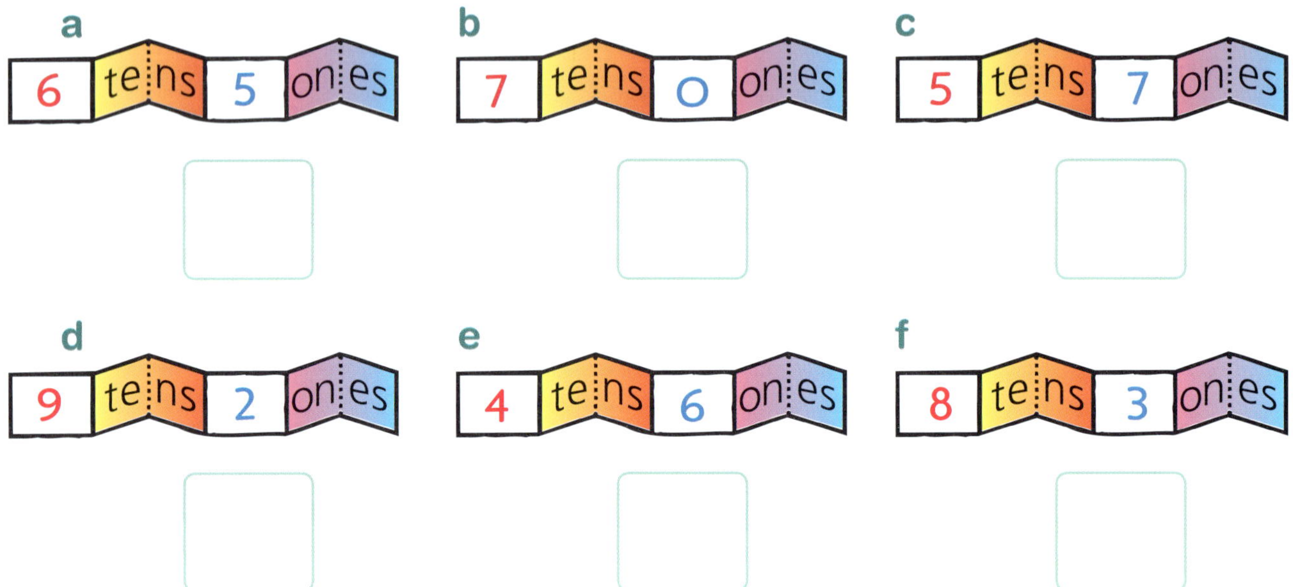


**2** Complete:

a 78 = ☐ tens ☐ ones  b 80 = ☐ tens ☐ ones

c 54 = ☐ tens ☐ ones  d 61 = ☐ tens ☐ one

**3** Circle the smaller number.

a 91 or 89  b 62 or 67  c 49 or 54

FUN SPOT

Three number cards are turned over. One student uses two of these to write a secret number. The other student tries to guess the secret number.

Start

1 Write the number shown by each numeral expander.

a 

b 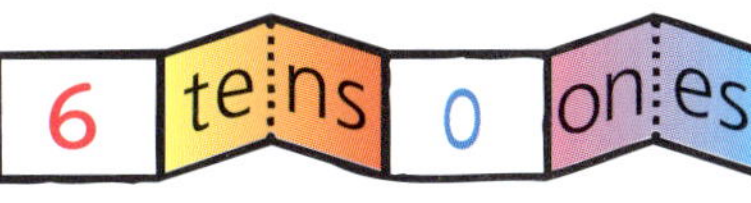


c 

d 

2 Expand the numbers.

a 90 = ☐ tens ☐ ones

b 73 = ☐ tens ☐ ones

c 112 = ☐ tens ☐ ones

3 Write the numeral.

a one hundred and five ☐

b eighty-three ☐

c one hundred and fifteen ☐

d one hundred ☐

Every 10th bead around this page is coloured, starting at the top.
Count the beads. Colour the beads at these numbers:

a 16 b 35 c 48 d 67 e 88 f 99 g 110

For each number say how many tens and how many ones.

120 110 100

 *AUSTRALIAN SIGNPOST MATHS 1* • ISBN 9780655708759

# Place value

1. Complete each numeral expander and write the number.

a, b, c

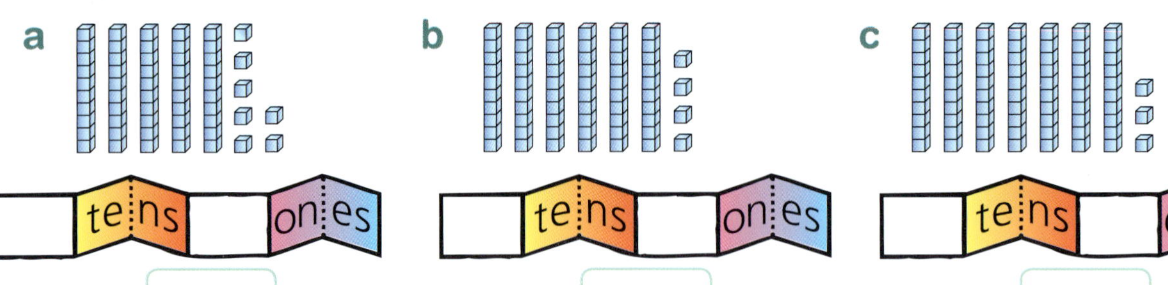


d, e, f

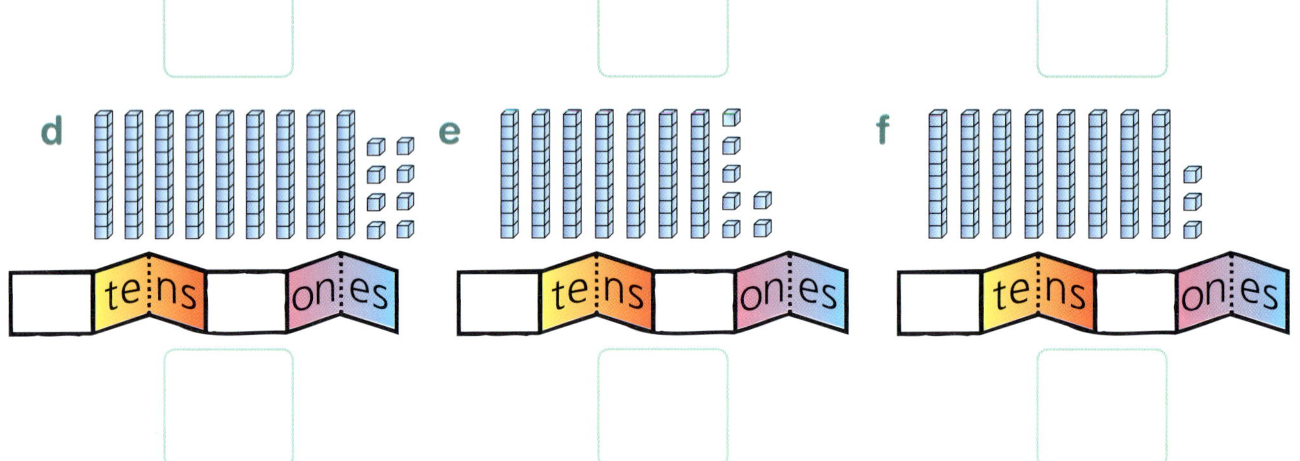


2. Write the numeral.

a fifty-one

b thirty-eight

c eighty-two

d forty-seven

e ninety-four

f fourteen

We write 24.

twenty-four

3. Write the numbers before (one less than) and after (one more than).

a

| before | | after |
|---|---|---|
| | 78 | |
| | 35 | |

b

| before | | after |
|---|---|---|
| | 80 | |
| | 56 | |


 • *AUSTRALIAN SIGNPOST MATHS 1* • ISBN 9780655708759

# 19D Finding the nearest ten

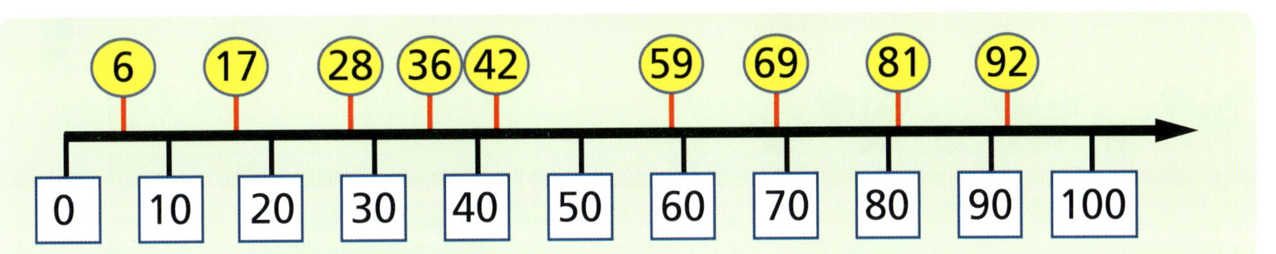

1 Use the number line above to write the nearest ten to the number:

a 6 ☐ b 17 ☐ c 28 ☐

d 36 ☐ e 42 ☐ f 59 ☐

g 69 ☐ h 81 ☐ i 92 ☐

2

Use this number line to write the nearest ten to the number:

a 51 ☐ b 57 ☐ c 59 ☐

d 54 ☐ e 52 ☐ f 56 ☐

3 Use the beads around the page to write the nearest ten to the number:

a 58 ☐ b 23 ☐ c 72 ☐

d 86 ☐ e 44 ☐ f 97 ☐

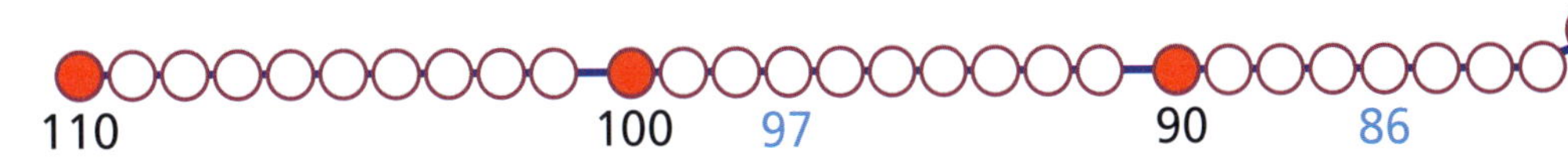

 • *AUSTRALIAN SIGNPOST MATHS 1* • ISBN 9780655708759

# Subtraction by counting on

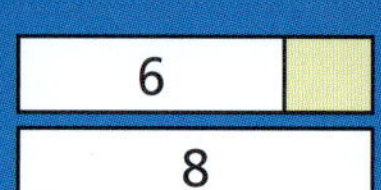

CONCEPT

How many more make 8?

- I count on from 6 to make 8.
- I need 2 more to make 8.

6 + ☐ = 8

8 – 6 = ☐

**1** Draw the missing objects and complete.

**a**

How many more to make 8?

6 + ☐ = 8 | 8 – 6 = ☐

**b**

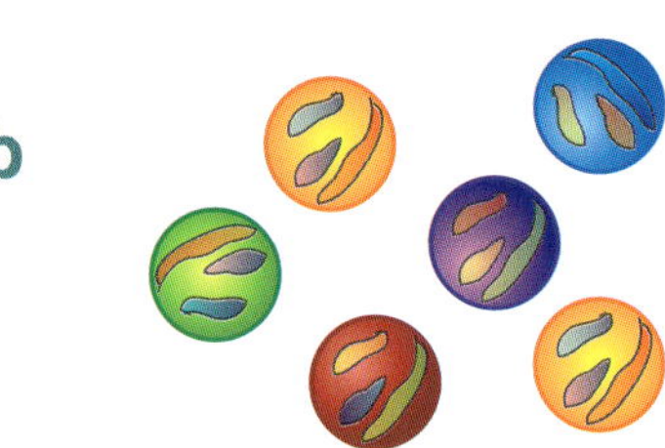

How many more to make 7?

6 + ☐ = 7 | 7 – 6 = ☐

**c**

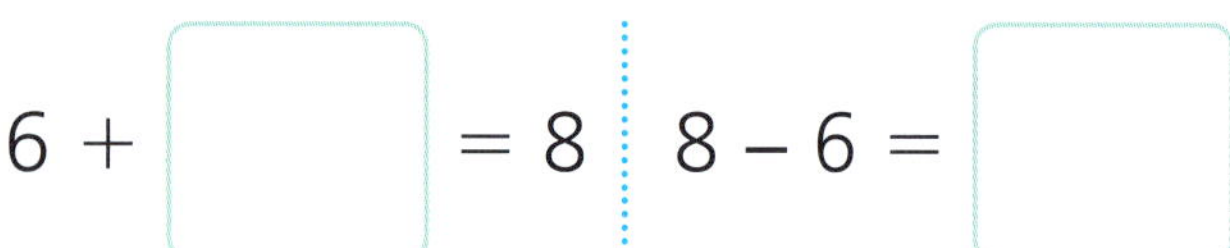

How many more to make 9?

6 + ☐ = 9 | 9 – 6 = ☐

**d**

How many more to make 10?

7 + ☐ = 10 | 10 – 7 = ☐

**e**

How many more to make 8?

5 + ☐ = 8 | 8 – 5 = ☐

**f**

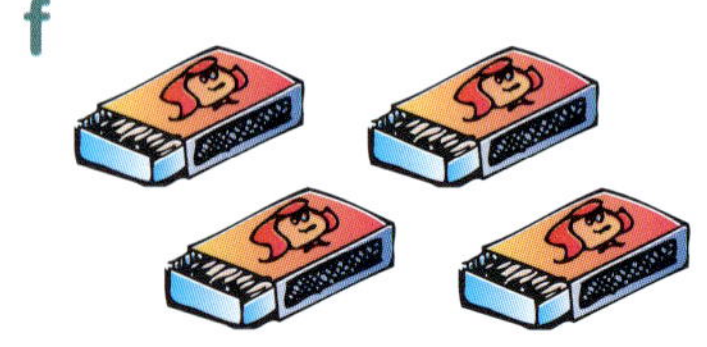

How many more to make 7?

4 + ☐ = 7 | 7 – 4 = ☐

 • *AUSTRALIAN SIGNPOST MATHS 1* • ISBN 9780655708759

# 20B Finding the difference

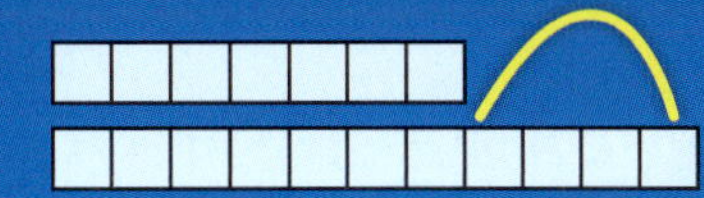

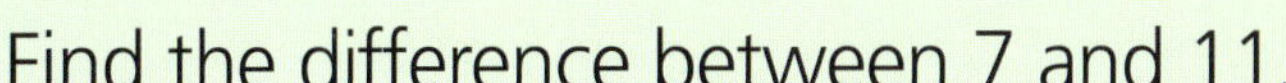

Find the difference between 7 and 11.

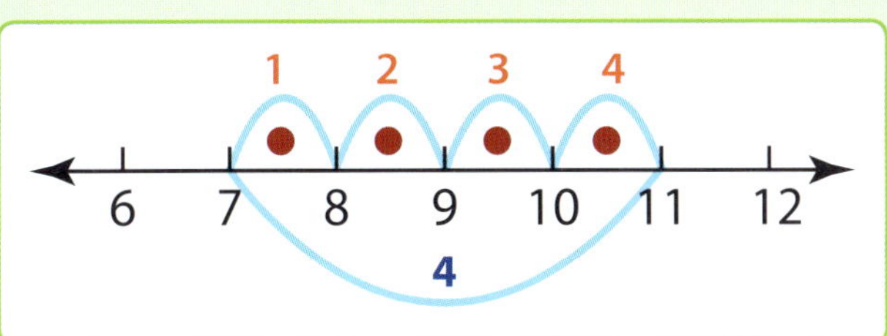

- I need 4 more to make 11.

1. Find the difference between:

**a** 14 and 8

**b** 16 and 19

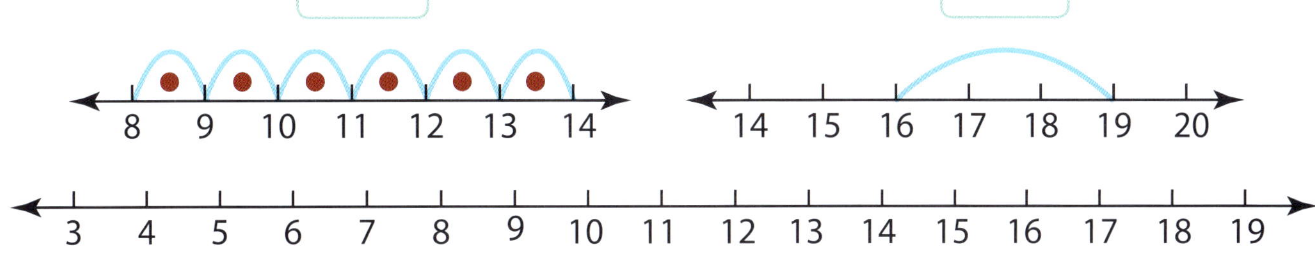


2. Use the number line to find the difference between:

**a** 8 and 3 

**b** 5 and 11 

**c** 8 and 12 

**d** 13 and 9 

**e** 18 and 12 

**f** 17 and 14 

**g** 19 and 17 

**h** 16 and 11 

**i** 15 and 9 

**j** 14 and 17 

**k** 18 and 13 

**l** 14 and 19

**m** 9 and 16 

**n** 15 and 11 

**o** 12 and 16

| before | | after |
|---|---|---|
| 27 | 28 | 29 |

On the number chart:

- Count by **ones** to 100.
- Count by **twos** to 50.
- Count by **fives** to 100.
- Count by **tens** to 100.

Start at any number on the chart and count backwards or forwards by ones.

| 1 | 2 | 3 | 4 | 5 | 6 | 7 | 8 | 9 | 10 |
|---|---|---|---|---|---|---|---|---|---|
| 11 | 12 | 13 | 14 | 15 | 16 | 17 | 18 | 19 | 20 |
| 21 | 22 | 23 | 24 | 25 | 26 | 27 | 28 | 29 | 30 |
| 31 | 32 | 33 | 34 | 35 | 36 | 37 | 38 | 39 | 40 |
| 41 | 42 | 43 | 44 | 45 | 46 | 47 | 48 | 49 | 50 |
| 51 | 52 | 53 | 54 | 55 | 56 | 57 | 58 | 59 | 60 |
| 61 | 62 | 63 | 64 | 65 | 66 | 67 | 68 | 69 | 70 |
| 71 | 72 | 73 | 74 | 75 | 76 | 77 | 78 | 79 | 80 |
| 81 | 82 | 83 | 84 | 85 | 86 | 87 | 88 | 89 | 90 |
| 91 | 92 | 93 | 94 | 95 | 96 | 97 | 98 | 99 | 100 |

1 Use the number chart above to locate the nearest ten to each number.

**a** 43 

**b** 61 

**c** 39 

**d** 86 

**e** 70 

**f** 68 

**g** 34 

**h** 57 

**i** 72 

2 Write the numbers before (one less than) and after (one more than).

**a**

| before | | after |
|---|---|---|
| | 69 | |
| | 100 | |

**b**

| before | | after |
|---|---|---|
| | 83 | |
| | 55 | |

3 Write the numbers given in Question 1 parts **a** to **f** in order, smallest to largest.

Three dimensional

Two dimensional

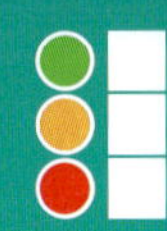

1 Colour the pictures that match the objects on the left. Discuss the choices.

| | | |
|---|---|---|
| Sphere  | **Ball-shaped object**<br>A *sphere* has 1 curved surface.<br>It can roll. | 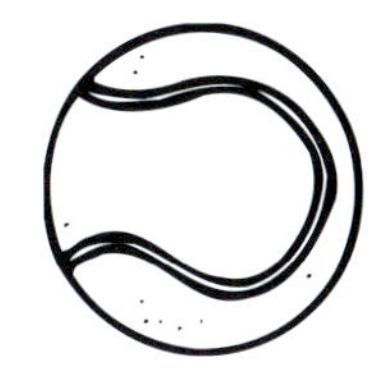  |
| Cylinder 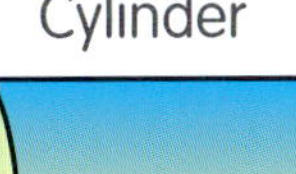 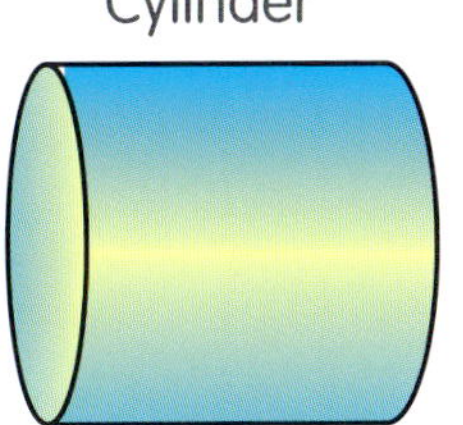 | **Can-shaped object**<br>A *cylinder* has 1 curved surface and 2 flat surfaces.<br>It can roll and slide. | 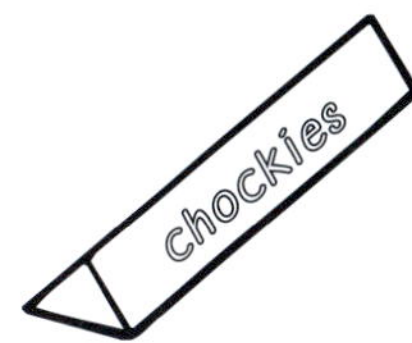  |
| Cube 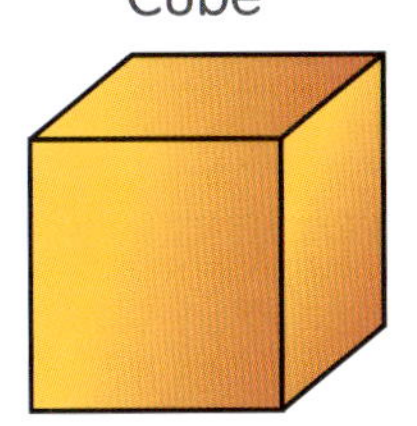 | **Box-shaped object**<br>A *cube* has 6 flat surfaces.<br>It can slide. All 6 surfaces are squares. |   |
| Cone 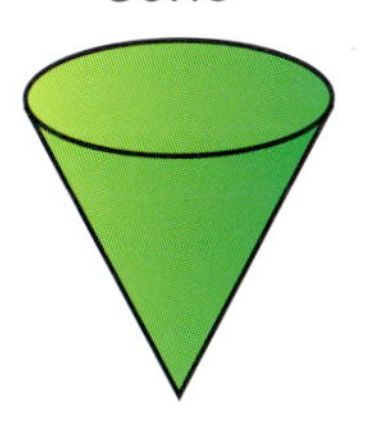 | **Cone-shaped object**<br>A *cone* has 1 curved surface and 1 flat surface.<br>It can roll and slide. | 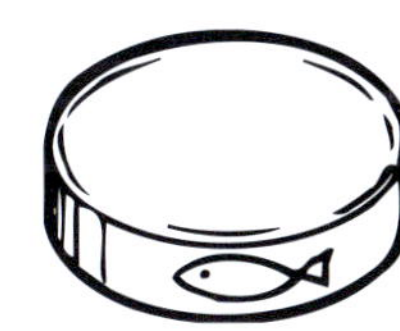  |
| Prism 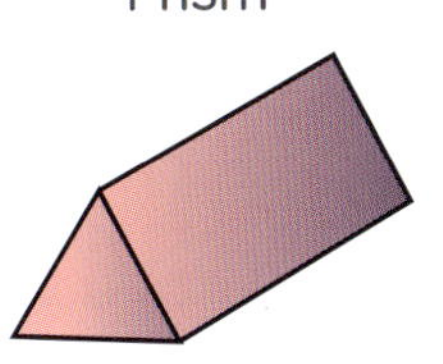 | **Box-shaped object**<br>A *prism* has flat surfaces.<br>It has 2 identical ends.<br>The other surfaces are rectangles. It can slide. |  |
| Rectangular prism 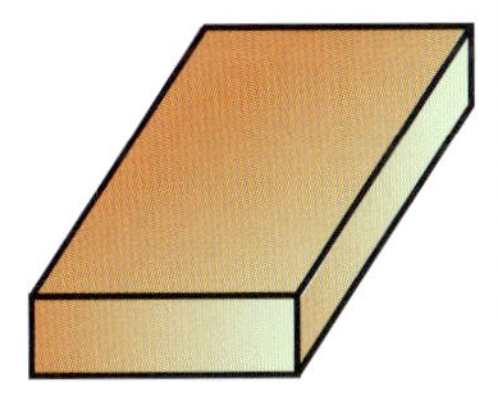 | **Box-shaped object**<br>A *rectangular prism* is a prism that has rectangular ends.<br>All surfaces are rectangles. |  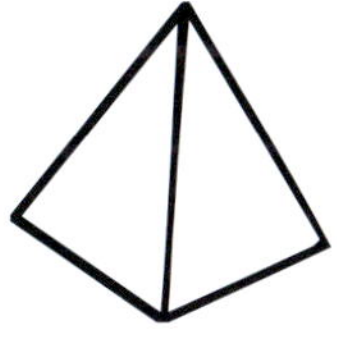 |

 ISBN 9780655708759

# 21A Equal groups

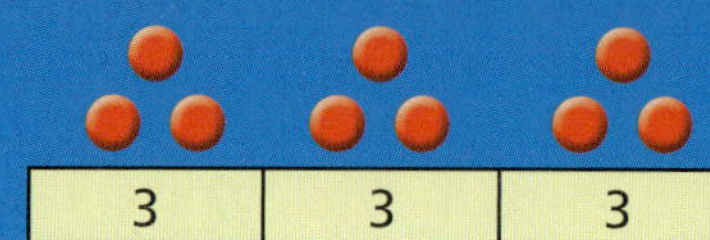

5 + 5 + 5

3 groups of 5 = 15

| 5 | 5 | 5 |
|---|---|---|
| 15 | | |

**1** a

☐ + ☐

☐ groups of ☐ = ☐

b

☐ + ☐ + ☐

☐ groups of ☐ = ☐

c

| 3 | | | |
|---|---|---|---|

☐ + ☐ + ☐ + ☐

☐ groups of ☐ = ☐

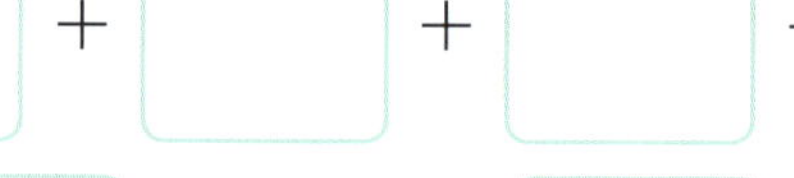

d

| 6 | | |
|---|---|---|

☐ + ☐ + ☐

☐ groups of ☐ = ☐

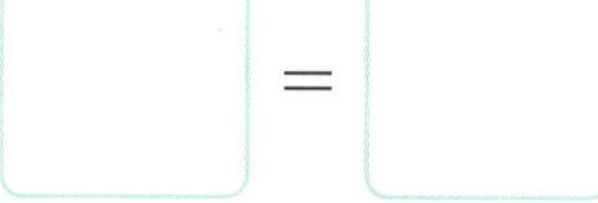

e 4 groups of 2 trees

☐ + ☐ + ☐ + ☐

☐ groups of ☐ = ☐

f 3 groups of 4 worms

☐ + ☐ + ☐

☐ groups of ☐ = ☐



ISBN 9780655708759

Number

# 21B Using groups

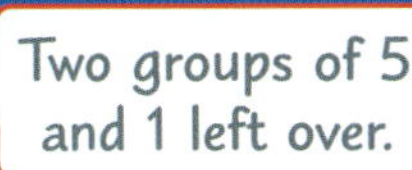

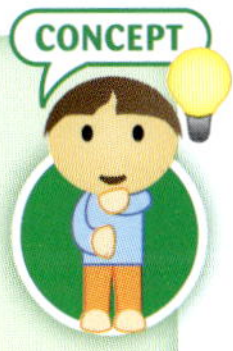

CONCEPT

Use counters to model this problem.

12 apples. Put 4 in each box.
How many boxes do we need?

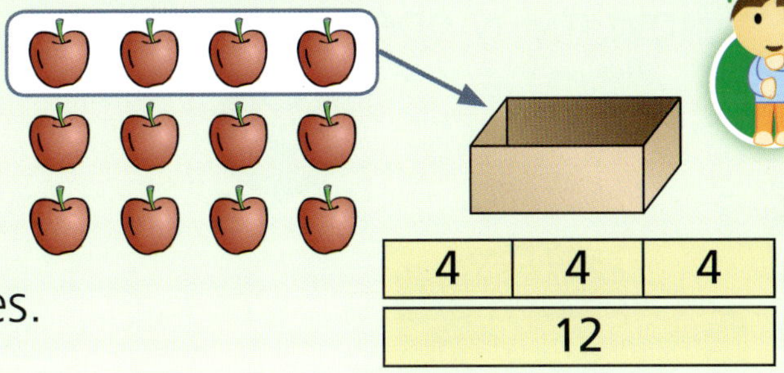

| 4 | 4 | 4 |
|---|---|---|
| 12 | | |

Answer: We would need ☐ boxes.

**1** Draw circles to show these groups or rows.

**a** groups of 3 frogs

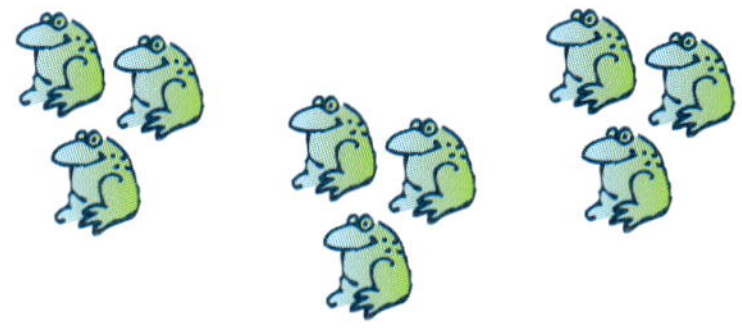

How many frogs? ☐ How many groups of 3? ☐

**b** groups of 4 jugs

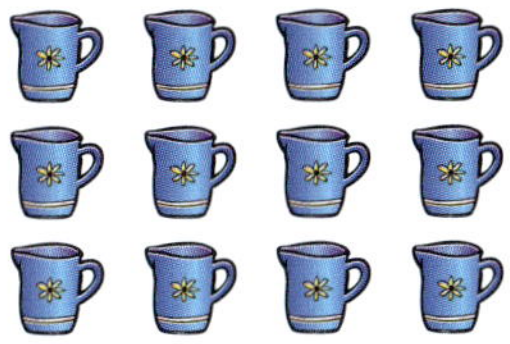

How many jugs? ☐ How many groups of 4? ☐

**c** groups of 8 fish

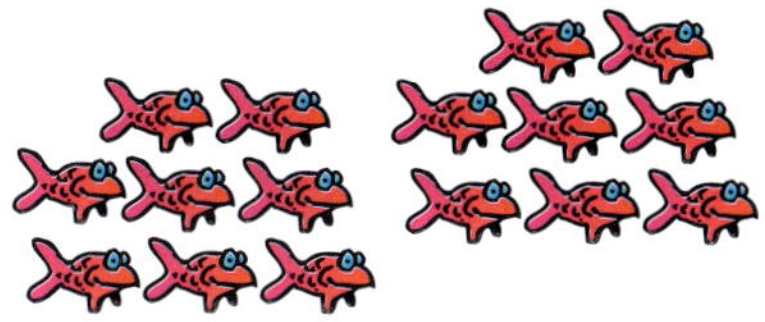

How many fish? ☐ How many groups of 8? ☐

**d**

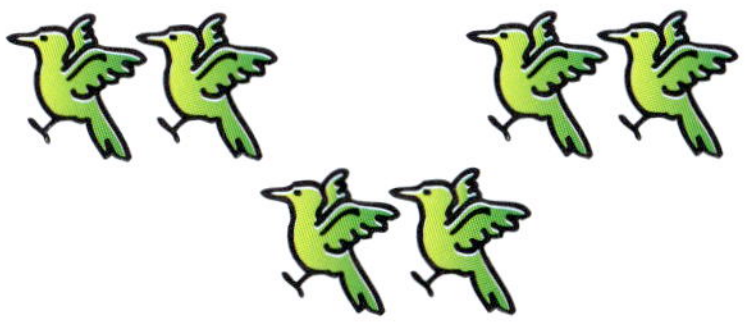

How many birds? ☐ How many groups of 2? ☐

**e**

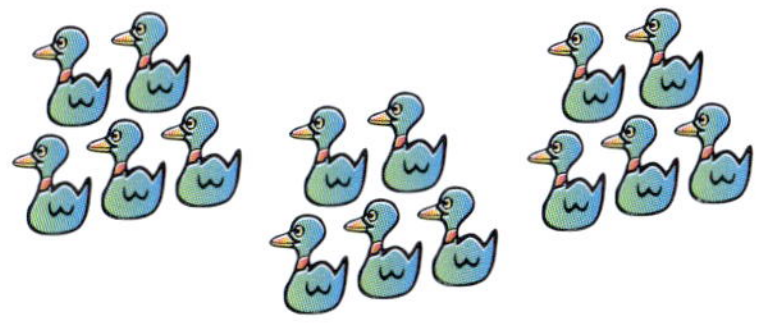

How many ducks? ☐ How many groups of 5? ☐

**f**

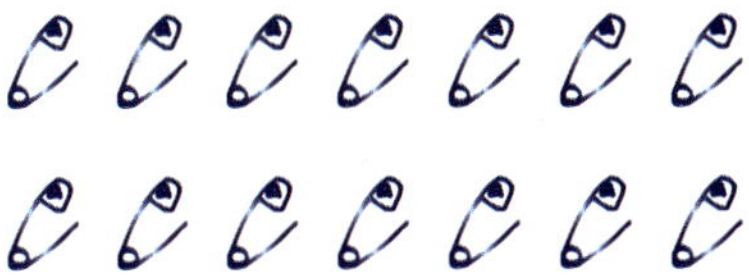

How many pins? ☐ How many groups of 7? ☐

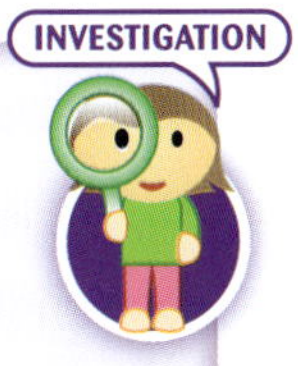

INVESTIGATION

Use 20 counters. How many students can be given:

**a** 3 counters? ☐ students with ☐ counters left over.

**b** 6 counters? ☐ students with ☐ counters left over.

# 21C Capacity and volume

Volume is how much space an object takes up.

INVESTIGATION

Capacity is how much a container can hold.

1 How many does each hold?

a Use blocks.

Fitwell Shoes — Guess | Check

Lunch — Guess | Check

b Use marbles.

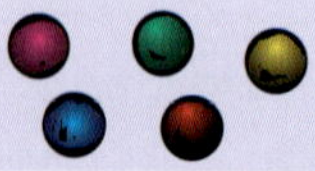

YOGHURT — Guess | Check

Guess | Check

c Use place-value ones blocks.

Guess | Check

Guess | Check

d Use place-value tens blocks.

CHAMP dog food — Guess | Check

TOOTHPASTE SMILEY — Guess | Check

2 In each part of Question 1, circle the object that has the larger capacity. Which unit is easiest to use?

3 If there are gaps when packing, would this make it hard to compare capacities?

# Capacity and volume

No gaps is better.
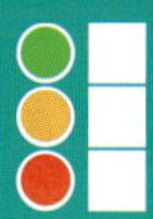

❶ Record the number of blocks in containers A, B and C.

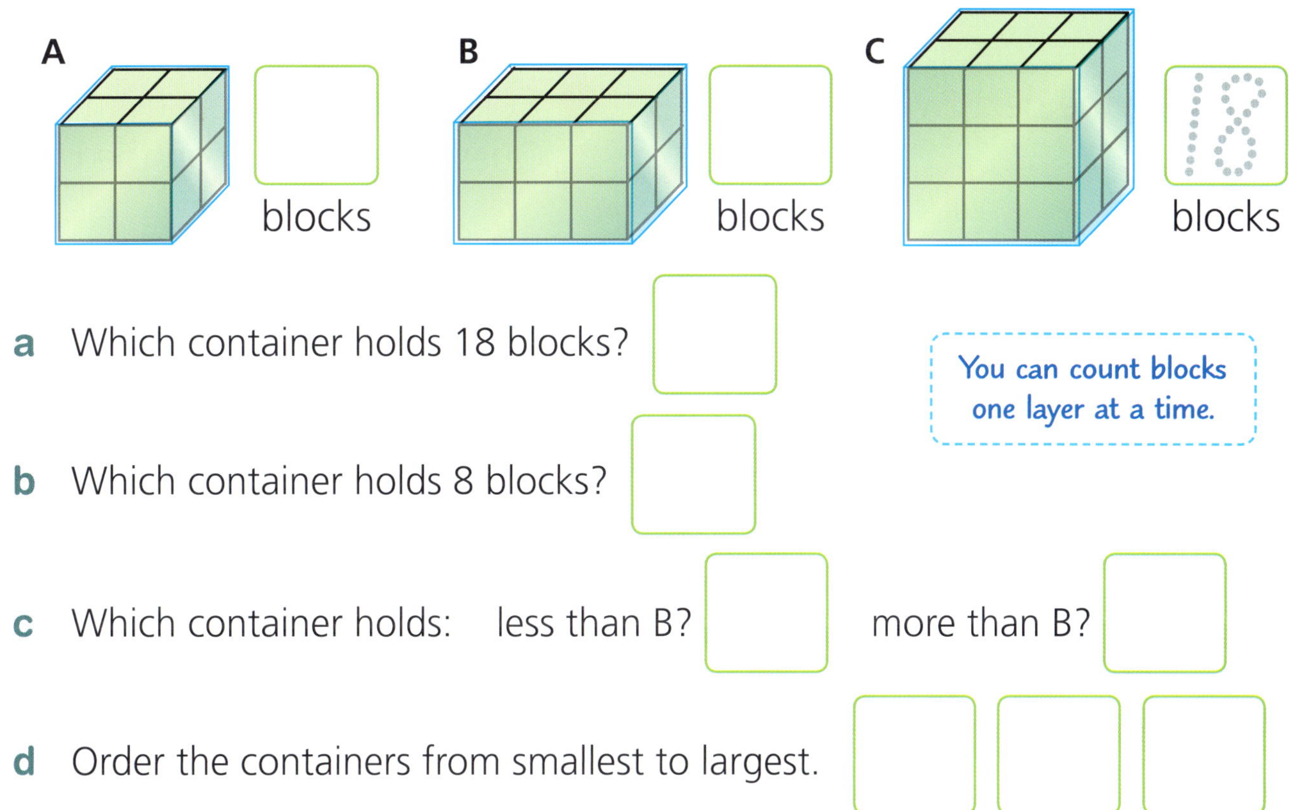


**a** Which container holds 18 blocks? ☐

**b** Which container holds 8 blocks? ☐

**c** Which container holds: less than B? ☐ more than B? ☐

**d** Order the containers from smallest to largest. ☐ ☐ ☐

ACTIVITY

Pack blocks into two boxes. Record the number of blocks needed to fill each box.

| Container | Guess | Volume | Holds less or more? |
|---|---|---|---|
| 1 | ☐ blocks | ☐ blocks | |
| 2 | ☐ blocks | ☐ blocks | |

The number between 27 and 29 is 28.

**1** Write the missing numbers.

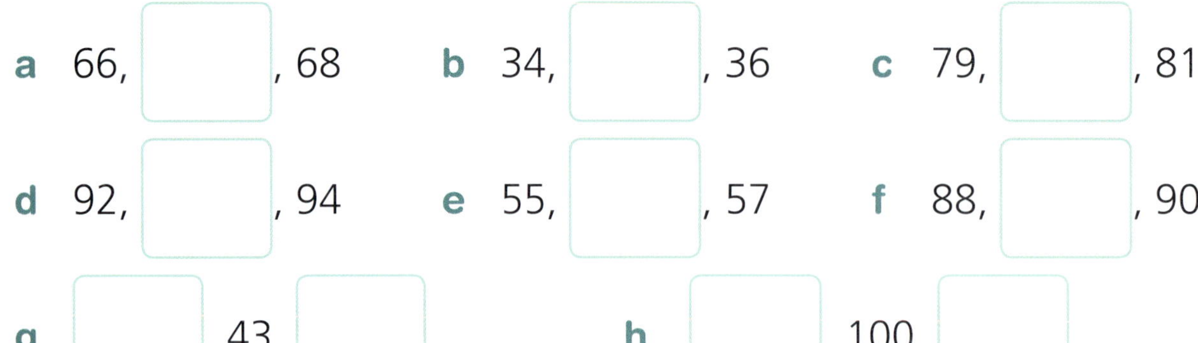

a 66, ☐, 68    b 34, ☐, 36    c 79, ☐, 81

d 92, ☐, 94    e 55, ☐, 57    f 88, ☐, 90

g ☐, 43, ☐    h ☐, 100, ☐

**2** Write the next two numbers.

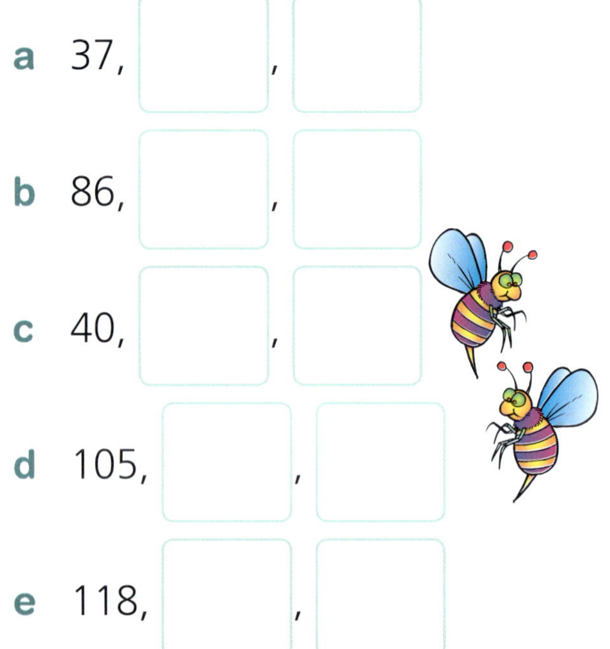

a 37, ☐, ☐

b 86, ☐, ☐

c 40, ☐, ☐

d 105, ☐, ☐

e 118, ☐, ☐

Practise counting to 120.

**3** Colour your answers from Questions 1 and 2 on the chart.

| 1 | 2 | 3 | 4 | 5 | 6 | 7 | 8 | 9 | 10 |
|---|---|---|---|---|---|---|---|---|---|
| 11 | 12 | 13 | 14 | 15 | 16 | 17 | 18 | 19 | 20 |
| 21 | 22 | 23 | 24 | 25 | 26 | 27 | 28 | 29 | 30 |
| 31 | 32 | 33 | 34 | 35 | 36 | 37 | 38 | 39 | 40 |
| 41 | 42 | 43 | 44 | 45 | 46 | 47 | 48 | 49 | 50 |
| 51 | 52 | 53 | 54 | 55 | 56 | 57 | 58 | 59 | 60 |
| 61 | 62 | 63 | 64 | 65 | 66 | 67 | 68 | 69 | 70 |
| 71 | 72 | 73 | 74 | 75 | 76 | 77 | 78 | 79 | 80 |
| 81 | 82 | 83 | 84 | 85 | 86 | 87 | 88 | 89 | 90 |
| 91 | 92 | 93 | 94 | 95 | 96 | 97 | 98 | 99 | 100 |
| 101 | 102 | 103 | 104 | 105 | 106 | 107 | 108 | 109 | 110 |
| 111 | 112 | 113 | 114 | 115 | 116 | 117 | 118 | 119 | 120 |

**4** Count by tens to join the dots.

a

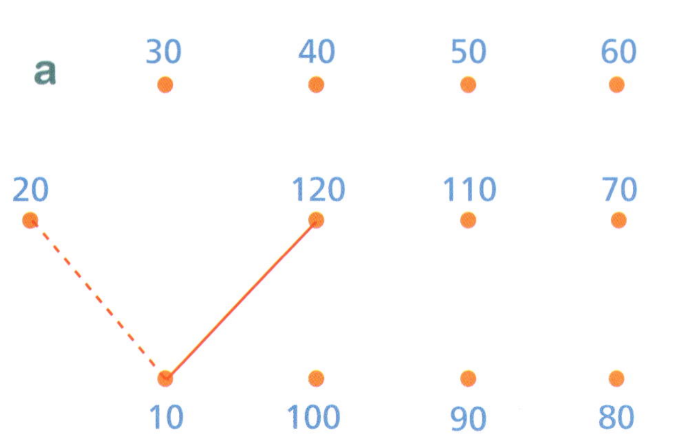


b

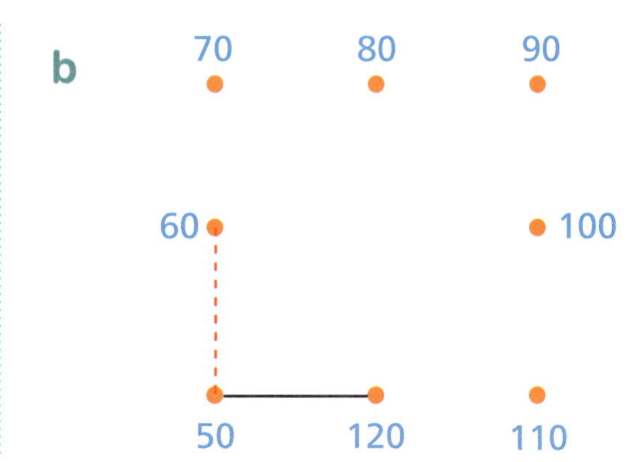




 • *AUSTRALIAN SIGNPOST MATHS 1* • ISBN 9780655708759

# 22B Skip counting patterns

Skip counting by 2 — 2, 4, 6, 8, 10, ...

Skip counting by 5 — 5, 10, 15, 20, 25, ...

Skip counting by 10 — 10, 20, 30, 40, 50, ...

20, 18, 16, 14 ... counting by 2 backwards

25, 20, 15, 10 ... counting by 5 backwards

1. Do these patterns count by 2, 5 or 10?

   a 8, 10, 12, 14, ... ☐

   b 20, 30, 40, 50, ... ☐

   c 5, 10, 15, 20, ... ☐

   d 12, 14, 16, 18, ... ☐

2. Write the missing numbers in each skip counting pattern.

   a 2, 4, 6, 8, 10, 12, ☐, ☐, ☐, 20

   b 10, 20, 30, 40, 50, ☐, ☐, ☐, 90, 100

   c 5, 10, 15, 20, 25, ☐, ☐, ☐, 45, 50

   d 90, 80, 70, 60, 50, ☐, ☐, ☐, 10

   e 50, 45, 40, 35, 30, ☐, ☐, ☐, 10

   How did you continue the pattern in part **a**? ☐

   How did you continue the pattern in part **b**? ☐

# 22C Area

Area is the part inside a shape.

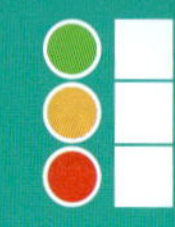

Area is the amount of surface.

The blue shape has more area.
The green square has the same area as the red square.

The $20 takes up more space.

A $20 note has more area than a $5 note.

My hand is smaller than the pencil case.

**1** Circle the larger area in each part.

**a**

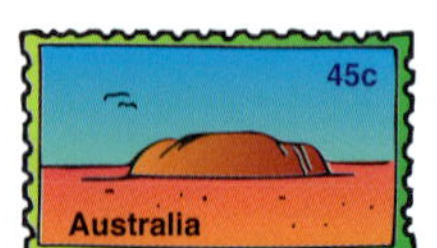


**b**

**2** Write the smallest and the largest top surface area in each group.

**3** Circle the object that has the smaller top area.

**a** this page or your hand

**b** a matchbox or an envelope

**c** a tea towel or a table

**d** a newspaper or a desk

**e** art paper or a book

**f** a newspaper or a plastic lid

Compare the areas of shapes in your room.
Name an object that has a small top area.

# 22D Comparison of areas

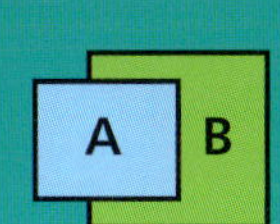

Area is the measure of the amount of surface.

The red square has more area than the green square.

1 Write the letter or colour of the shape with the larger area.

a A, B

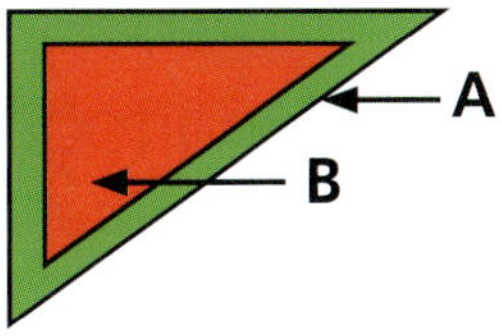

b 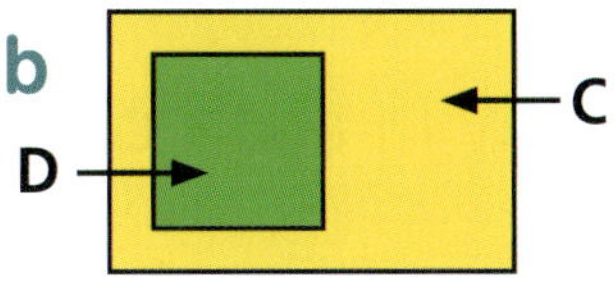 C, 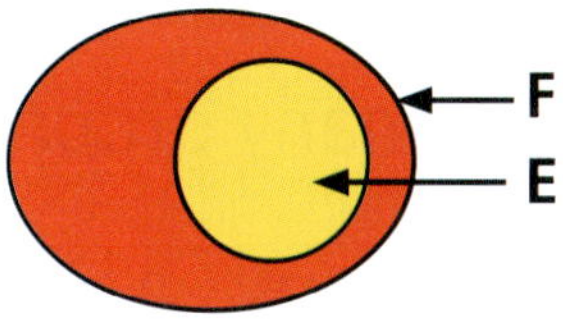 D

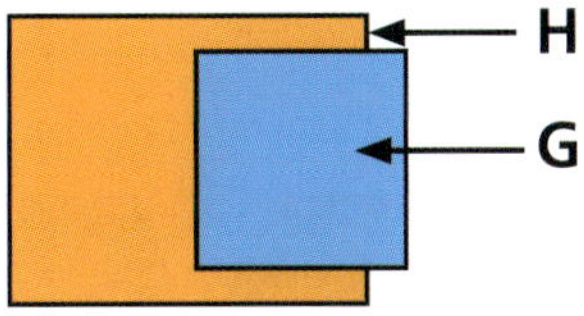

c F, E

d H, G

e J, K

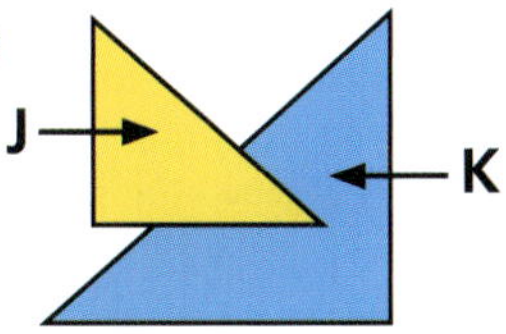

f L, M

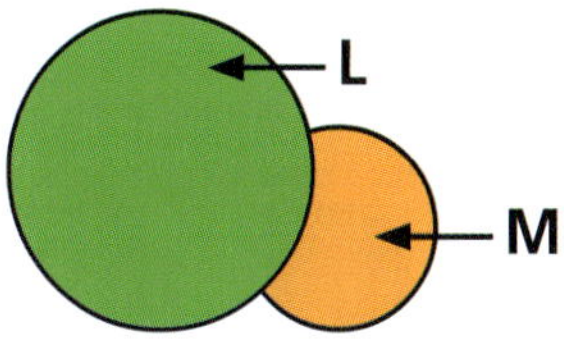

g N, P

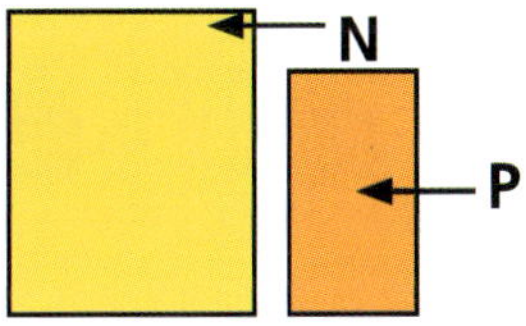

h R, Q

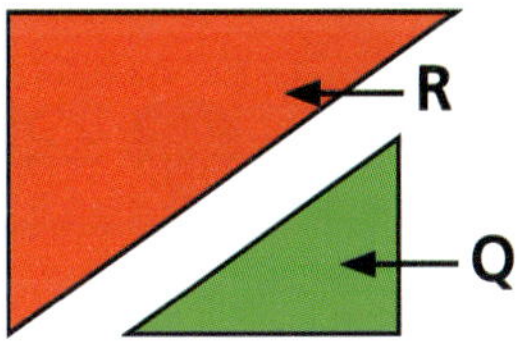

i S, T

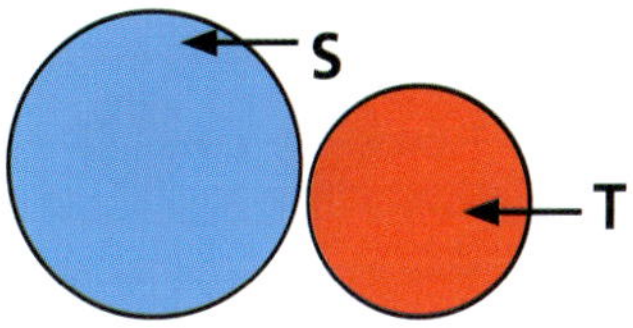

2 Use the letters in Question 1 to compare areas.

Choose three flat objects.

By placing one object on top of another, order their top areas from smallest to largest.

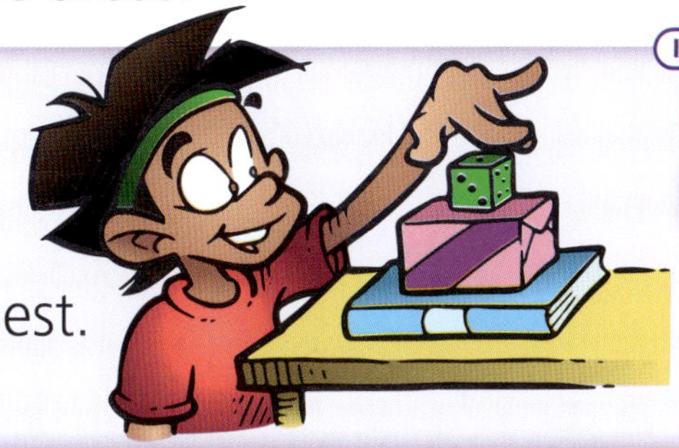

# 23A Equal groups

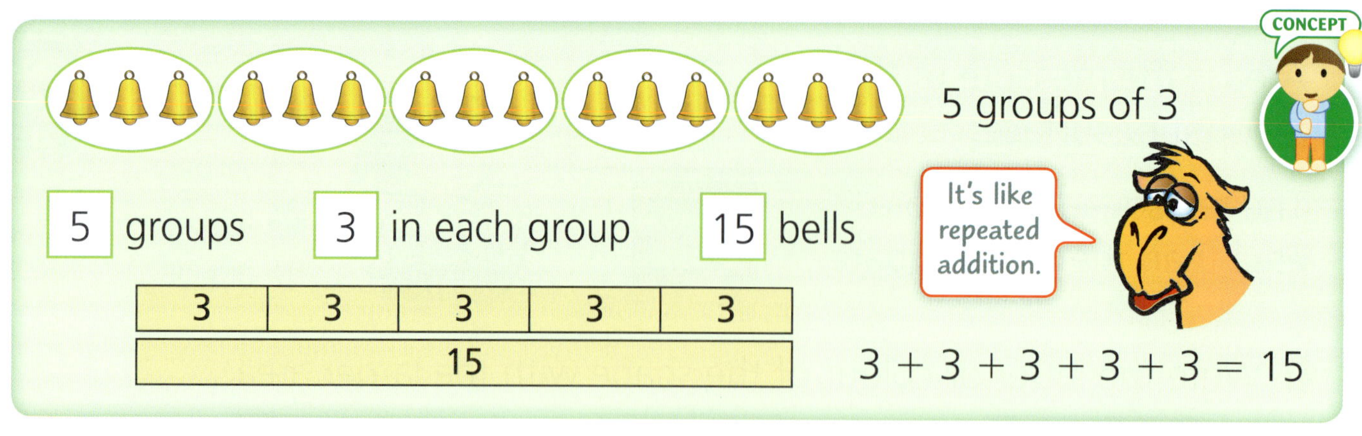


1 How many groups? How many in each group? How many altogether?

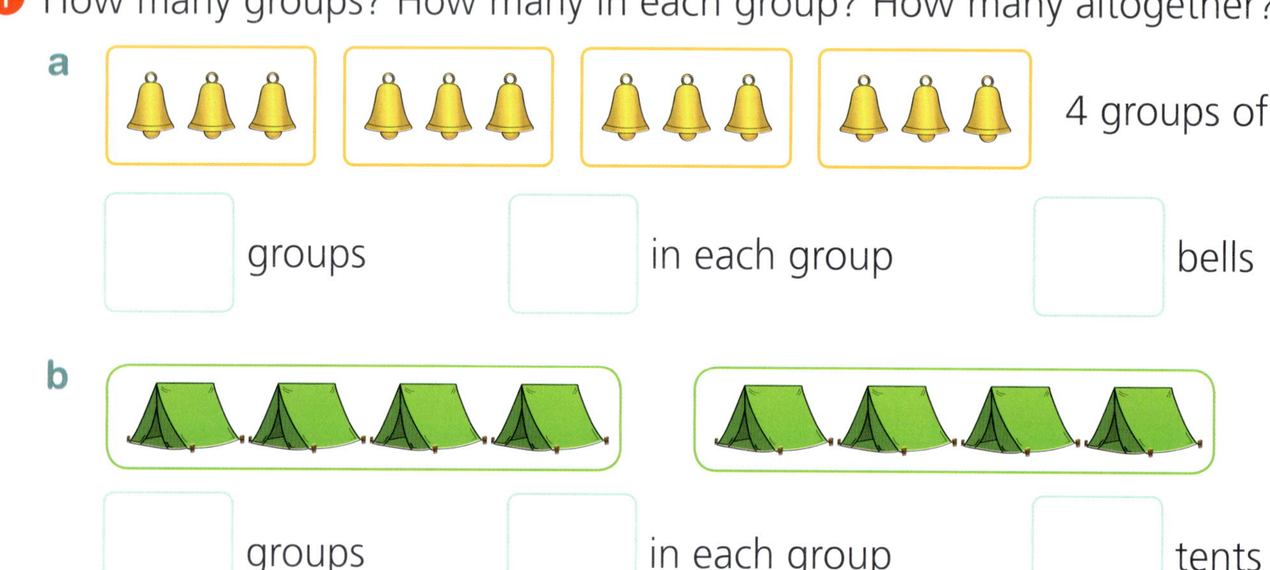

a 4 groups of 3

☐ groups ☐ in each group ☐ bells

b

☐ groups ☐ in each group ☐ tents

c

☐ groups ☐ in each group ☐ bats

d

☐ groups ☐ in each group ☐ balls

2 a 5 groups of 2 = ☐   b 2 groups of 5 = ☐

# 23B Using groups

four groups of 2

4 groups of 5 is the same as 20.

Skip counting: 5, 10, 15, 20 … or 5 + 5 + 5 + 5 = 20

1 Use skip counting to find the total number of objects in:

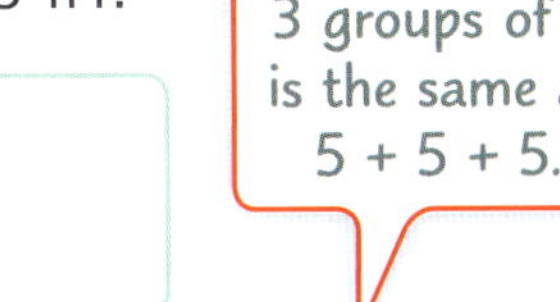

3 groups of 5 is the same as 5 + 5 + 5.

a 3 groups of 5 

b 5 groups of 5 

c 6 groups of 5 

d 7 groups of 5

2 Use counters to make these groups. Skip count to find the total.

a 3 groups of 2

b 6 groups of 2

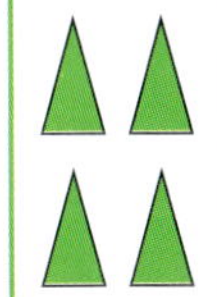

c 2 groups of 10

d 5 groups of 10

e 2 groups of 4 

f 4 groups of 2

2 groups of 4

3 a

How many groups?

How many in each group?

How many altogether?

b

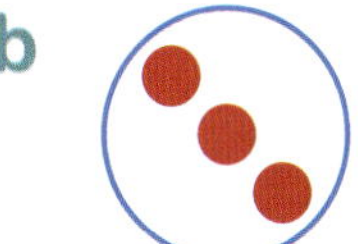
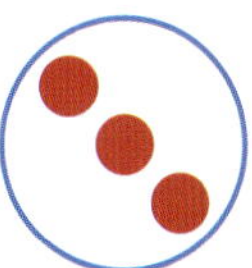
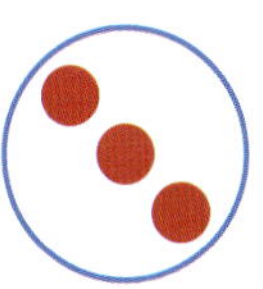

How many groups?

How many in each group?

How many altogether?

 • *AUSTRALIAN SIGNPOST MATHS 1* • ISBN 9780655708759

# 23C Angles

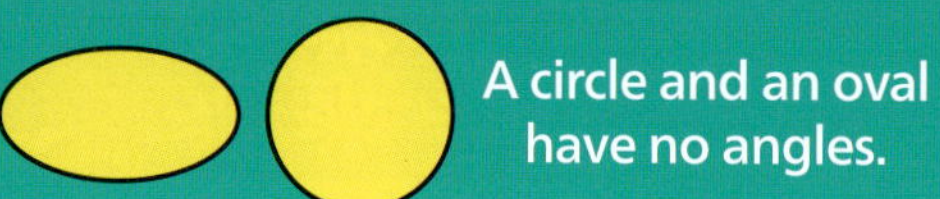


This is an angle.

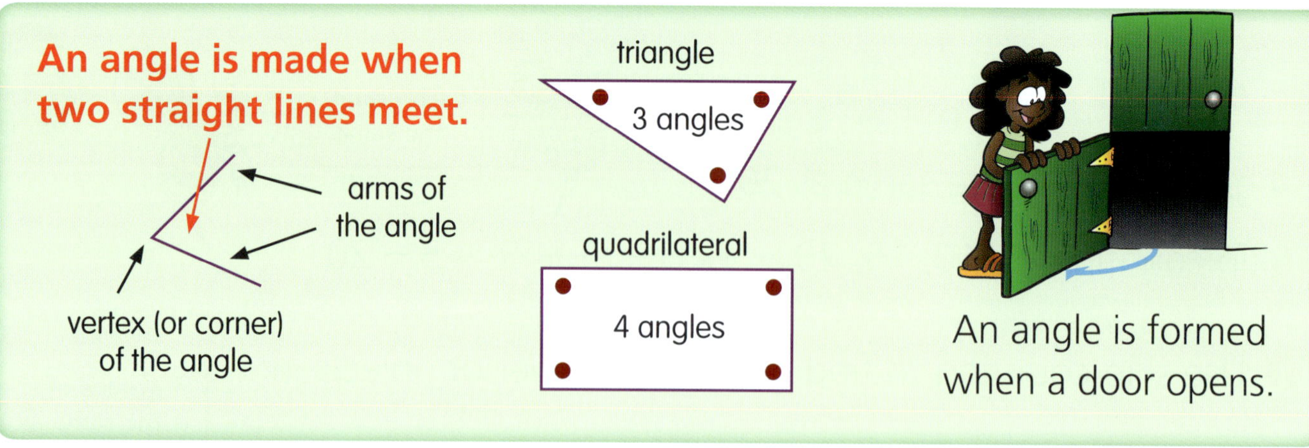


1 Trace the angles made in these pictures.

a 

b 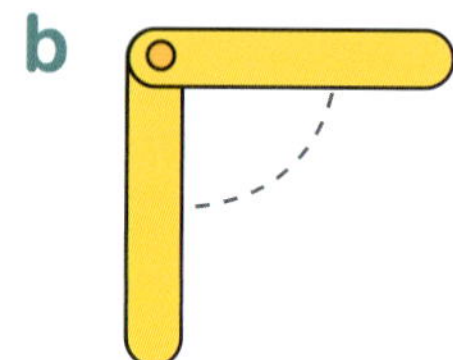

c 

2 How many angles has each shape?

a 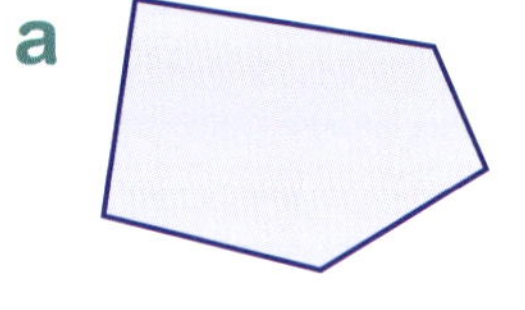 

b 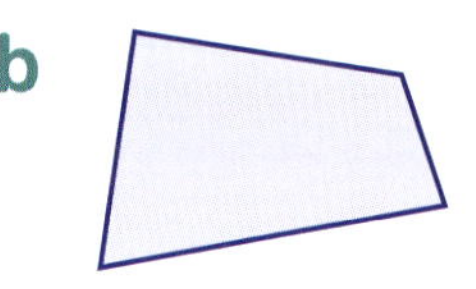 

c 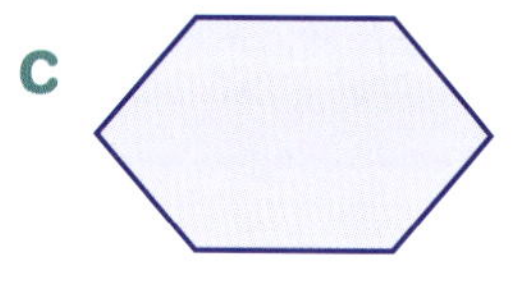 

d 

e  

f 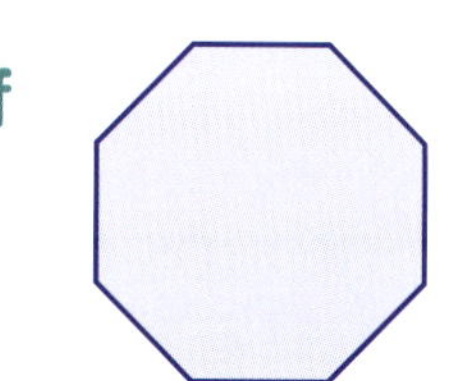 

3 Mark each angle in Question 2 with a large dot.

4 Here angles have been made. Mark each angle with a large dot.

a 

b 

c 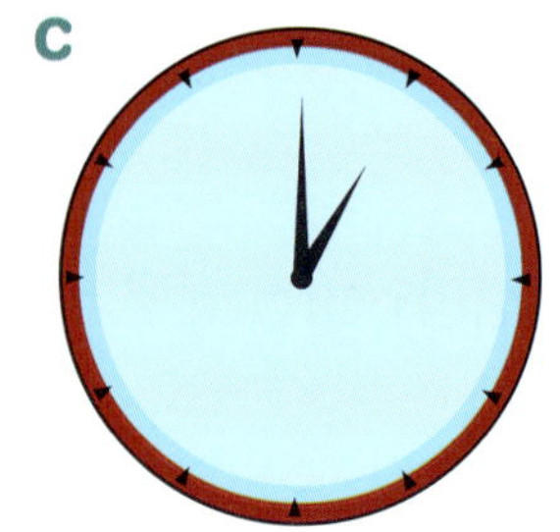

d 

# 23D Angles in our world

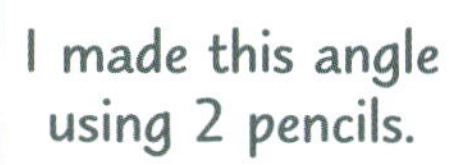

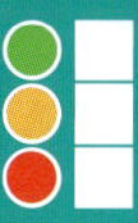

1 Draw dots in 3 angles in each picture.

a 
b 
c 
d 

2 Draw and label angles you can see in your classroom.

3 Draw three more angles on this pin holder.

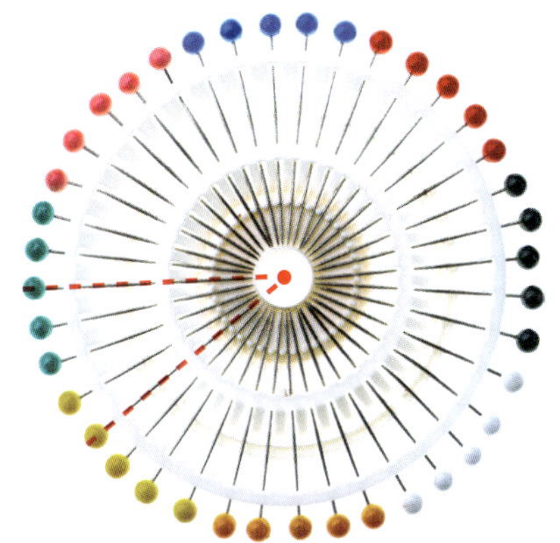

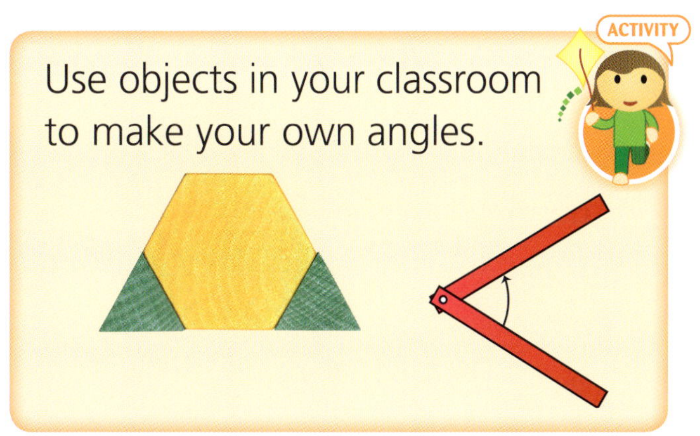

# 24A Skip counting

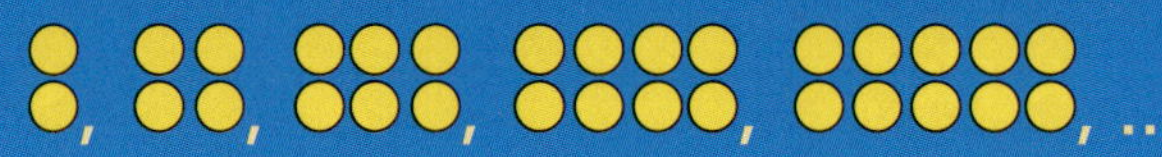

Skip counting by 2:
2, 4, 6, 8, 10, 12, 14, …

Skip counting by 5:
5, 10, 15, 20, 25, 30, 35, …

Skip counting by 3:

| 3 | 6 | 9 | 12 | 15 | 18 | 21 | 24 |
|---|---|---|---|---|---|---|---|

CONCEPT

Try rhythmic counting.

**1** Do these patterns count by 2, 3, 5 or 10?

**a** 12, 14, 16, 18, … ☐

**b** 10, 15, 20, 25, … ☐

**c** 3, 6, 9, 12, 15, … ☐

**d** 10, 20, 30, 40, … ☐

**2** Write the next four numbers in each skip counting pattern.

**a** 5, 10, 15, 20, 25, ☐, ☐, ☐, ☐

**b** 10, 20, 30, 40, 50, ☐, ☐, ☐, ☐

**c** 2, 4, 6, 8, 10, 12, ☐, ☐, ☐, ☐

**3** Use the bells above and skip counting by 3 to find the total.

**a** 2 groups of 3 ☐

**b** 5 groups of 3 ☐

**c** 4 groups of 3 ☐

**d** 3 groups of 3 ☐

**e** 7 groups of 3 ☐

**f** 9 groups of 3 ☐


 • *AUSTRALIAN SIGNPOST MATHS 1* • ISBN 9780655708759

# Number patterns

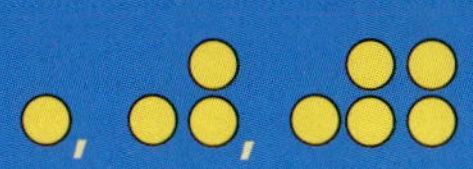

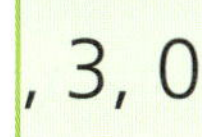


4, 10, 16, ☐, 28, 34

4 add 6 makes 10.
10 add 6 makes 16.
16 add 6 makes 22,
**so 22 is the missing number.**
**Check:** 22 + 6 = 28 and 28 + 6 = 34

**add 6**

15, 12, 9, ☐, 3, 0

15 take away 3 leaves 12.
12 take away 3 leaves 9.
9 take away 3 leaves 6,
**so 6 is the missing number.**
**Check:** 6 – 3 = 3 and 3 – 3 = 0

**subtract 3**

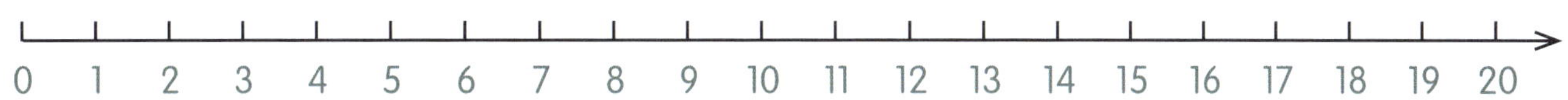


**1** Complete each number pattern.

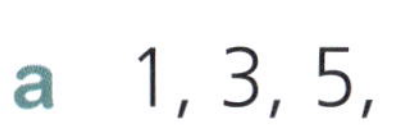

**a** 1, 3, 5, 

**b** 8, 11, 14, 

**c** 9, 7, 5, ☐

**d** 15, 10, 5, 

Discuss how you found the answer to part **d**.

**2** Complete each number pattern and write the rule.

**a** 2, 4, , 8, 10 The rule is: add .

**b** 9, 7, , 3, 1 The rule is: subtract .

**c** 3, 6, , 12, 15 The rule is: add .

**d** 0, 4, , 12, 16 The rule is: add .

**e** 20, , 10, 5, 0 The rule is: subtract .

 • *AUSTRALIAN SIGNPOST MATHS 1* • ISBN 9780655708759

# 24C Months of the year

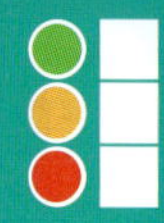

January, February, March, April, May, June, July, August, September, October, November, December

There are 12 months in one year.

1 Discuss the calendar below.

| January | February | March | April |
|---|---|---|---|
| | School starts | Tom's birthday | Easter holidays |
| **May** | **June** | **July** | **August** |
| | Ella's birthday | | |
| **September** | **October** | **November** | **December** |
| | | Speech night | Christmas holidays |

a Which month is Tom's birthday?

b How many months from Tom's birthday until Christmas?

c How many months from January to Easter holidays?

d If it is August now, how many months ago was Ella's birthday?

Use a real calendar to find the number of months until or after Christmas.

# 24D Gather and display data

## Find our favourite colour.

- Put many counters of 4 colours into a container.
- Each student chooses one counter and puts it into another container.
- Place the counters chosen into 4 lines to make a data display.

## Steps to gather and organise data.

- Make up a question and list the possible answers.

Question: What is our favourite colour?

4 possible answers:

- Show the data in a data display.

  Write the colours in the left column below.
  Record the numbers chosen next to each colour.

Our favourite colour

- Make a picture graph using the data we have gathered.

  Write the colours in spaces at the bottom of the graph.
  Colour a face for each person who chose that colour.

 • *AUSTRALIAN SIGNPOST MATHS 1* • ISBN 9780655708759

# 25A Number patterns

Even numbers end in 0, 2, 4, 6 or 8.

Odd numbers end in 1, 3, 5, 7 or 9.

We can use the columns to add 10,
**3, 13, 23, 33, ...**
or to take away 10,
**49, 39, 29, 19.**

| 1 | 2 | 3 | 4 | 5 | 6 | 7 | 8 | 9 | 10 |
|---|---|---|---|---|---|---|---|---|---|
| 11 | 12 | 13 | 14 | 15 | 16 | 17 | 18 | 19 | 20 |
| 21 | 22 | 23 | 24 | 25 | 26 | 27 | 28 | 29 | 30 |
| 31 | 32 | 33 | 34 | 35 | 36 | 37 | 38 | 39 | 40 |
| 41 | 42 | 43 | 44 | 45 | 46 | 47 | 48 | 49 | 50 |

**1** Write the next two numbers in each pattern.

**a** 4, 14, 24, ☐, ☐

**b** 7, 17, 27, ☐, ☐

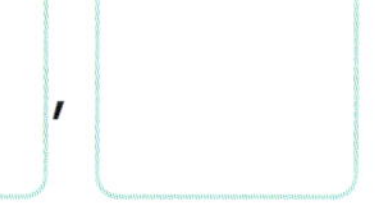

**c** 45, 35, 25, ☐, ☐

**d** 14, 16, 18, ☐, ☐

**e** 50, 49, 48, ☐, ☐

**f** 3, 6, 9, ☐, ☐

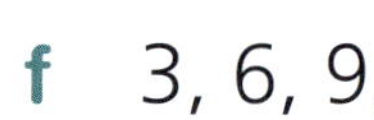

**2** Complete each pattern for 8 more hops.

**a**

0 2 4 6 8 10 12 14 16 18 20 22 24 26 28 30

This is counting by twos.
What is the rule being used?

**b**

This is counting by tens.
What is the rule being used?

**3** Use the number chart at the top of the page.

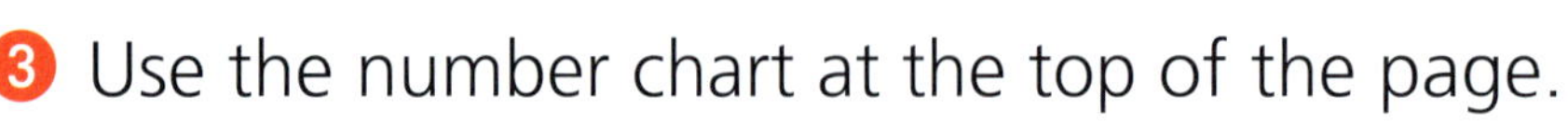

**a** Colour the even numbers red. Circle the smallest even number.

**b** Colour the odd numbers green. Tick the largest odd number.

# Counting by 2s, 5s and 10s

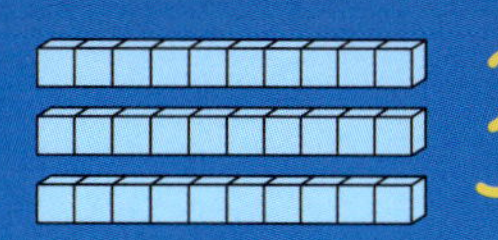

Start

10 20 30 40 50 60 70 80 90 100 110 120

CONCEPT

| 1 | 2 | 3 | 4 | 5 | 6 | 7 | 8 | 9 | 10 |
|---|---|---|---|---|---|---|---|---|---|
| 11 | 12 | 13 | 14 | 15 | 16 | 17 | 18 | 19 | 20 |
| 21 | 22 | 23 | 24 | 25 | 26 | 27 | 28 | 29 | 30 |
| 31 | 32 | 33 | 34 | 35 | 36 | 37 | 38 | 39 | 40 |
| 41 | 42 | 43 | 44 | 45 | 46 | 47 | 48 | 49 | 50 |

**1** Count by twos to finish this pattern.

$2, $4, $6, ____, ____, ____, ____, ____, ____

| 1 | 2 | 3 | 4 | 5 | 6 | 7 | 8 | 9 | 10 |
|---|---|---|---|---|---|---|---|---|---|
| 11 | 12 | 13 | 14 | 15 | 16 | 17 | 18 | 19 | 20 |
| 21 | 22 | 23 | 24 | 25 | 26 | 27 | 28 | 29 | 30 |
| 31 | 32 | 33 | 34 | 35 | 36 | 37 | 38 | 39 | 40 |
| 41 | 42 | 43 | 44 | 45 | 46 | 47 | 48 | 49 | 50 |

**2** Count by fives to finish this pattern.

$5, $10, $15, ____, ____, ____, ____, ____, ____

**3** Count by tens to finish this pattern.

$10, $20, $30, ____, ____, ____, ____, ____, ____

**4** Look at the beads around the page. Colour every 5th bead black.

# 2D shapes

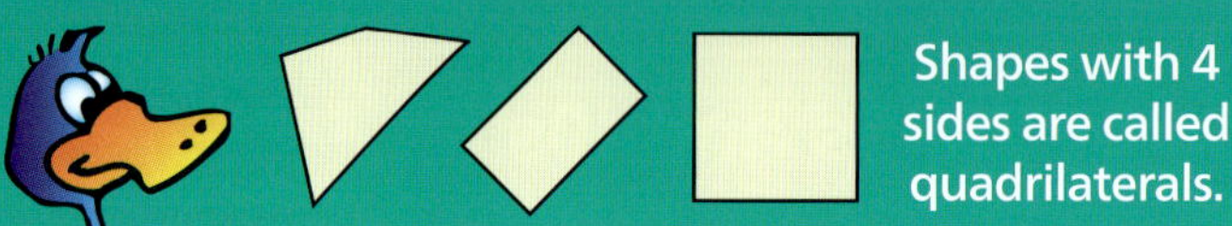

Shapes with 4 sides are called quadrilaterals.

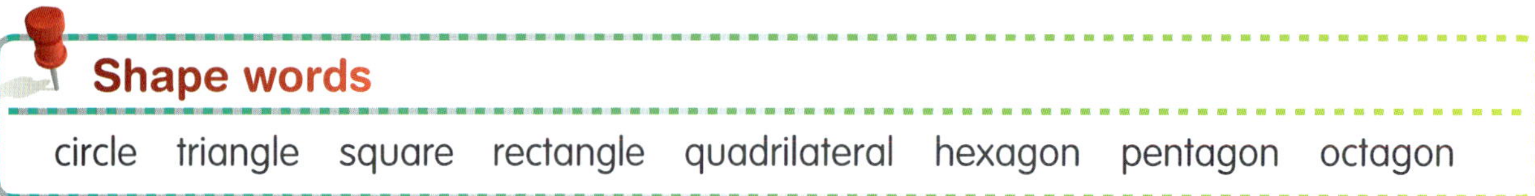

## Shape words

circle triangle square rectangle quadrilateral hexagon pentagon octagon

1 Join the dots. Write the shape name and the number of angles, sides and vertices (corners).

**a**

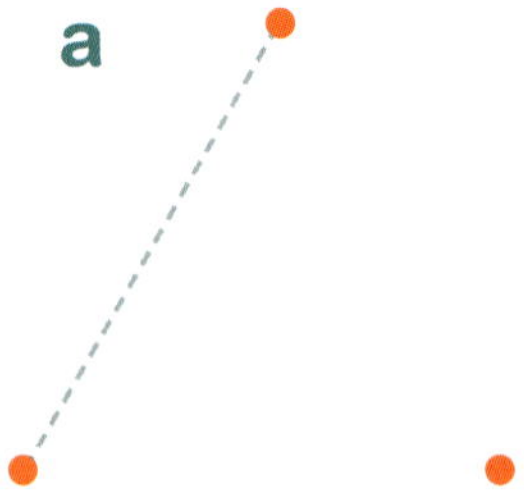

Angles

Sides Vertices

Shape name:

**b**

Angles

Sides Vertices

Shape name:

**c**

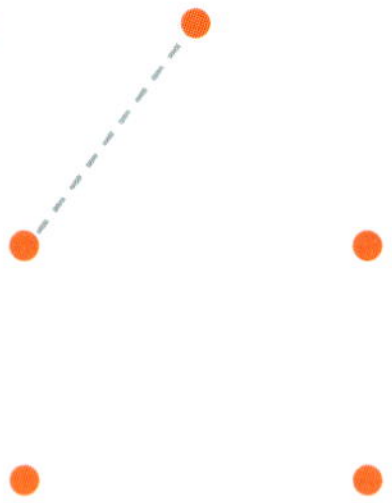

Angles

Sides Vertices

Shape name:

**d**

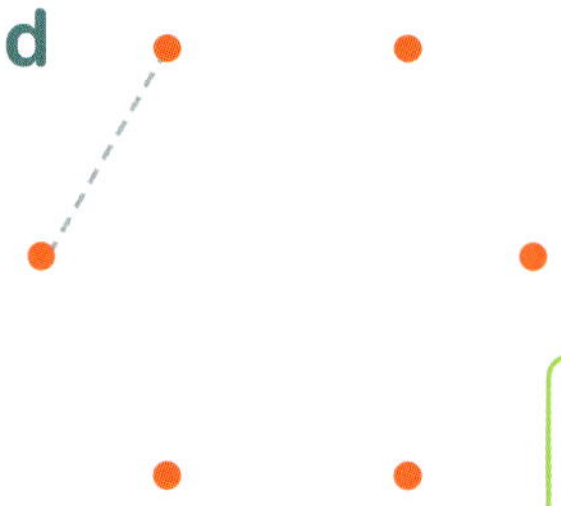

Angles

Sides Vertices

Shape name:

INVESTIGATION

Draw a square and a rectangle. These shapes are quadrilaterals.

 ISBN 9780655708759

# 25D Properties of shapes

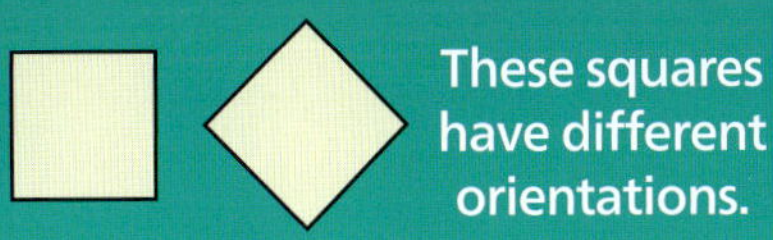

1 a Complete this table. (A vertex is a corner. Vertices are corners.)

| Shape | Name | Number of | | |
|---|---|---|---|---|
| | | vertices | sides | angles |
| triangle | | | | |
| square | | 4 | | |
| rectangle | | | | |
| pentagon | | | | 5 |
| hexagon | | | | |
| circle | circle | | | |
| octagon | | | 8 | |

Hexagons have 6 sides, 6 vertices and 6 angles.

Describe a shape. Ask a classmate to name the shape.

b Colour in the shapes that have all sides equal.

c Circle the shapes that have four sides. These are quadrilaterals.

d Write the name of the shape that has:

3 vertices ______ 6 sides ______

e Name another shape, like the hexagon, that can make a pattern with no gaps or overlaps. ______

INVESTIGATION

Find out what you can about these shapes.

oval kite parallelogram

 • *AUSTRALIAN SIGNPOST MATHS 1* • ISBN 9780655708759

# 26A Problems with equal groups

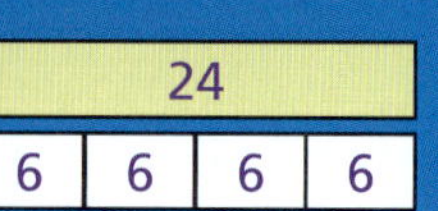

How many students can sit at four tables if two can sit on each longer side and one can sit at each end?

4 groups of 6
= 6 + 6 + 6 + 6
= 24

We can sit 24 students altogether.

What if the ends are not used?

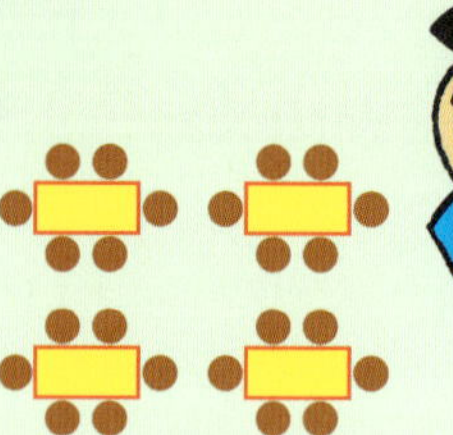

CONCEPT

No ends used:

4 groups of 4
= 4 + 4 + 4 + 4
= ☐

1. If 6 can sit at a table, how many can sit at:

a 2 tables? ☐

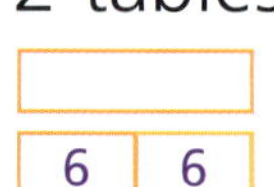


b 3 tables? ☐

c 5 tables? ☐

Tom decided to place the tables end to end like this. How many students can sit at:

d 2 tables? ☐

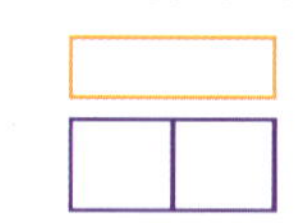

e 3 tables? ☐

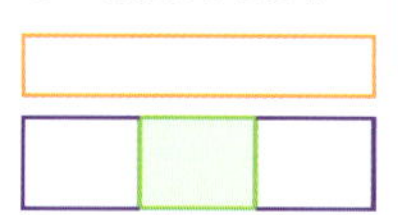

f 4 tables? ☐

2. Alan gave 4 oranges to each of his 5 children.

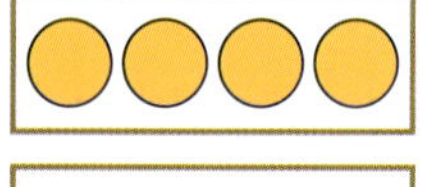
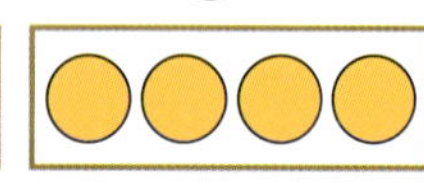
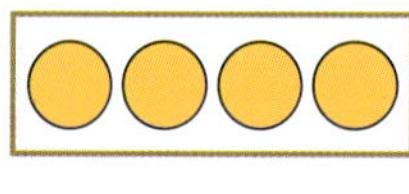

How many oranges did he give them altogether? ☐

How many oranges would he give away if he gave each of them:

a 2 oranges? ☐ b 3 oranges? ☐ c 5 oranges? ☐

3. Nana bought 6 packets of pins. There were 10 pins in each packet. How many pins did she buy?

☐ groups of ☐ pins = ☐ pins

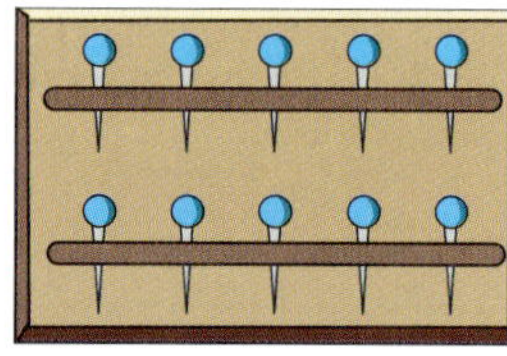

# 26B Number relationships

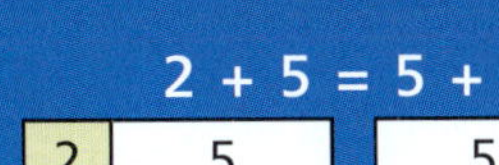

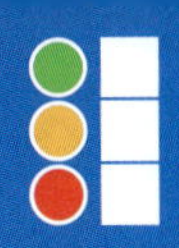

= can mean **is the same as**, **equals** or **is equal to**.

$2 + 2 = 1 + 3 = 4$

**1** a $1 + 4 =$ ☐ $2 + 3 =$ ☐

SO $1 + 4 = 2 + 3 =$ ☐

b $5 + 2 =$ ☐ $3 + 4 =$ ☐

SO $5 + 2 = 3 + 4 =$ ☐

c $3 + 1 =$ ☐ $1 + 3 =$ ☐

SO $3 + 1 = 1 + 3 =$ ☐

d $6 + 2 =$ ☐ $2 + 6 =$ ☐

SO $6 + 2 = 2 + 6 =$ ☐

e $4 + 5 =$ ☐ $5 + 4 =$ ☐

SO $4 + 5 = 5 + 4 =$ ☐

f $7 + 3 =$ ☐ $3 + 7 =$ ☐

SO $7 + 3 = 3 + 7 =$ ☐

**2** True (T) or false (F)?

a $8 + 5 = 4 + 9$ ☐

b $5 + 4 = 3 + 6$ ☐

**3** Match those that have the same answer.

| 6 + 7 | 6 + 4 | 7 + 5 | 9 + 5 | 8 + 7 | 7 + 4 |
|---|---|---|---|---|---|
| 4 + 6 | 5 + 7 | 7 + 6 | 7 + 8 | 4 + 7 | 5 + 9 |

 • *AUSTRALIAN SIGNPOST MATHS 1* • ISBN 9780655708759

# 26C Calendar

Which month has the least number of days?

CONCEPT

Thirty days has September,
April, June and November,
All the rest have thirty-one
Except February alone
Which has twenty-eight days clear,
And twenty-nine days each leap year.

1 How many days are there in these months?

a September ☐
b May ☐
c February ☐
d January ☐
e April ☐
f July ☐

| March | | | | | | |
|---|---|---|---|---|---|---|
| Sun | Mon | Tue | Wed | Thu | Fri | Sat |
| | | 1 | 2 | 3 | 4 | 5 |
| 6 | 7 | 8 | 9 | 10 | 11 | 12 |
| 13 | 14 | 15 | 16 | 17 | 18 | 19 |
| 20 | 21 | 22 | 23 | 24 | 25 | 26 |
| 27 | 28 | 29 | 30 | 31 | | |

Use a real calendar to mark important dates.

2 a How many days are in March? ☐

b On what day does this March begin? ☐

c On what day does this March end? ☐

d How many Wednesdays are in March? ☐



 • *AUSTRALIAN SIGNPOST MATHS 1* • ISBN 9780655708759

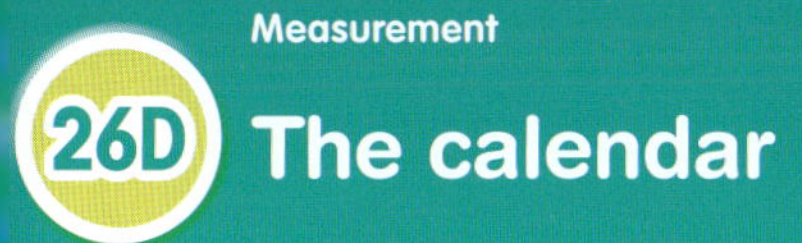

Measurement

# 26D The calendar

Practise using a calendar at home.

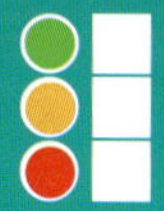

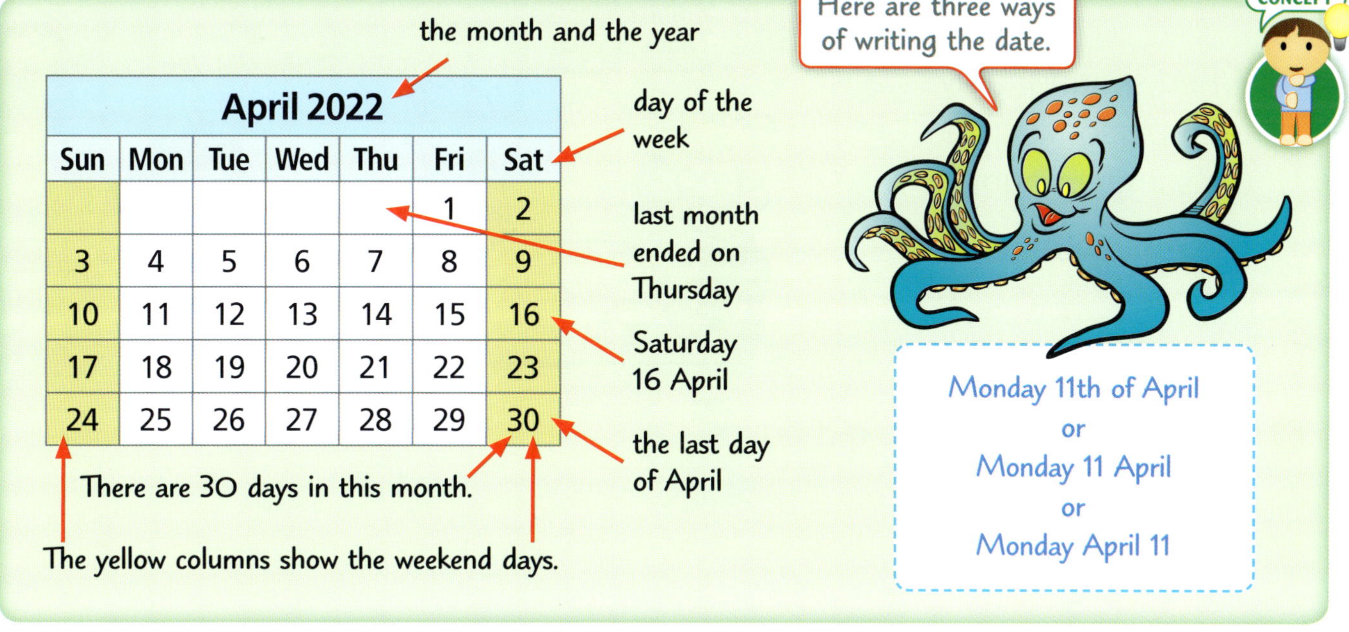

| April 2022 | | | | | | |
|---|---|---|---|---|---|---|
| Sun | Mon | Tue | Wed | Thu | Fri | Sat |
| | | | | | 1 | 2 |
| 3 | 4 | 5 | 6 | 7 | 8 | 9 |
| 10 | 11 | 12 | 13 | 14 | 15 | 16 |
| 17 | 18 | 19 | 20 | 21 | 22 | 23 |
| 24 | 25 | 26 | 27 | 28 | 29 | 30 |



Sunday, Monday, Tuesday, Wednesday, Thursday, Friday, Saturday

**1** On the calendar, colour these dates blue.

a Monday 4th of April

b Friday 8th of April

c Tuesday April 12

d Thursday April 14

e Wednesday 20 April

f Thursday 21 April

**2** On the calendar, circle these dates.

a Sunday 3rd of April

b Saturday 9th April

c the first day of the month

d the last day of the month

e the first Wednesday

f the last Tuesday

**3** What day of the week is:

a April 13? ______

b April 1? ______

c April 24? ______

d April 10? ______

e 19 April? ______

f 11 April? ______

# 27A Sharing

CONCEPT

When sharing fairly, each person is given the same amount.

There may be some left over.

1 Share 6 counters among 3 boxes.

One share = ☐

2 Share 8 blocks between 2 groups.

One share = ☐

3 Share 10 blocks between 2 groups.

One share = ☐

INVESTIGATION

Share 12 counters:

a between 2.
One share = ☐

b between 3.
One share = ☐

c between 4.
One share = ☐

d between 6.
One share = ☐

# Sharing

CONCEPT

When we share, each person gets the same number of items.

(One could be left over.)

Five each.

Half of 10 is 5.

1 Share 9 counters among these boxes.

How many are in each box?

2 Share 8 counters among these boxes.

How many are in each box?

3

Is this a fair share?

Circle the group with the unequal share.

INVESTIGATION

Share 14 counters into 3 equal groups.

How many did you put in each group?

What was left over?

 • *AUSTRALIAN SIGNPOST MATHS 1* • ISBN 9780655708759

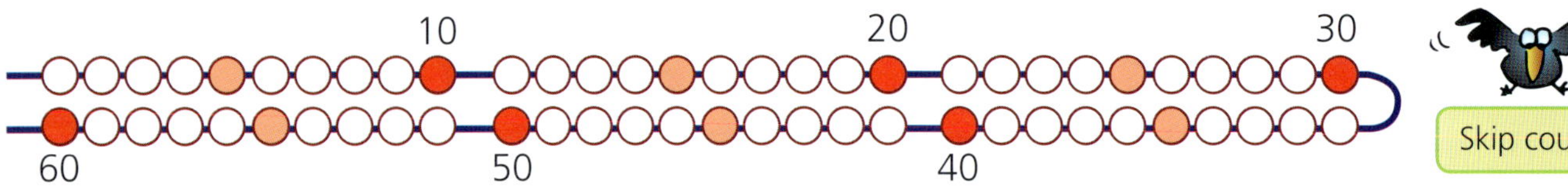


1 Find the value of each group of coins.

a $

b $

c c

d c

e c

f c

g c

2 Find the value of each group of coins.

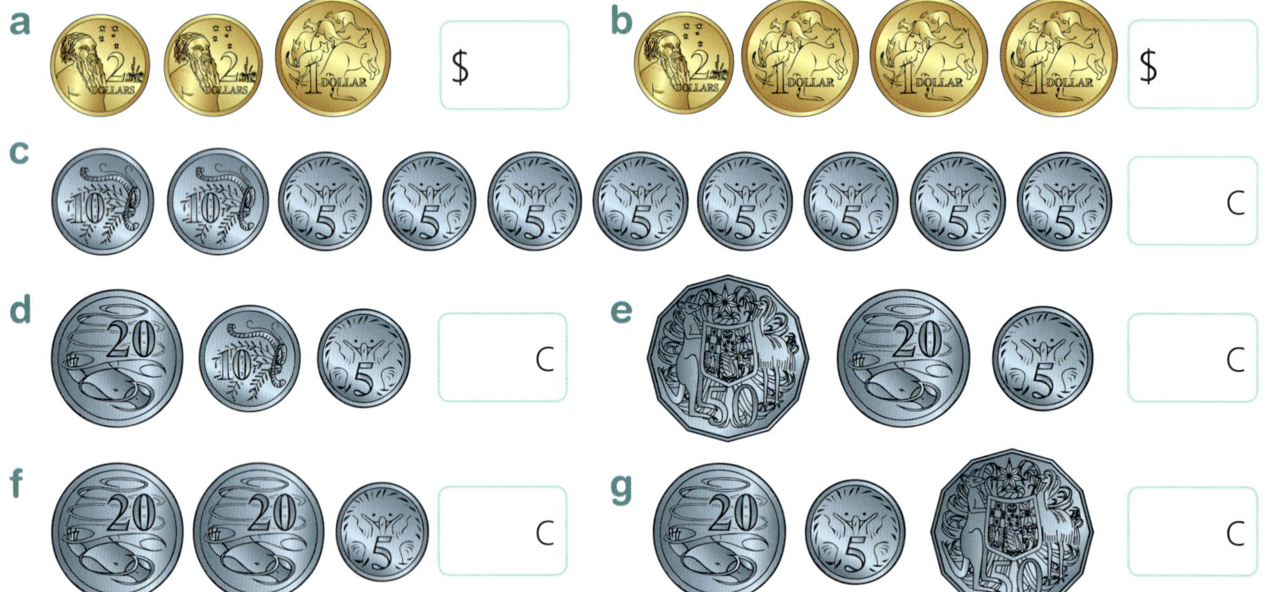

a $

b $

c c

d c

e c

f c

g c

3 Find the value of this group of notes.

$

# Giving directions

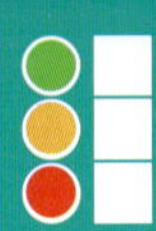

FUN SPOT

1 Use a counter to follow the instructions.

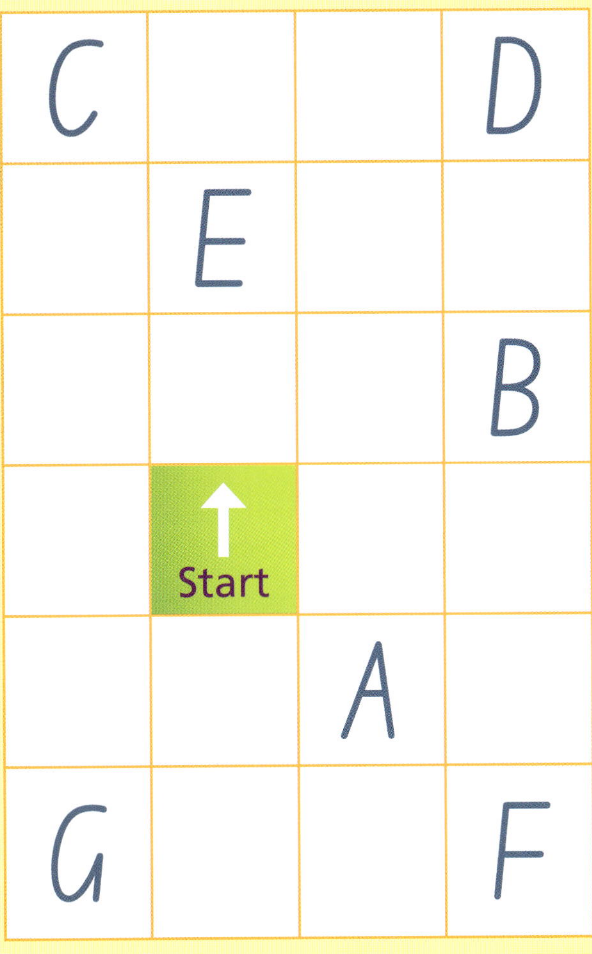


1 Place your counter on the space marked Start.

2 Move the counter 3 spaces up. Colour that square red.

3 From the red square, move the counter 2 spaces right. Colour that square blue.

4 From the blue square, move the counter 5 spaces down. Colour that square green.

5 From the green square, move the counter 3 spaces left.

The counter is now at ☐.

2 Follow these directions from Start on the diagram above. Where do you finish?

a 2 up, 2 right, 3 down, 1 left ☐

b 1 up, 1 left, 3 down, 3 right ☐

3 Work with a partner.

Take turns to give each other directions.

## Challenge

4 You are at the Start. Write the letter where you finish if you:

a move 2 forward, turn to your right, move 2 forward, turn right, move 4 forward, turn right, move 3 forward. ☐

b move 1 backward, turn to your left, move 1 forward, turn right, move 4 forward, turn right, move 3 forward. ☐

# 28A Grouping to share

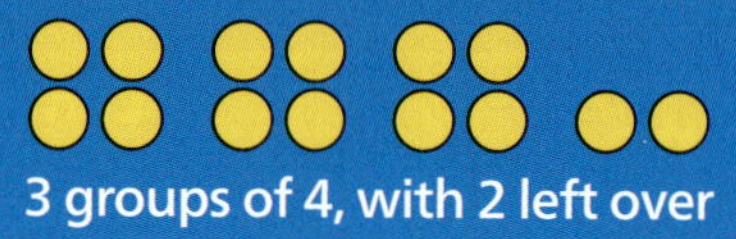

14 eggs

How many groups of 3 eggs can be given away?

4 groups of 3 2 left over

1 How many groups of 4 students can play tennis at the same time?

☐ groups of 4 with ☐ left over.

2 

a How many teachers can be given 4 tennis balls? ☐ teachers

b How many girls can be given 3 tennis balls? ☐ girls

c How many boys can be given 2 tennis balls? ☐ boys

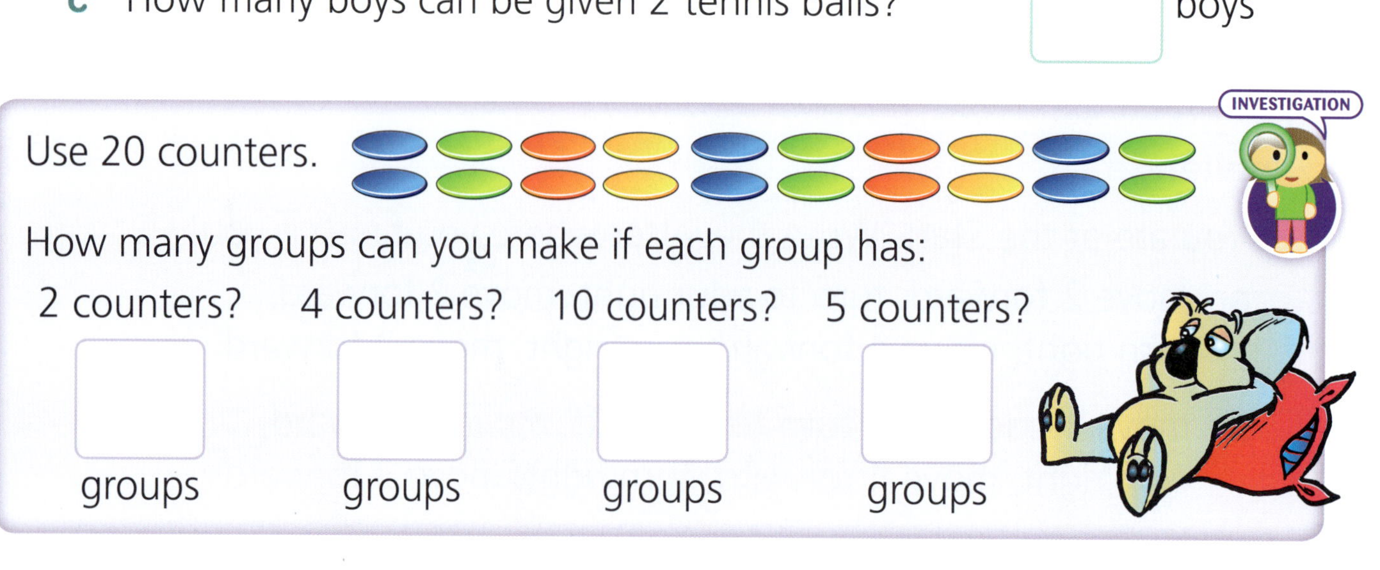


Use 20 counters.

How many groups can you make if each group has:

| 2 counters? | 4 counters? | 10 counters? | 5 counters? |
|---|---|---|---|
| ☐ groups | ☐ groups | ☐ groups | ☐ groups |

# 28B How many groups?

How many times can I take 3 grapes from a bunch of 15?

CONCEPT

We have 12 tennis balls. How many girls can be given 2 tennis balls?

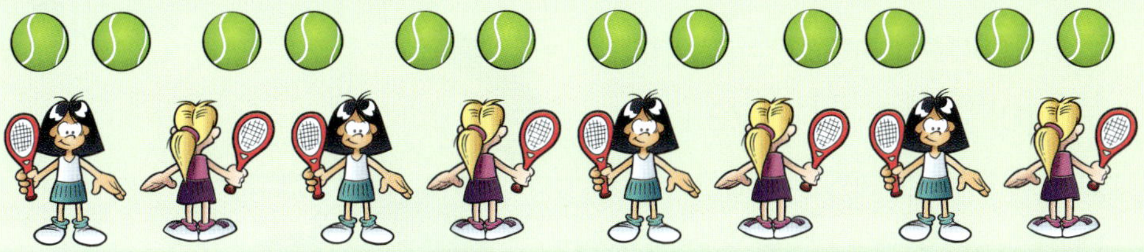

6 girls

1 a 8 counters. How many girls can be given 2 counters? ☐ girls

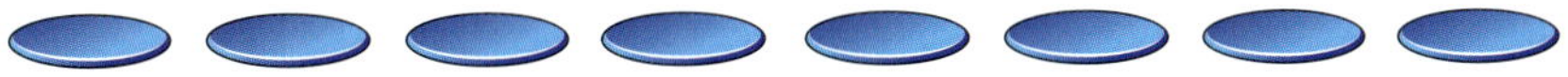

b 9 counters. How many boys can be given 3 counters? ☐ boys

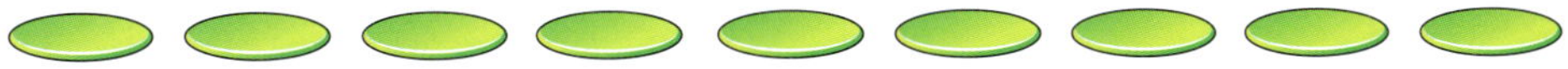

c 20 marbles. How many students can be given 5 marbles? ☐ students

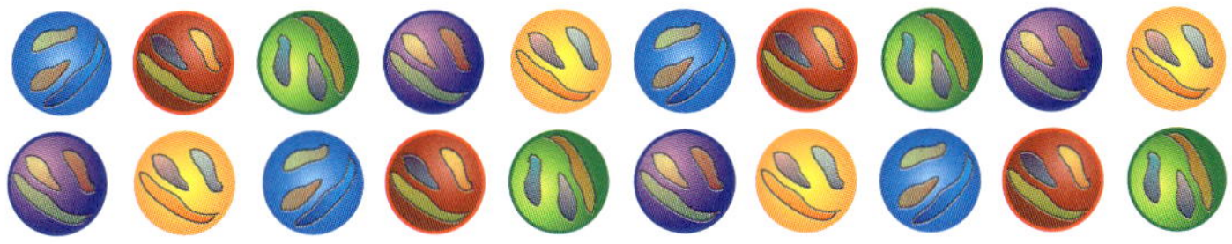

2

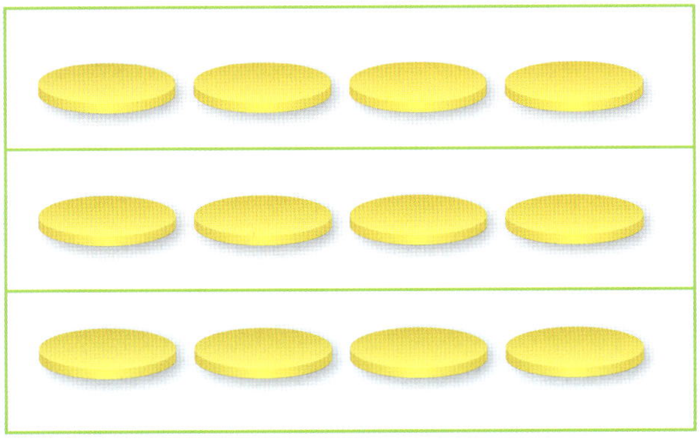

How many altogether? ☐

How many groups? ☐

How many in each group? ☐

3 Circle the groups. How many groups are there?

a 10 hats, 2 in each group. ☐ groups

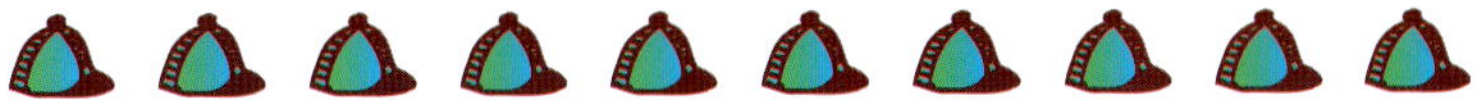

b 12 carrots, 3 in each group. ☐ groups

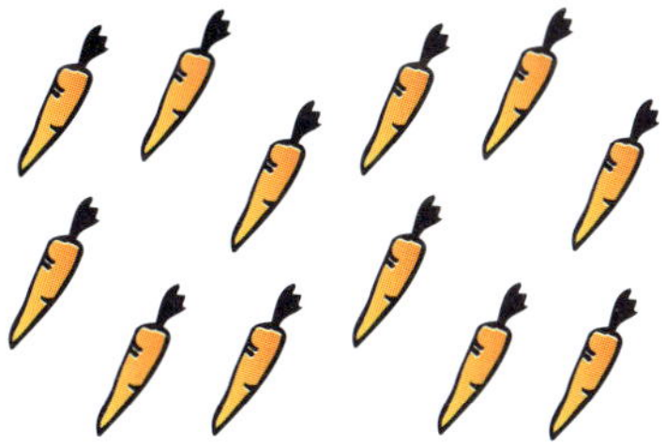

# 28C Comparing areas

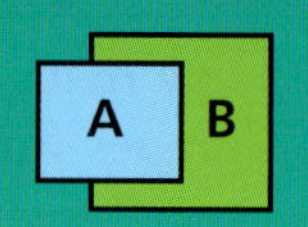

Which has the bigger area?

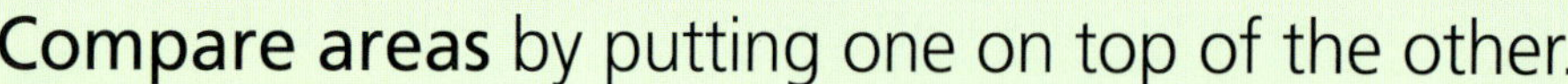

CONCEPT

**Compare areas** by putting one on top of the other.

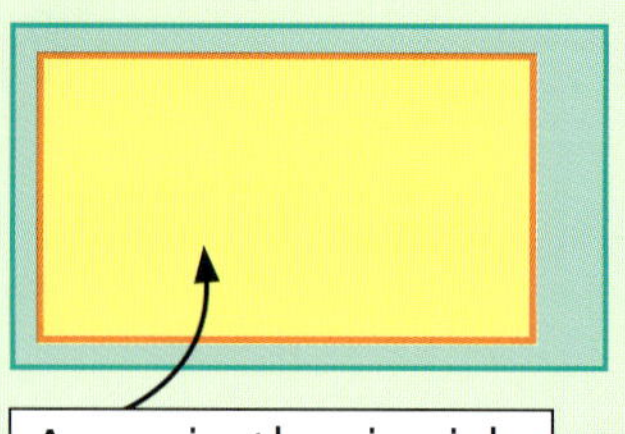

Area is the inside part of a shape.

- The blue paper has the larger area. The yellow paper has less area.
- We can trace an area on paper and put it on top of another area.

1. Find objects in the classroom and draw to complete the table. Check by covering.

| | Smaller area | About the same area | Larger area |
|---|---|---|---|
| newspaper | | | |
| book | | | |

2. Predict which shape has the larger area. Check by tracing one area and placing the tracing over the other shape. Then write an **L** on the larger area.

a

b

ACTIVITY

Compare the area of two surfaces by cutting paper to cover one surface, then placing the cut paper on top of the other surface.

 • *AUSTRALIAN SIGNPOST MATHS 1* • ISBN 9780655708759

# 28D Area using units

Area is the amount of surface on a shape.

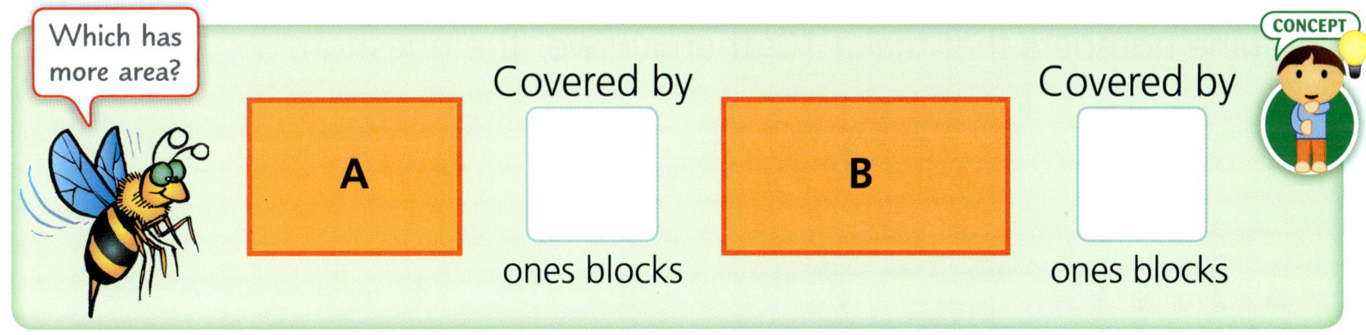


1. Use small sticky notes and then 50c coins to cover the green square.

a ☐ sticky notes  b ☐ 50c coins

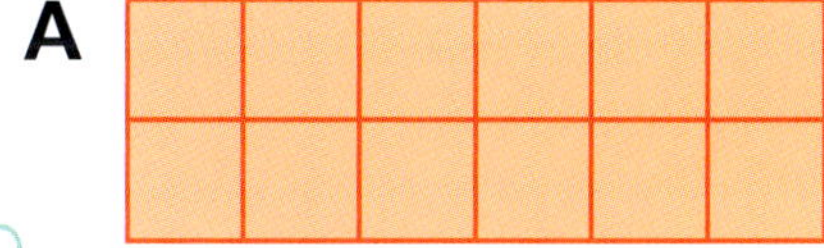


2. Shraven used 12 tiles to make pattern A. He then used the tiles to make pattern B.

Do the patterns have the same area? ☐

- Colour a different pattern on the tiles below that has the same area as Shravan's patterns.

| | | | | | | | | | | | | | | | | |
|---|---|---|---|---|---|---|---|---|---|---|---|---|---|---|---|---|

Why is it better to measure area using shapes that do not leave spaces or have overlaps?

 • *AUSTRALIAN SIGNPOST MATHS 1* • ISBN 9780655708759

# 29A Looking for tens

7 + 4 + 8 + 6 + 3
= 2 tens + 8 = 28

Combine numbers that make 10, then answer the question.

**1** **a** 3 + 4 + 7 **b** 8 + 5 + 2 **c** 5 + 3 + 5

**d** 7 + 6 + 4 **e** 1 + 9 + 8 **f** 6 + 3 + 7

**g** 2 + 4 + 6 **h** 9 + 9 + 1 **i** 8 + 7 + 3

**2** **a** 8 cows, 5 sheep,
2 goats.
How many animals?

**b** 8 cars, 3 trucks,
7 bikes.
What is the total?

**3** **a** 9 + 2 + 1 + 4 **b** 7 + 1 + 8 + 3

**c** 3 + 6 + 3 + 4 **d** 6 + 5 + 4 + 5

**e** 3 + 4 + 5 + 7 **f** 4 + 3 + 7 + 5

Combine numbers that make 10, then add.

**4** **a** \$3 + \$2 + \$6 + \$4 \$ **b** \$2 + \$7 + \$8 + \$3 \$

**c** \$5 + \$4 + \$1 + \$6 \$ **d** \$8 + \$3 + \$1 + \$7 \$

**5** **a** 8 + 9 + 2 + 1 + 6 **b** 6 + 5 + 5 + 4 + 2

**c** 6 + 3 + 4 + 2 + 7 **d** 1 + 5 + 8 + 9 + 5

# 29B Relating addition and subtraction

10 = 3 + 7

❶ Use the number bonds to find the answers.

**a** 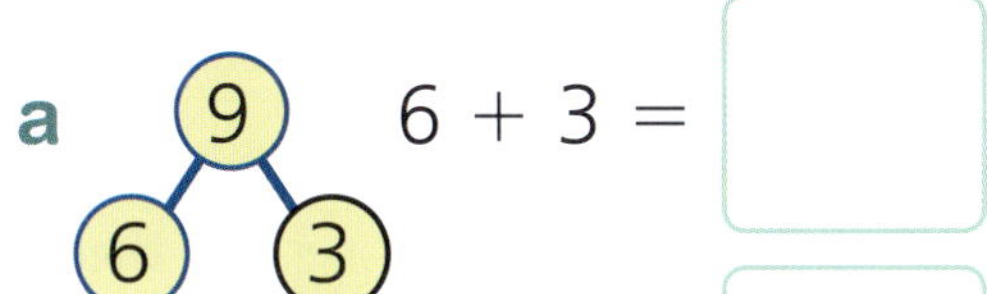

6 + 3 = ☐

9 − 6 = ☐

9 − 3 = ☐

**b** 

7 − 4 = ☐

7 − 3 = ☐

4 + 3 = ☐

We write three number sentences for each number bond.

**c** (12: 5, 7)

5 + 7 = ☐

12 − 7 = ☐

12 − 5 = ☐

**d** 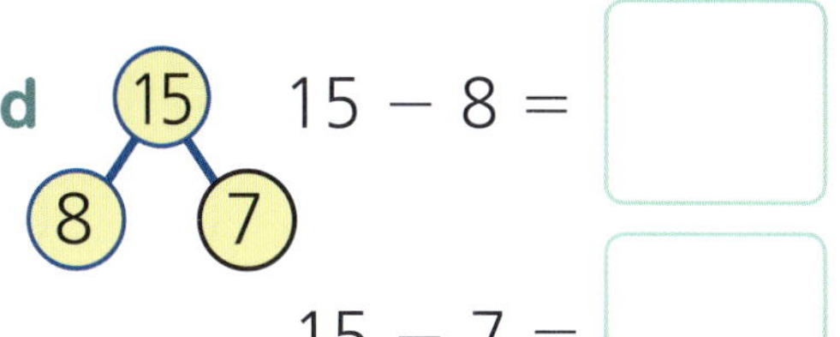

15 − 8 = ☐

15 − 7 = ☐

8 + 7 = ☐

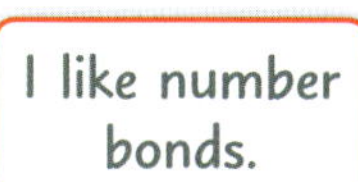

**e** 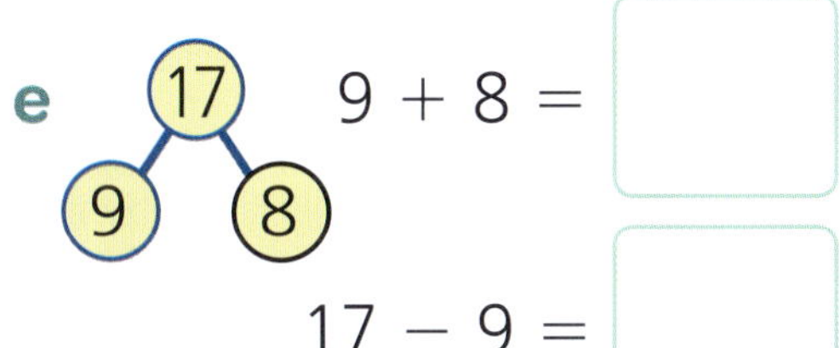

9 + 8 = ☐

17 − 9 = ☐

17 − 8 = ☐

**f** (13: 8, 5)

13 − 8 = ☐

13 − 5 = ☐

8 + 5 = ☐

**g** 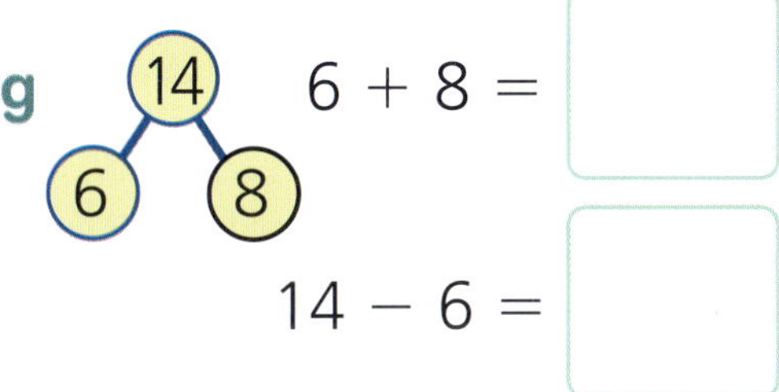

6 + 8 = ☐

14 − 6 = ☐

14 − 8 = ☐

**h** (16: 7, 9)

16 − 7 = ☐

16 − 9 = ☐

7 + 9 = ☐

 • *AUSTRALIAN SIGNPOST MATHS 1* • ISBN 9780655708759

# Relating addition and subtraction

**1** Complete the number bonds and answer the number sentences.

**a** 

5 + 3 = ☐

8 − 3 = ☐

8 − 5 = ☐

**b** 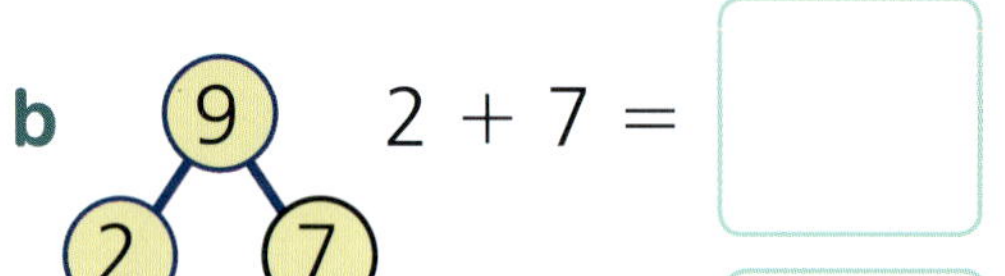


2 + 7 = ☐

9 − 2 = ☐

9 − 7 = ☐

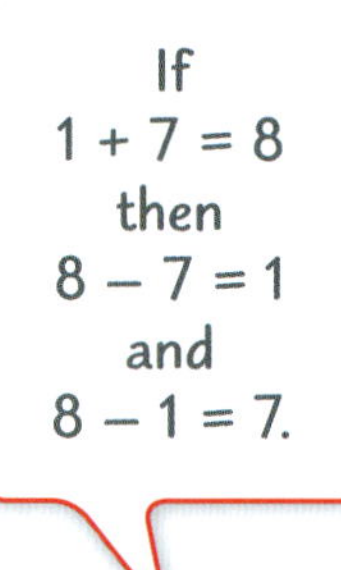

**c** 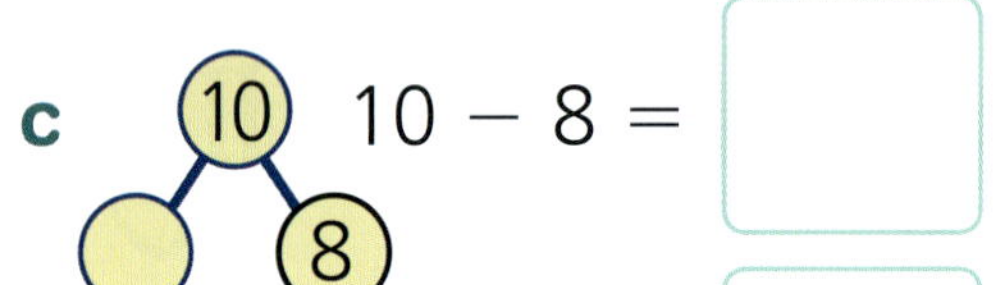


10 − 8 = ☐

8 + 2 = ☐

10 − 2 = ☐

**d** 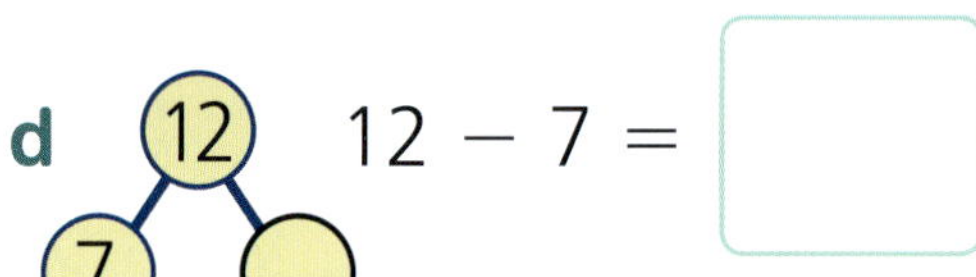


12 − 7 = ☐

5 + 7 = ☐

12 − 5 = ☐

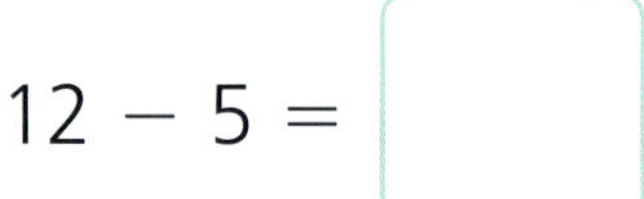

In part h write the number sentences.

**e** 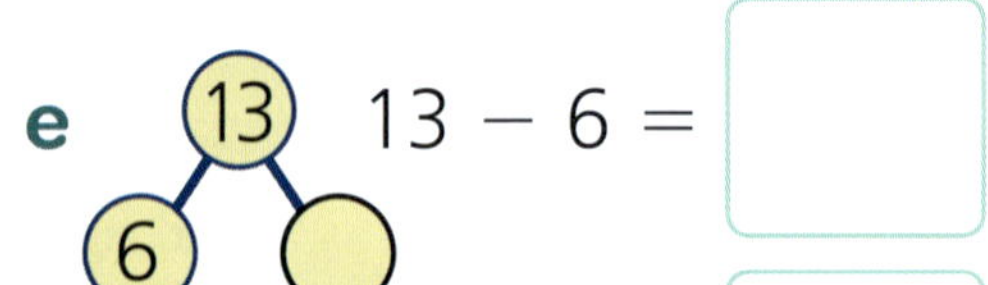


13 − 6 = ☐

6 + 7 = ☐

13 − 7 = ☐

**f** 

18 − 8 = ☐

8 + 10 = ☐

18 − 10 = ☐

**g** 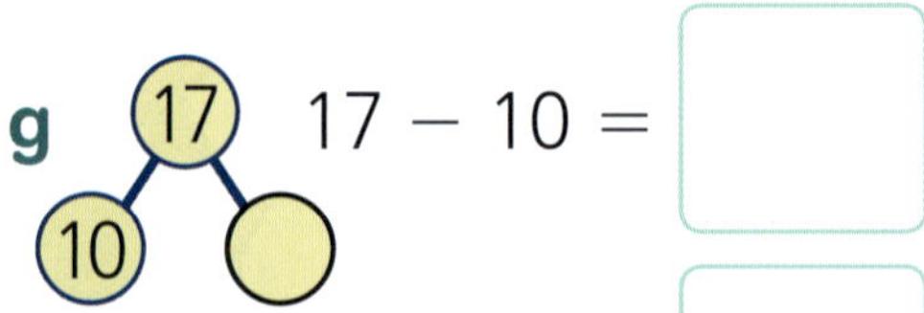


17 − 10 = ☐

10 + 7 = ☐

17 − 7 = ☐

**h** 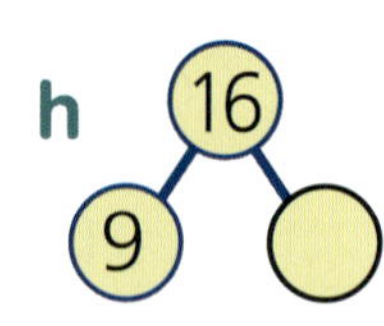

=

=

=



 • *AUSTRALIAN SIGNPOST MATHS 1* • ISBN 9780655708759

# 29D Comparing mass

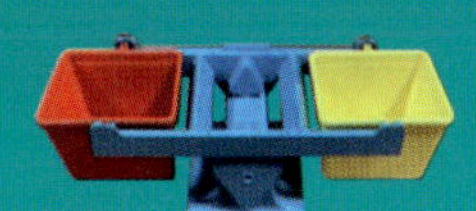

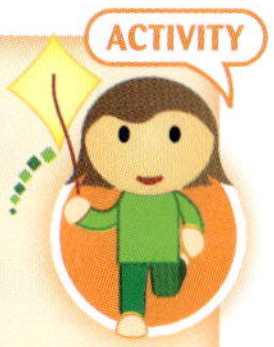

ACTIVITY

1 Compare the masses of these objects by hefting.

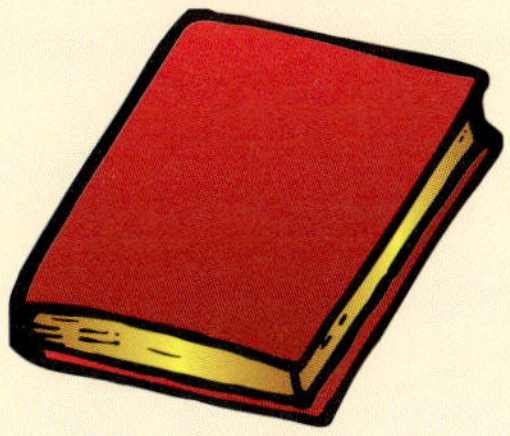

book 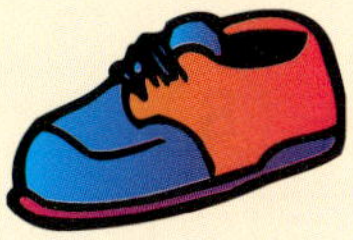 shoe 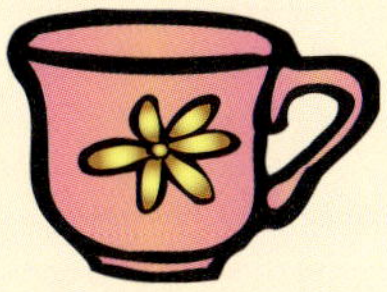 cup

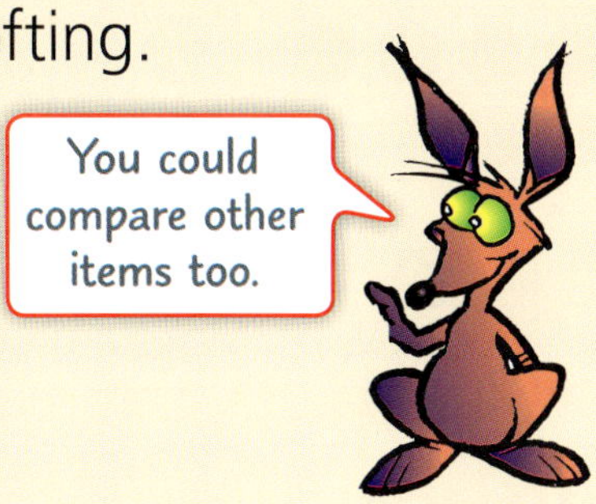

You could compare other items too.

The [ ] is heaviest. The [ ] is lightest.

**Use balance scales to check.**

2 Find two collections of objects that balance. Draw them below.

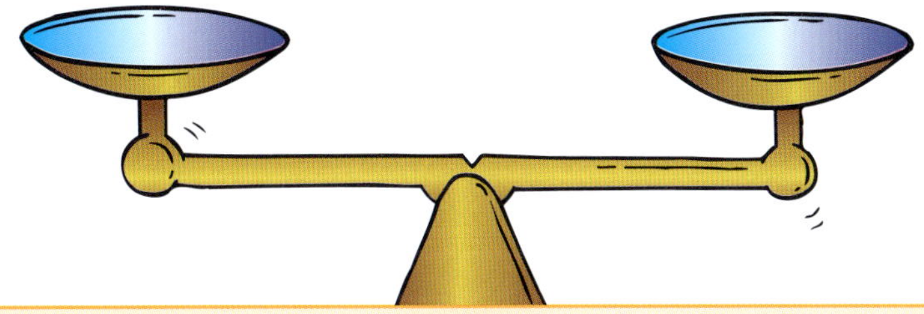

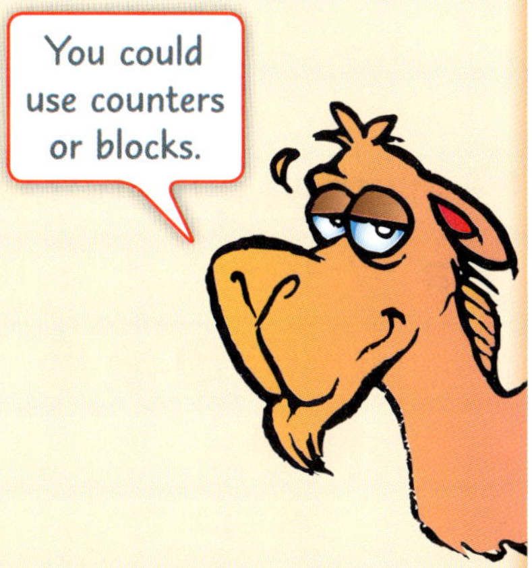

You could use counters or blocks.

3 Use balance scales to answer these questions.

a 1 tens block has a mass equal to [ ] ones blocks.

b 2 tens blocks have a mass equal to [ ] ones blocks.

c 3 tens blocks have a mass equal to [ ] ones blocks.

4 How many marbles balance 10 tens blocks? [ ]

# 30A Bridging to 10

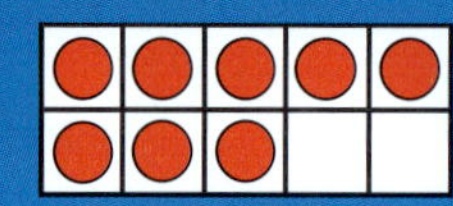

CONCEPT

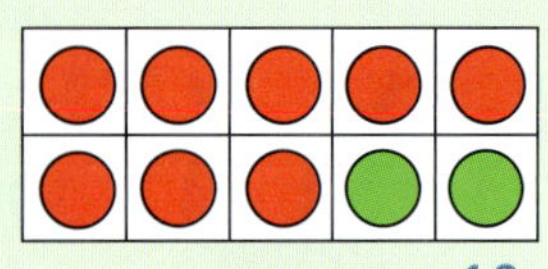

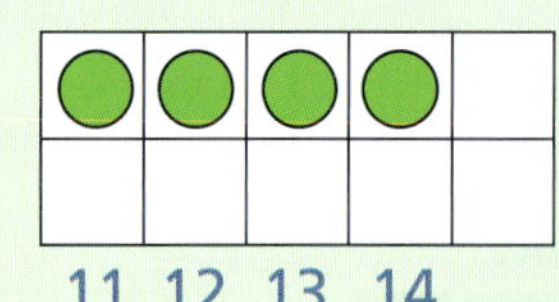

10 11 12 13 14

$8 + 6$
$= 8 + 2 + 4$
$= 10 + 4$
$= 14$

Make a group of 10, then count on.

This is called bridging to 10.

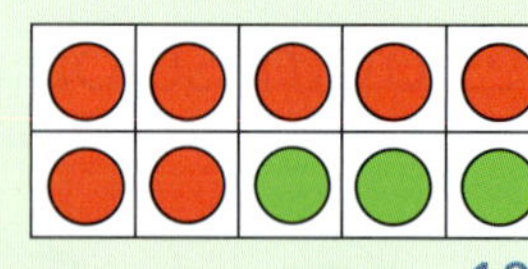

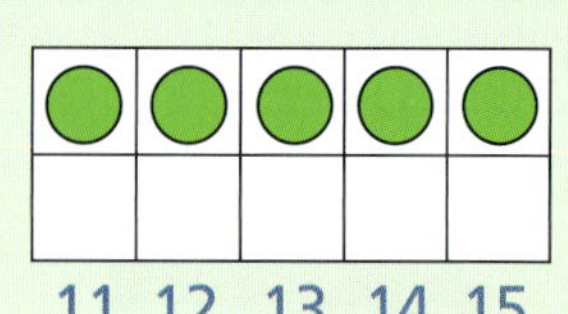

10 11 12 13 14 15

$7 + 8$
$= 7 + 3 + 5$
$= 10 + 5$
$= 15$

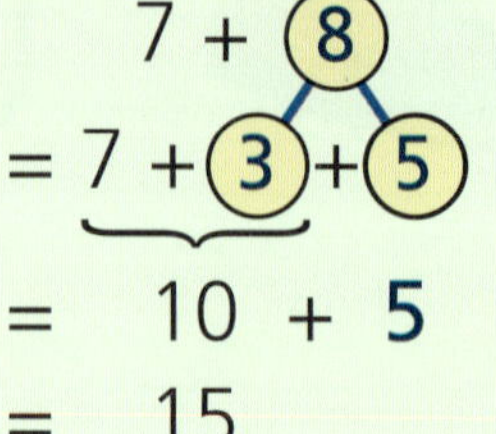

1. Finish each question.

   a $9 + 5 = 9 + 1 + 4$

   $= 10 + \square = \square$

   b $8 + 8 = 8 + 2 + 6$

   $= 10 + \square = \square$

2. Fill the first ten frame, then draw the rest in the second ten frame.

   a $7 + 5$

   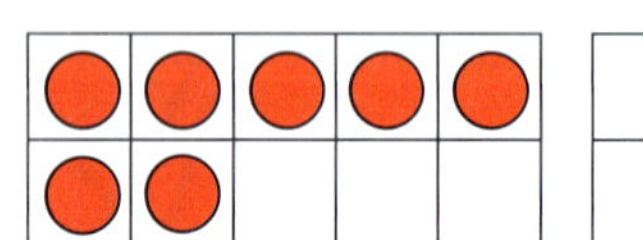

   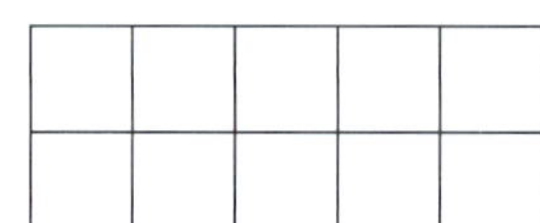

   $7 + 5$
   $= 7 + \bigcirc + \bigcirc$
   $= 10 + \square$
   $= \square$

   b $9 + 8$

   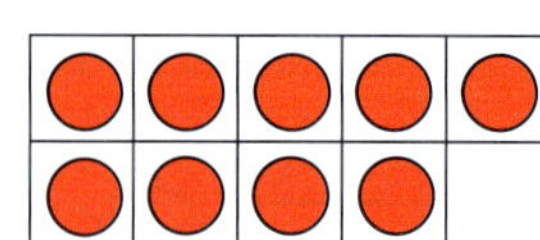

   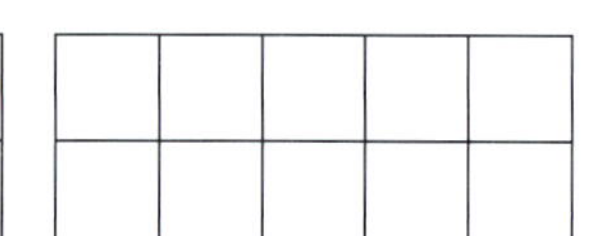

   $9 + 8$
   $= 9 + \bigcirc + \bigcirc$
   $= 10 + \square$
   $= \square$

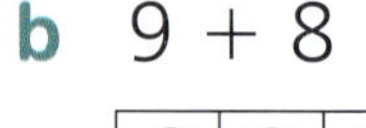

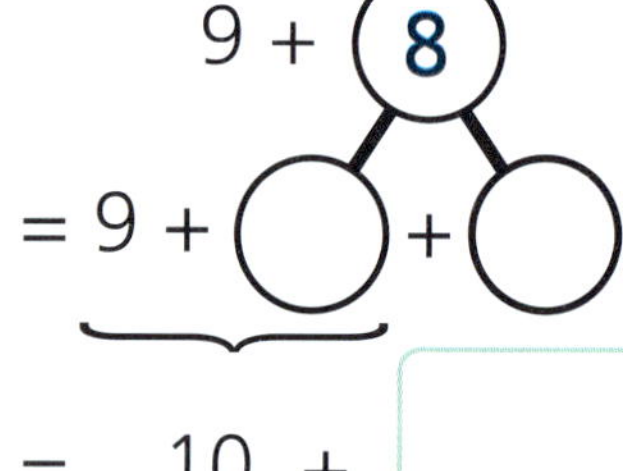

3. Use bridging to ten to answer these questions.

   a $7 + 6$ $\square$

   b $8 + 5$ $\square$

   c $9 + 4$ $\square$

   d $8 + 5$ $\square$

 • *AUSTRALIAN SIGNPOST MATHS 1* • ISBN 9780655708759

# Bridging to 10s

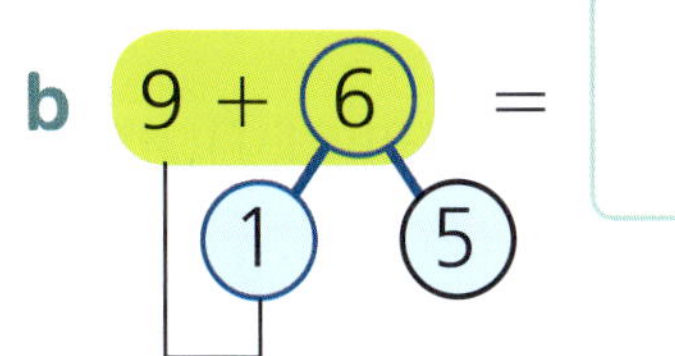

1. Use the number bonds to make the first 10.

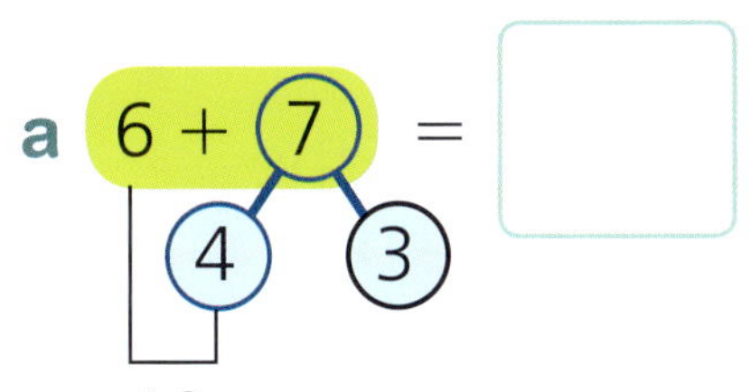


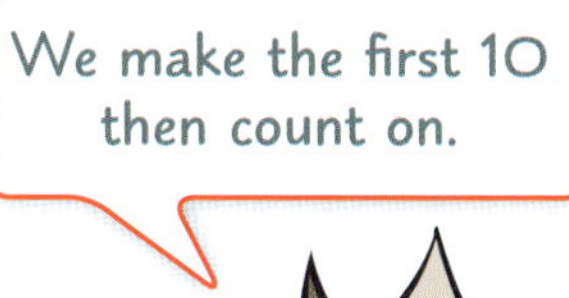


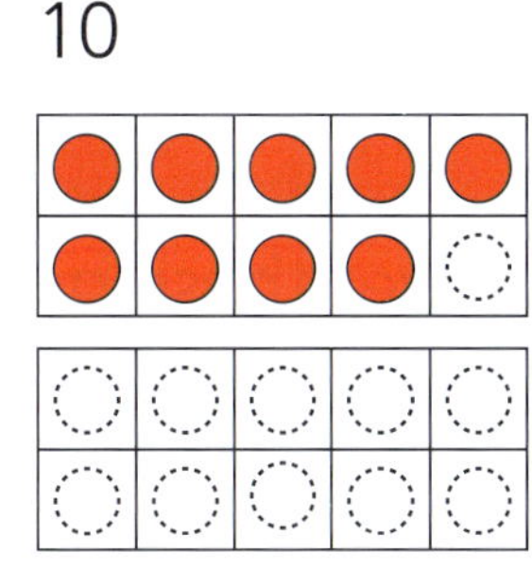

2. Use the number bonds to bridge to the next 10.

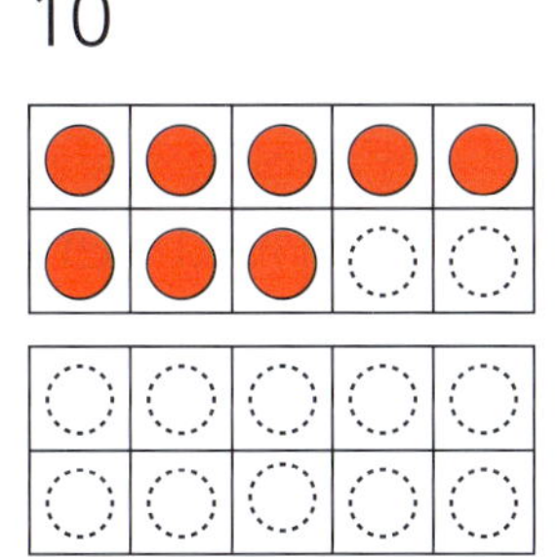


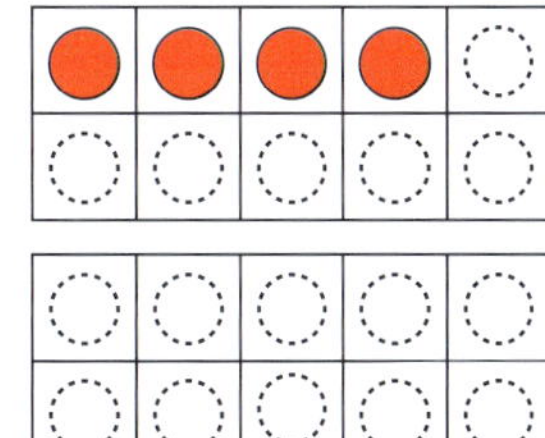

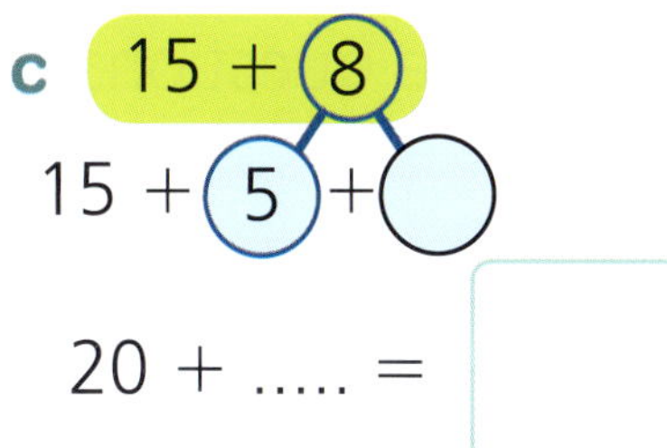


3. Use the number bonds to bridge to the next 10.

a 18 + 7
18 + 2 + 5
20 + 5 =

b 24 + 9
24 + 6 +
30 + ..... =

c 15 + 8
15 + 5 +
20 + ..... =

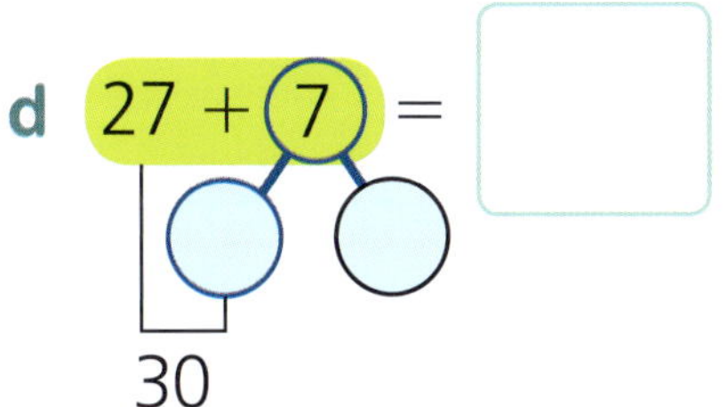


e 26 + 9 =
30

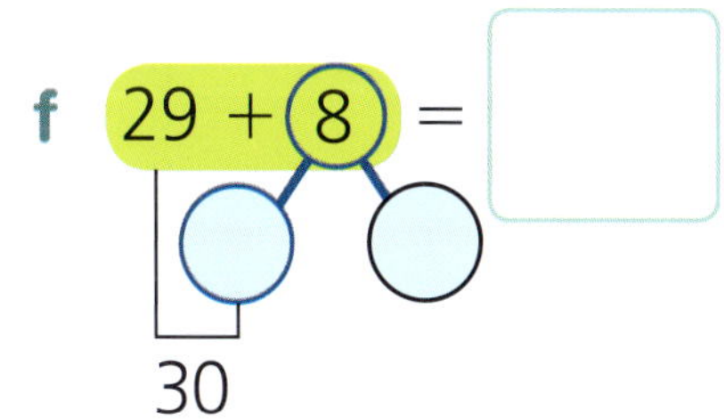

# Bridging to 10s

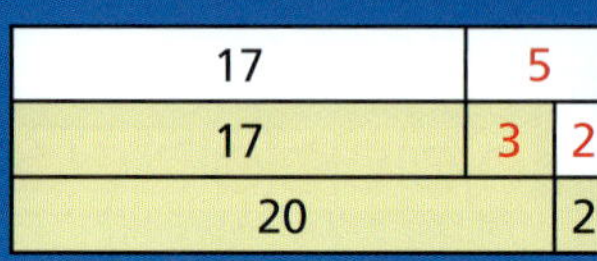

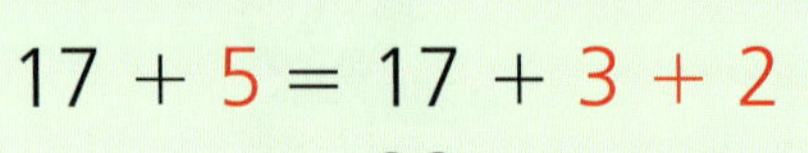

## Bridging to ten

We can break up (partition) the smaller number to bridge to the next ten.

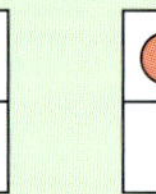
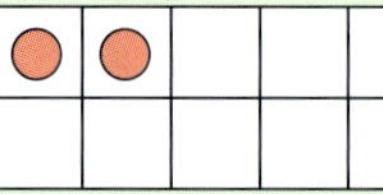

$17 + 5 = 17 + 3 + 2$
$= 22$

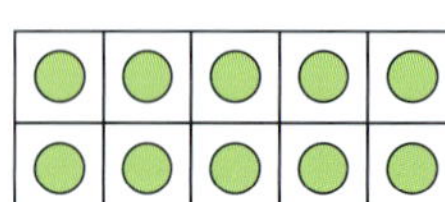
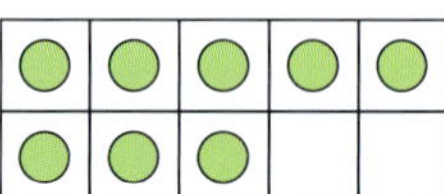
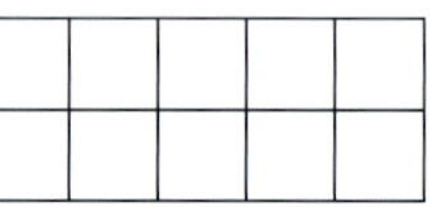

17 and 3 is 20, and 2 more makes 22.

1. Use the tens frames to answer these questions.

a 18 + 7 = ☐

b 15 + 6 = ☐

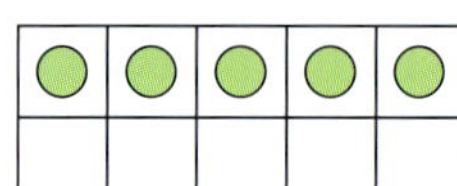
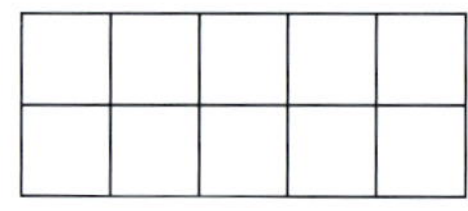

c 19 + 5 = ☐

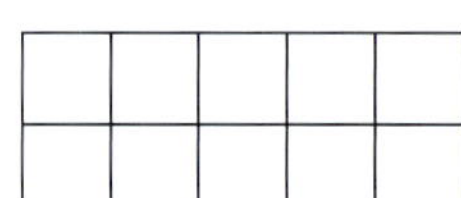
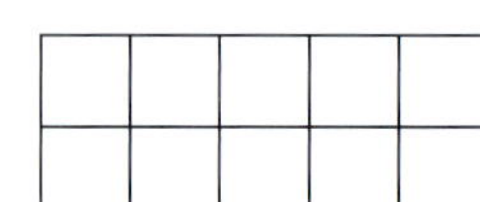
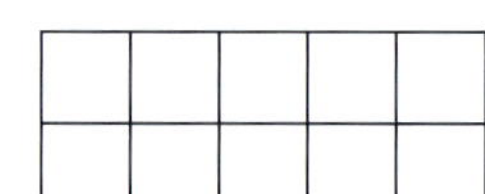

## Using the number line

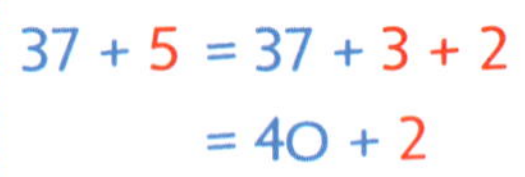

37 + 5 = 37 + 3 + 2
= 40 + 2
= 42

Break up the number to bridge to the next ten.

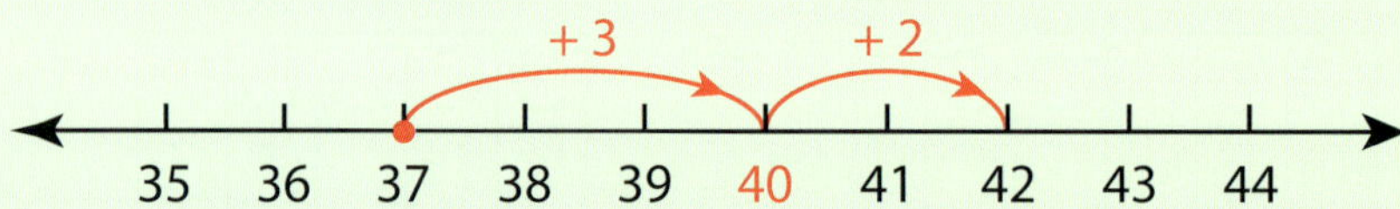


2. Use the number line to bridge to the next ten and answer these questions.

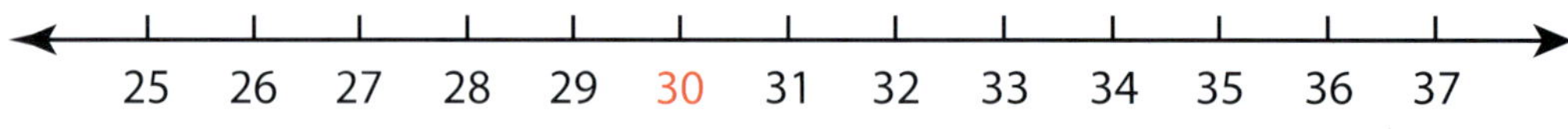


a 28 + 4 = 28 + ☐ + ☐
= ☐ + ☐
= ☐

b 27 + 6 = 27 + ☐ + ☐
= ☐ + ☐
= ☐

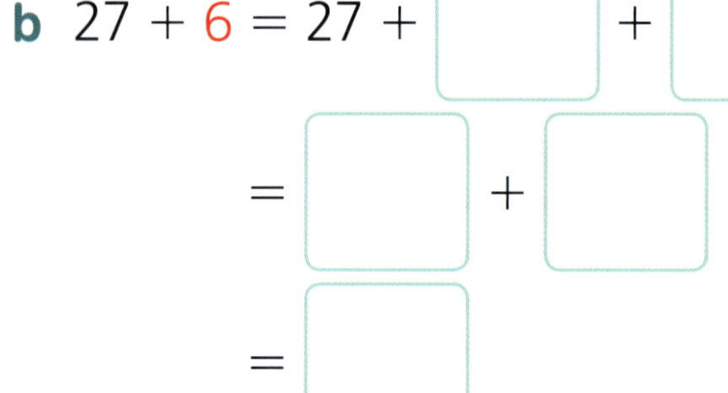

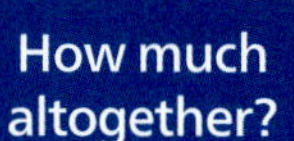

1. Find the value of each group of notes.

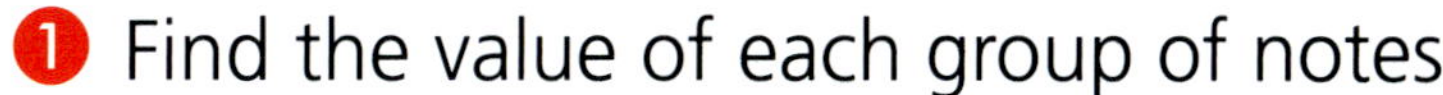

a  $ ____

b  $ ____

c  $ ____

d  $ ____

e  $ ____

In Question 2 the notes are mixed.

2. Find the value of each group of notes.

a     $ ____

b    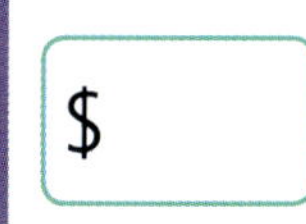 $ ____

c   $ ____

# Subtraction strategies

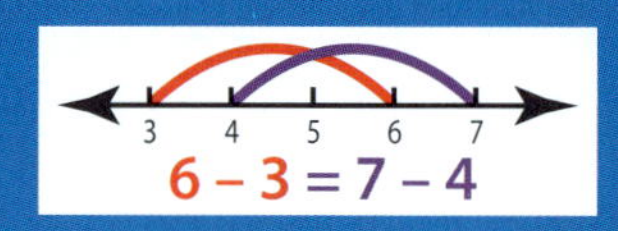

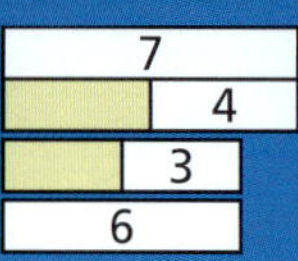

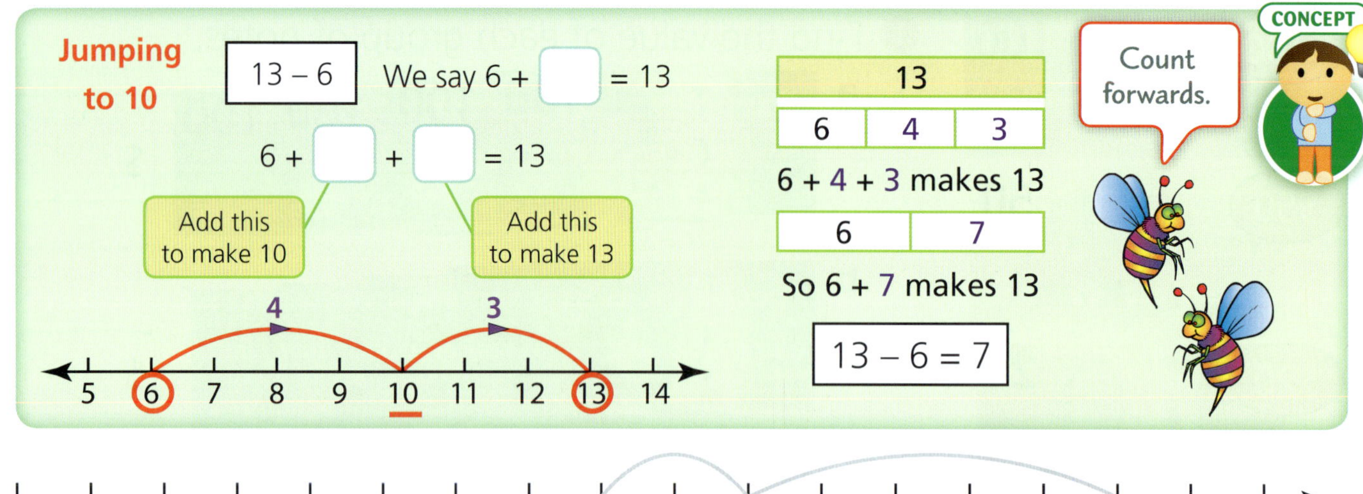


0 1 2 3 4 5 6 7 8 9 10 11 12 13 14 15 16 17

**1** Jump to the next 10 and then to the larger number.

a 15 – 8 8 and 2 and 5 makes 15. So 15 – 8 = 2 + 5 = ☐

b 16 – 7 = ☐ c 16 – 9 = ☐ d 17 – 8 = ☐

e 14 – 9 = ☐ f 13 – 7 = ☐ g 15 – 9 = ☐

**Subtracting by adding the same number to each part**

15 – 8 becomes 17 – 10 if we add 2 to each part.
We do this because it is easier to take away 10.

**15 – 8**
**= (15 + 2) – (8 + 2)**
**= 17 – 10**
**= 7**

**2** Add the same number to each part so you can take away 10.

Example: 17 – 9 = (17 + 1) – (9 + 1) = 18 – 10 = 8

a 17 – 8 = ☐ b 15 – 7 = ☐ c 13 – 8 = ☐

d 14 – 8 = ☐ e 18 – 9 = ☐ f 13 – 9 = ☐

# 31B Addition facts (extension)

## Are you a tables champion?

- Match questions to answers using a pencil.
- Get someone to time you.

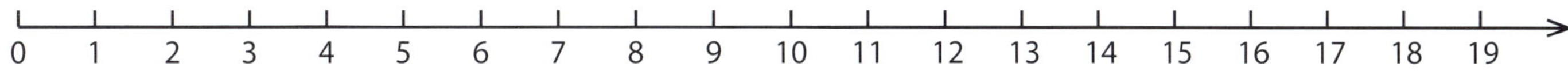


1 Join each question to the correct answer using a pencil and ruler. Practise your addition facts by rubbing out your answers and doing them again and again.

**a**

| + | |
|---|---|
| 1 + 2 | 1 |
| 2 + 2 | 2 |
| 0 + 1 | 3 |
| 1 + 1 | 4 |
| 4 + 2 | 5 |
| 2 + 5 | 6 |
| 3 + 2 | 7 |
| 6 + 3 | 8 |
| 2 + 6 | 9 |
| 5 + 5 | 10 |
| Scores: | |

**b**

| + | |
|---|---|
| 2 + 3 | 4 |
| 4 + 3 | 5 |
| 2 + 1 | 7 |
| 3 + 7 | 10 |
| 0 + 4 | 8 |
| 5 + 3 | 3 |
| 2 + 9 | 12 |
| 7 + 6 | 11 |
| 3 + 9 | 9 |
| 5 + 4 | 13 |
| Scores: | |

**c**

| + | |
|---|---|
| 4 + 6 | 8 |
| 5 + 2 | 13 |
| 4 + 4 | 10 |
| 5 + 8 | 7 |
| 4 + 7 | 11 |
| 7 + 5 | 6 |
| 9 + 6 | 15 |
| 3 + 3 | 12 |
| 1 + 4 | 5 |
| 7 + 7 | 14 |
| Scores: | |

**d**

| + | |
|---|---|
| 4 + 9 | 5 |
| 3 + 8 | 15 |
| 4 + 1 | 13 |
| 6 + 9 | 11 |
| 2 + 4 | 6 |
| 5 + 2 | 12 |
| 4 + 8 | 7 |
| 7 + 3 | 9 |
| 4 + 5 | 8 |
| 7 + 1 | 10 |
| Scores: | |

**e**

| + | |
|---|---|
| 5 + 9 | 10 |
| 6 + 4 | 14 |
| 3 + 6 | 9 |
| 6 + 1 | 11 |
| 5 + 6 | 7 |
| 8 + 4 | 13 |
| 8 + 8 | 12 |
| 6 + 7 | 16 |
| 7 + 8 | 8 |
| 1 + 7 | 15 |
| Scores: | |

**f**

| + | |
|---|---|
| 3 + 4 | 14 |
| 6 + 5 | 11 |
| 9 + 5 | 7 |
| 8 + 2 | 13 |
| 5 + 7 | 12 |
| 8 + 5 | 10 |
| 2 + 7 | 16 |
| 7 + 9 | 9 |
| 9 + 6 | 17 |
| 10 + 7 | 15 |
| Scores: | |

**g**

| + | |
|---|---|
| 9 + 7 | 9 |
| 8 + 1 | 16 |
| 7 + 4 | 10 |
| 6 + 6 | 17 |
| 8 + 2 | 11 |
| 9 + 8 | 13 |
| 6 + 7 | 12 |
| 10 + 5 | 14 |
| 6 + 8 | 18 |
| 9 + 9 | 15 |
| Scores: | |

**h**

| + | |
|---|---|
| 7 + 9 | 13 |
| 6 + 7 | 16 |
| 2 + 7 | 11 |
| 8 + 3 | 9 |
| 2 + 4 | 14 |
| 8 + 6 | 12 |
| 9 + 9 | 18 |
| 7 + 5 | 6 |
| 8 + 7 | 17 |
| 8 + 9 | 15 |
| Scores: | |

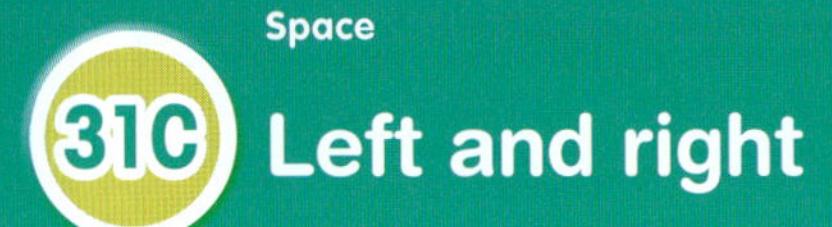

# 31C Left and right

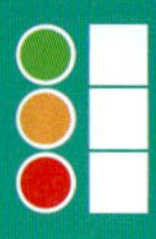

CONCEPT

If a friend is facing me, their **right hand side** is on my **left**.

All the children have the bat in their right hand.

**1** Draw an arrow to show how each car will turn.

**a** Turn right. **b** Turn left. **c** Turn right. **d** Turn left.

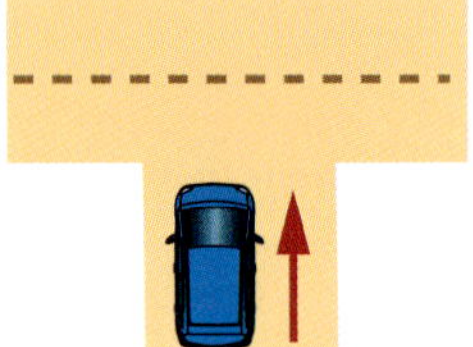

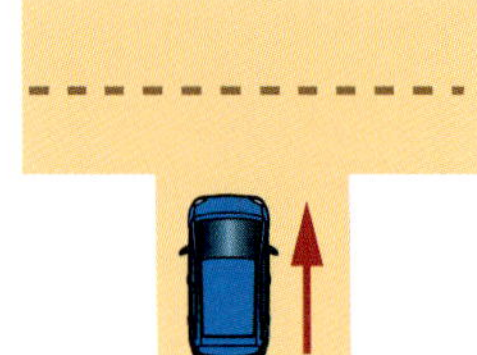

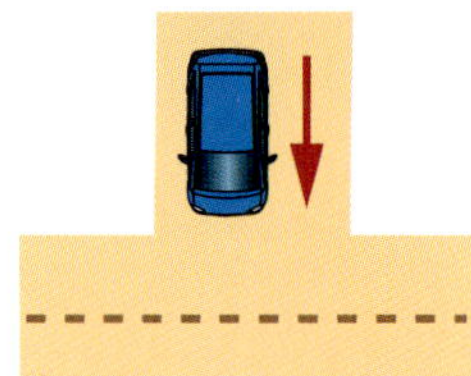

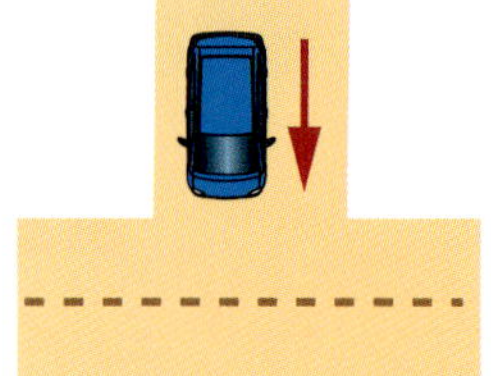

**2** Write the letters the truck will go through if **L** means the truck goes left, and **R** means it goes right.

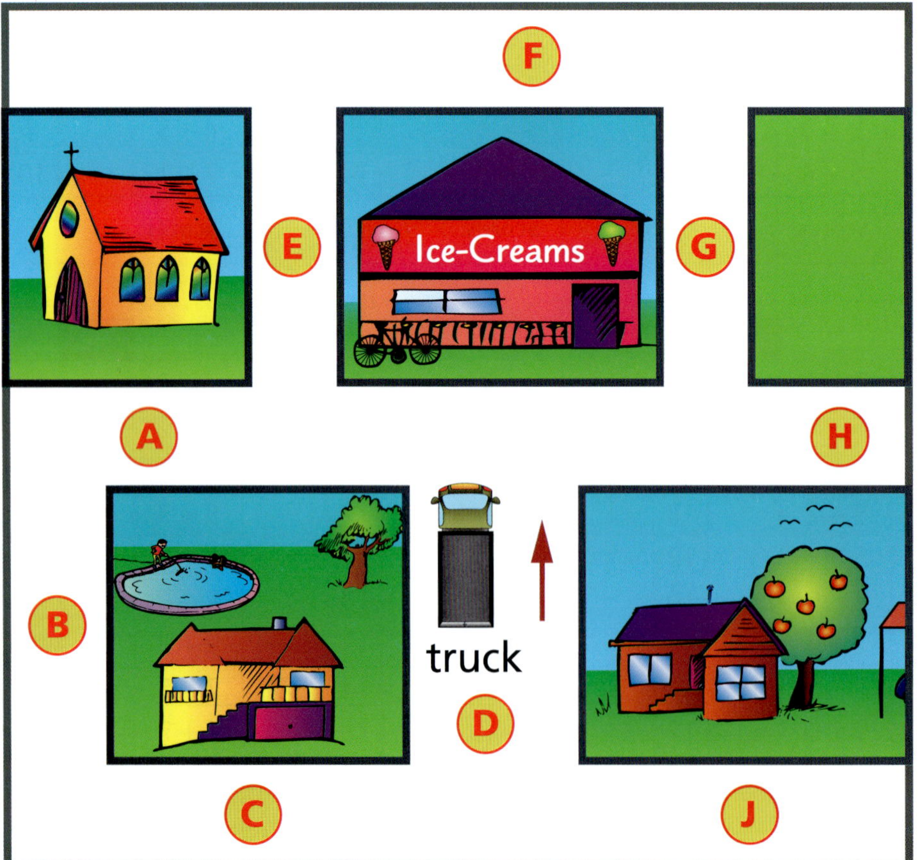


**a** **L**, **L**

**b** **L**, **L**, **L**

**c** **L**, **L**, **L**, **L**

**d** **L**, **R**, **R**, **R**

**e** **L**, **R**, **R**, **R**, **L**

# Subtraction facts (extension)

## Are you a tables champion?

15 – 7 We ask:

7 plus what makes 15?

7 + ☐ = 15

0 1 2 3 4 5 6 7 8 9 10 11 12 13 14 15 16 17 18 19

**1** Join each question to the correct answer using a pencil and ruler. You could practise your tables facts by rubbing out your answers and doing them again and again.

**a**

| – | |
|---|---|
| 2 – 1 | 0 |
| 7 – 7 | 1 |
| 9 – 5 | 3 |
| 7 – 2 | 4 |
| 9 – 6 | 5 |
| 8 – 2 | 6 |
| 9 – 0 | 7 |
| 10 – 2 | 8 |
| 9 – 2 | 9 |
| 6 – 4 | 2 |
| Scores: | |

**b**

| – | |
|---|---|
| 5 – 3 | 4 |
| 10 – 5 | 5 |
| 7 – 3 | 2 |
| 12 – 4 | 10 |
| 6 – 3 | 8 |
| 13 – 3 | 3 |
| 16 – 9 | 6 |
| 12 – 6 | 7 |
| 11 – 2 | 9 |
| 5 – 4 | 1 |
| Scores: | |

**c**

| – | |
|---|---|
| 4 – 2 | 3 |
| 12 – 9 | 4 |
| 13 – 9 | 2 |
| 3 – 2 | 7 |
| 13 – 6 | 1 |
| 12 – 7 | 6 |
| 13 – 4 | 5 |
| 14 – 8 | 9 |
| 14 – 6 | 0 |
| 7 – 7 | 8 |
| Scores: | |

**d**

| – | |
|---|---|
| 5 – 2 | 5 |
| 7 – 5 | 9 |
| 9 – 4 | 3 |
| 12 – 3 | 2 |
| 10 – 4 | 6 |
| 9 – 8 | 8 |
| 11 – 3 | 1 |
| 10 – 3 | 10 |
| 11 – 7 | 7 |
| 16 – 6 | 4 |
| Scores: | |

**e**

| – | |
|---|---|
| 10 – 8 | 0 |
| 2 – 2 | 2 |
| 9 – 2 | 3 |
| 10 – 7 | 10 |
| 14 – 4 | 7 |
| 11 – 5 | 6 |
| 15 – 6 | 8 |
| 15 – 7 | 1 |
| 13 – 8 | 9 |
| 4 – 3 | 5 |
| Scores: | |

**f**

| – | |
|---|---|
| 4 – 1 | 1 |
| 10 – 5 | 5 |
| 12 – 8 | 7 |
| 10 – 9 | 3 |
| 14 – 7 | 8 |
| 17 – 9 | 4 |
| 13 – 7 | 6 |
| 9 – 7 | 2 |
| 16 – 9 | 9 |
| 17 – 8 | 7 |
| Scores: | |

**g**

| – | |
|---|---|
| 5 – 1 | 8 |
| 11 – 3 | 0 |
| 4 – 4 | 9 |
| 3 – 0 | 4 |
| 18 – 9 | 6 |
| 11 – 4 | 3 |
| 15 – 9 | 7 |
| 14 – 9 | 2 |
| 4 – 2 | 5 |
| 8 – 7 | 1 |
| Scores: | |

**h**

| – | |
|---|---|
| 11 – 9 | 0 |
| 6 – 5 | 1 |
| 9 – 9 | 2 |
| 7 – 1 | 4 |
| 10 – 6 | 5 |
| 14 – 9 | 6 |
| 16 – 7 | 7 |
| 15 – 8 | 8 |
| 16 – 8 | 9 |
| 17 – 7 | 10 |
| Scores: | |

 • *AUSTRALIAN SIGNPOST MATHS 1* • ISBN 9780655708759

# 32A The halfway point (extension)

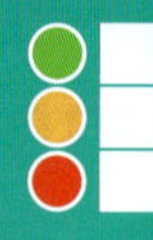

The halfway point is the middle.

1 Circle the halfway point of the see-saw.

From the halfway point, is the distance to the two ends the same?

2 Circle the halfway point of the rope.

3 Circle the child in the middle of the seat.

4 Is the child with the hat about halfway along the seat?

5 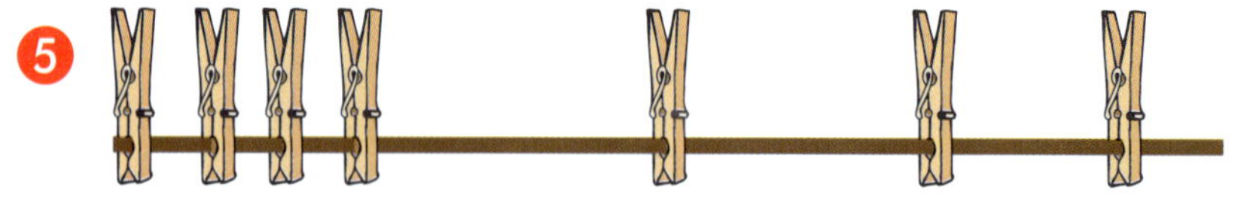

Circle the peg that is halfway along the rope.

6 Tick the bead in middle.

Circle the bead that is halfway along the string.

Cross a bead that is more than halfway along the string.

Hold the two ends of a piece of string together.

Use a pencil to mark the halfway point.

Cut the string at the halfway mark.

Do the halves have the same length?

Discuss.

# Making more patterns

CONCEPT

We can use a **code of letters** to show movement or sound patterns.

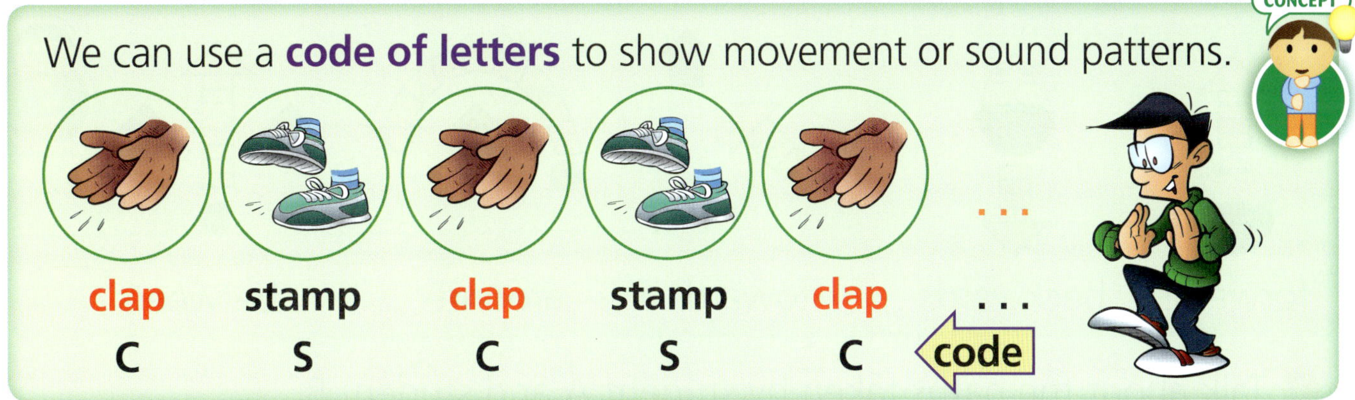


Continue the pattern then write the code.

1

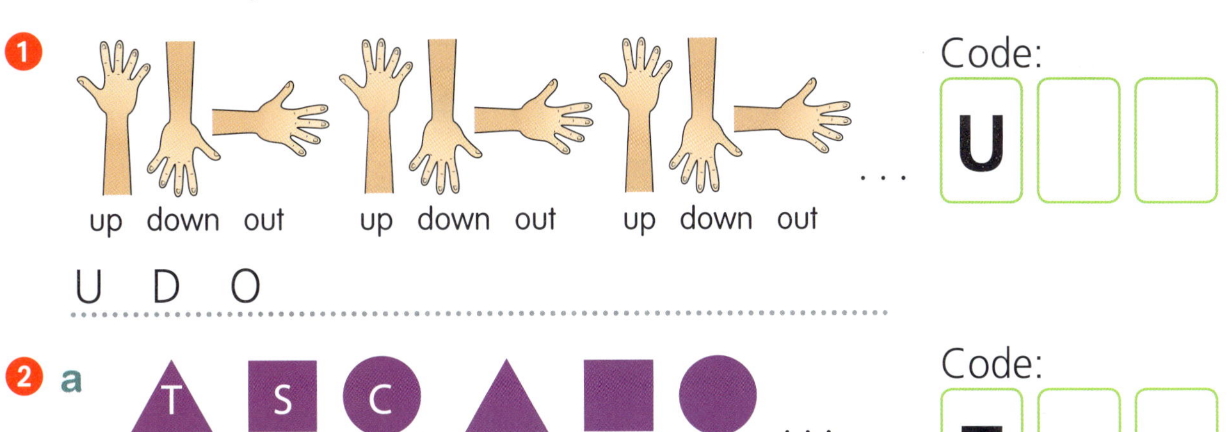


Code: U ☐ ☐

2 a

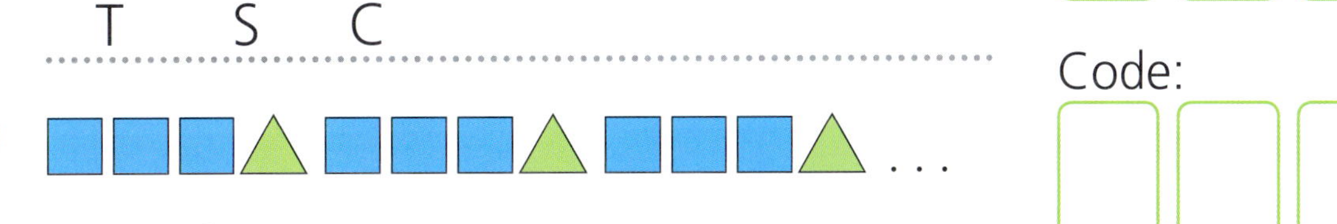


Code: T ☐ ☐

b

S S S T

Code: ☐ ☐ ☐ ☐

c

C

Code: ☐ ☐ ☐ ☐

ACTIVITY

**S** means **stamp your foot**, **C** means **clap** and **H** means **touch your head.** Make these sound and action patterns.

- SCC, SCC, SCC, ...
- CSH, CSH, CSH, ...
- HCCC, HCCC, HCCC, ...
- SSH, SSH, SSH, ...
- CSCCS, CSCCS, CSCCS, ...
- CCCHH, CCCHH, ...

# 32C Following directions

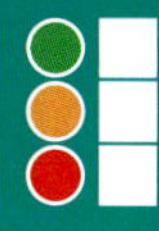

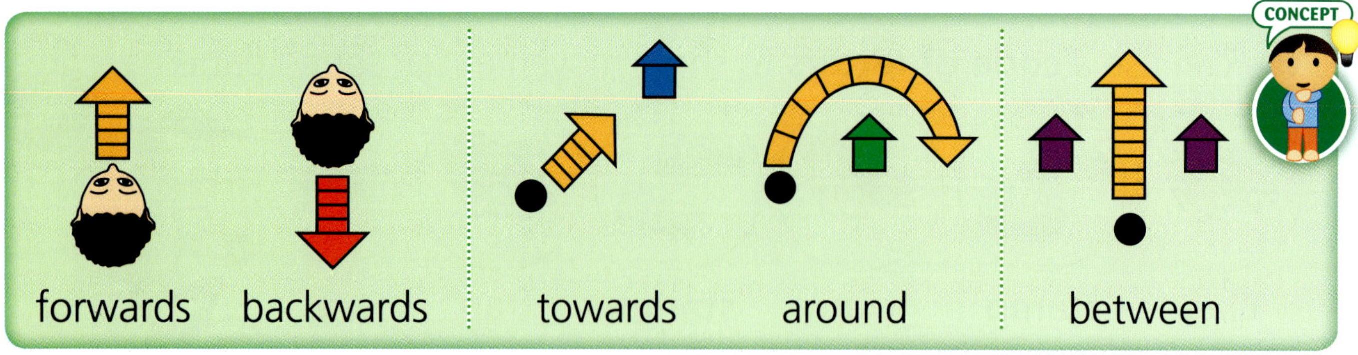


1 Talk about the paths taken by student A and student B. Give directions to student C to take them to the finish.

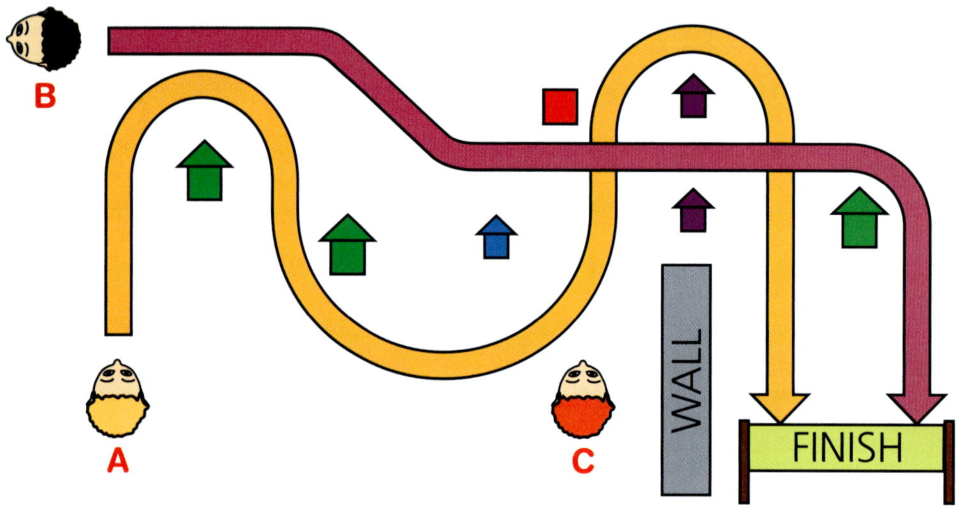


2 Talk about the paths taken by student D (forwards) and student E (backwards).

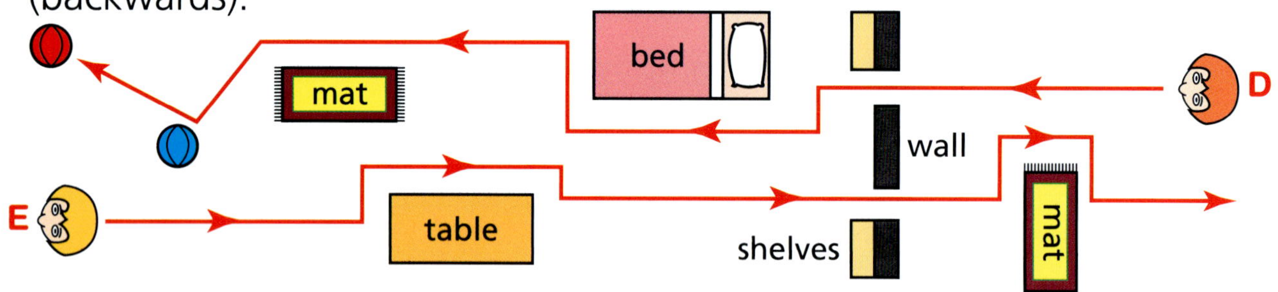


Give directions to a partner for moving around the room. Take turns.

 • *AUSTRALIAN SIGNPOST MATHS 1* • ISBN 9780655708759

# 32D Gather and organise data

A picture graph is a data display with pictures.

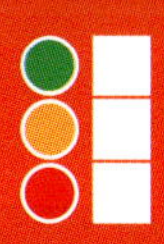

1. Make up a question and write 4 answers that 15 students in your class could choose.

Write your question here.

4 possible choices:

2. Collect information from 15 students. Show answers in this table.
Put your 4 possible choices in the left column.
Trace one line in black for each student.

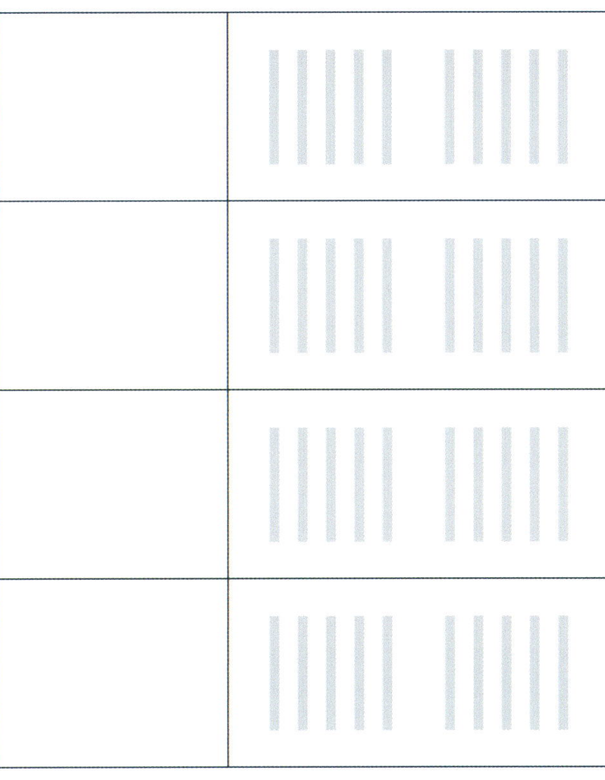

3. Make a picture graph on the right. Put your 4 possible choices in the spaces at the bottom of the graph.
Use the information above to colour a face for each student who chose that answer.

CONCEPT

**Tally marks**

Each mark stands for 1 choice.
Tallies are usually placed in groups of 5.

The fifth mark is often drawn across the other four marks.

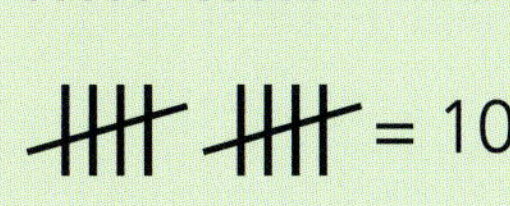


  ISBN 9780655708759

## Identifying and addressing areas of need

An essential part of a teacher's role is identifying and addressing areas of student need.

This includes recognising areas where memory is fading and discovering any concepts that have been missed or misunderstood.

**Testing is a great way to identify areas of need, but is only really useful when the results are used to help the student.**

It is important to build a strong foundation when teaching new concepts and skills.

It is also important to revise / re-teach areas of weakness you discover so that these areas will not be barriers to the future learning of related concepts.

## Progress tests and retests (see adjacent page)

Progress tests 1 to 5 are found in the online Teacher Resource.

After each test, notes and answers are supplied.

Progress test questions are cross-referenced to appropriate Student Book pages.

Progress retests 1 to 5 are also found in the online Teacher Resource.

**The remediation records pages** are used to provide a record of each student's progress.

These are found in the online Teacher Resource.

For each error recorded, the question should be discussed, and using the Student Book cross-reference provided, practice should occur. Retesting should follow using the progress retests.

### Summary

1 Test recent work.

2 Enter any mistakes in the remediation records.

3 Use this record to direct your revision / re-teaching.

4 Retest using the matching retest questions to ensure understanding.

## Teaching and learning

Successfully teaching content and skills is a complex process.

A **good textbook** is an important tool alongside **effective teaching and planning**.

Knowledge, understanding and skills must be embedded in the student's mind so that recall continues with time. This will be done using:

(1) instruction (2) practice (3) drill (4) review.

**Instruction** involves explicit explanation, investigation and the use of good educational resources.

**Practice** forms neural pathways within the brain.

**Drill** strengthens neural pathways. The stronger the pathways become, the longer the understanding or knowledge is retained. 'Overlearning' prolongs recall.

**Review** revitalises weakened neural pathways.

## Progress test

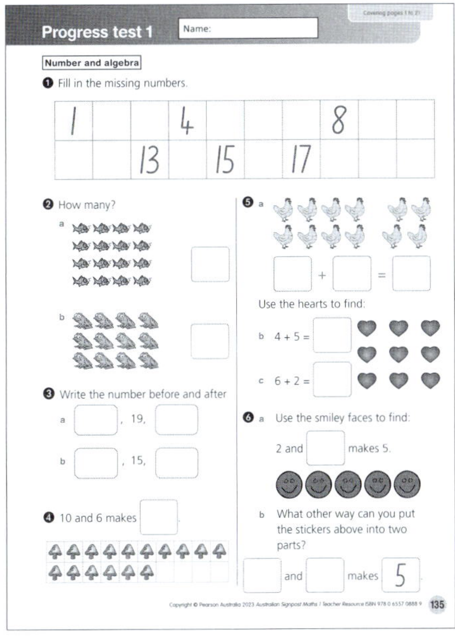

Covering pages 1 to 21

**Progress test 1** Name:

Number and algebra

1 Fill in the missing numbers.

| 1 | | | 4 | | | | 8 | | |
|---|---|---|---|---|---|---|---|---|---|
| | | 13 | | 15 | | 17 | | | |

2 How many?

a

b

3 Write the number before and after.

a ___, 19, ___

b ___, 15, ___

4 10 and 6 makes ___

5 a ___ + ___ = ___

Use the hearts to find:

b 4 + 5 =

c 6 + 2 =

6 a Use the smiley faces to find:

2 and ___ makes 5.

b What other way can you put the stickers above into two parts?

___ and ___ makes 5

Copyright © Pearson Australia 2023 Australian Signpost Maths 1 Teacher Resource ISBN 978 0 6557 0888 9 135

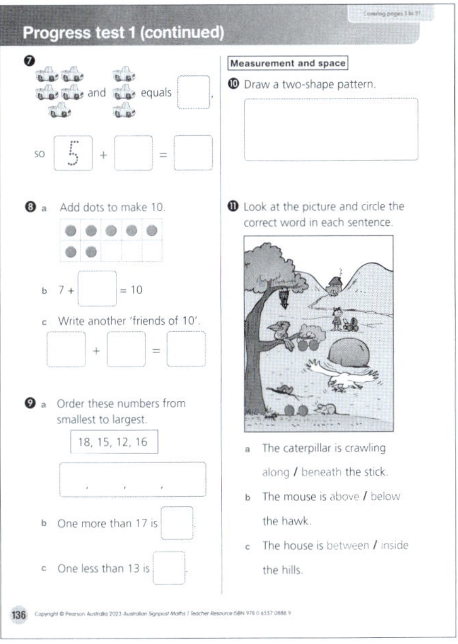

Covering pages 1 to 21

**Progress test 1 (continued)**

7 ___ and ___ equals ___,

so 5 + ___ = ___

8 a Add dots to make 10.

b 7 + ___ = 10

c Write another 'friends of 10'.

___ + ___ = ___

9 a Order these numbers from smallest to largest.

18, 15, 12, 16

___, ___, ___, ___

b One more than 17 is ___

c One less than 13 is ___

Measurement and space

10 Draw a two-shape pattern.

11 Look at the picture and circle the correct word in each sentence.

a The caterpillar is crawling along / beneath the stick.

b The mouse is above / below the hawk.

c The house is between / inside the hills.

136 Copyright © Pearson Australia 2023 Australian Signpost Maths 1 Teacher Resource ISBN 978 0 6557 0888 9

## Progress retest

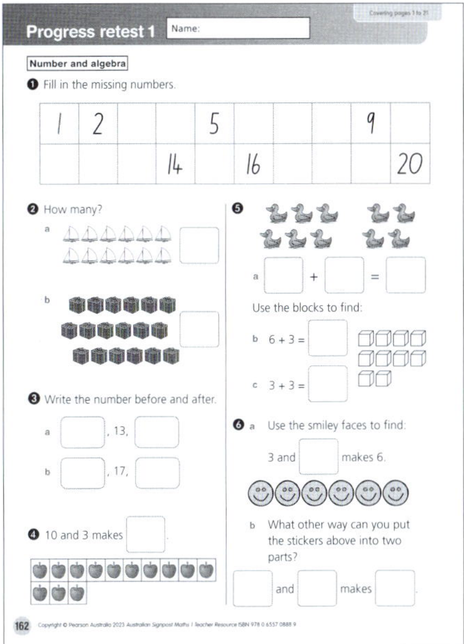

Covering pages 1 to 21

**Progress retest 1** Name:

Number and algebra

1 Fill in the missing numbers.

| 1 | 2 | | | 5 | | | 9 | |
|---|---|---|---|---|---|---|---|---|
| | | | 14 | | 16 | | | 20 |

2 How many?

a

b

3 Write the number before and after.

a ___, 13, ___

b ___, 17, ___

4 10 and 3 makes ___

5 a ___ + ___ = ___

Use the blocks to find:

b 6 + 3 =

c 3 + 3 =

6 a Use the smiley faces to find:

3 and ___ makes 6.

b What other way can you put the stickers above into two parts?

___ and ___ makes ___

162 Copyright © Pearson Australia 2023 Australian Signpost Maths 1 Teacher Resource ISBN 978 0 6557 0888 9

## Notes and answers for Progress test 1

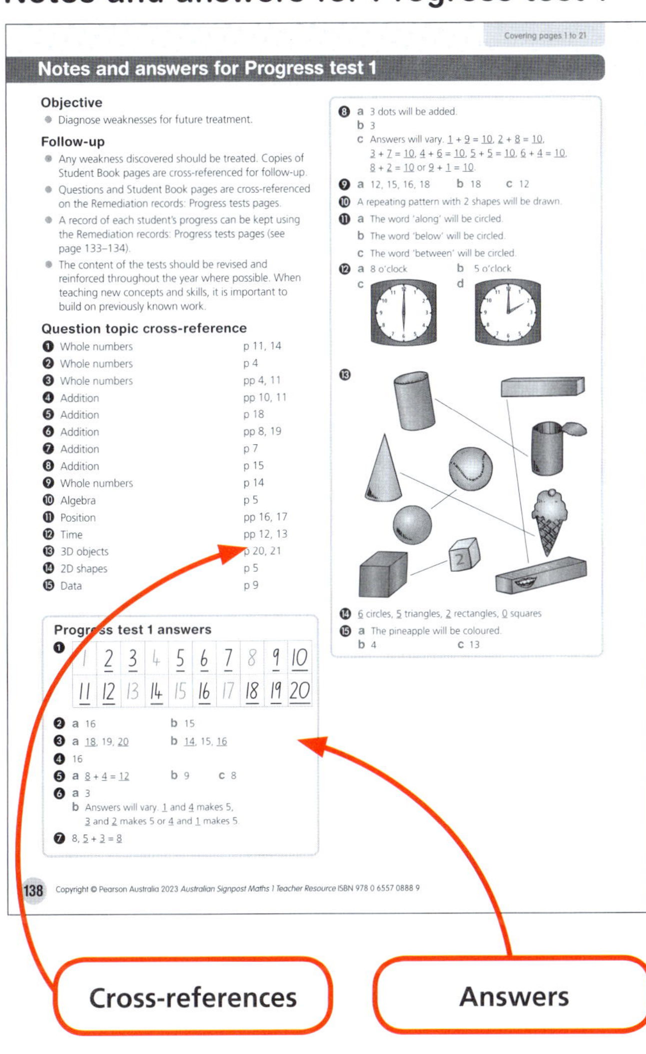

Covering pages 1 to 21

**Notes and answers for Progress test 1**

**Objective**

- Diagnose weaknesses for future treatment.

**Follow-up**

- Any weakness discovered should be treated. Copies of Student Book pages are cross-referenced for follow-up.
- Questions and Student Book pages are cross-referenced on the Remediation records: Progress tests pages.
- A record of each student's progress can be kept using the Remediation records: Progress tests pages (see page 133–134).
- The content of the tests should be revised and reinforced throughout the year where possible. When teaching new concepts and skills, it is important to build on previously known work.

**Question topic cross-reference**

| | Topic | Page |
|---|---|---|
| 1 | Whole numbers | p 11, 14 |
| 2 | Whole numbers | p 4 |
| 3 | Whole numbers | pp 4, 11 |
| 4 | Addition | pp 10, 11 |
| 5 | Addition | p 18 |
| 6 | Addition | pp 8, 19 |
| 7 | Addition | p 7 |
| 8 | Addition | p 15 |
| 9 | Whole numbers | p 14 |
| 10 | Algebra | p 5 |
| 11 | Position | pp 16, 17 |
| 12 | Time | pp 12, 13 |
| 13 | 3D objects | p 20, 21 |
| 14 | 2D shapes | p 5 |
| 15 | Data | p 9 |

**Progress test 1 answers**

1

| 1 | 2 | 3 | 4 | 5 | 6 | 7 | 8 | 9 | 10 |
|---|---|---|---|---|---|---|---|---|---|
| 11 | 12 | 13 | 14 | 15 | 16 | 17 | 18 | 19 | 20 |

2 a 16 b 15

3 a 18, 19, 20 b 14, 15, 16

4 16

5 a 8 + 4 = 12 b 9 c 8

6 a 3

b Answers will vary. 1 and 4 makes 5, 3 and 2 makes 5 or 4 and 1 makes 5.

7 8, 5 + 3 = 8

8 a 3 dots will be added.

b 3

c Answers will vary. 1 + 9 = 10, 2 + 8 = 10, 3 + 7 = 10, 4 + 6 = 10, 5 + 5 = 10, 6 + 4 = 10, 8 + 2 = 10 or 9 + 1 = 10.

9 a 12, 15, 16, 18 b 18 c 12

10 A repeating pattern with 2 shapes will be drawn.

11 a The word 'along' will be circled.

b The word 'below' will be circled.

c The word 'between' will be circled.

12 a 8 o'clock b 5 o'clock

c d

13

14 6 circles, 5 triangles, 2 rectangles, 0 squares

15 a The pineapple will be coloured.

b 4 c 13

138 Copyright © Pearson Australia 2023 Australian Signpost Maths 1 Teacher Resource ISBN 978 0 6557 0888 9

## Remediation records: Progress tests

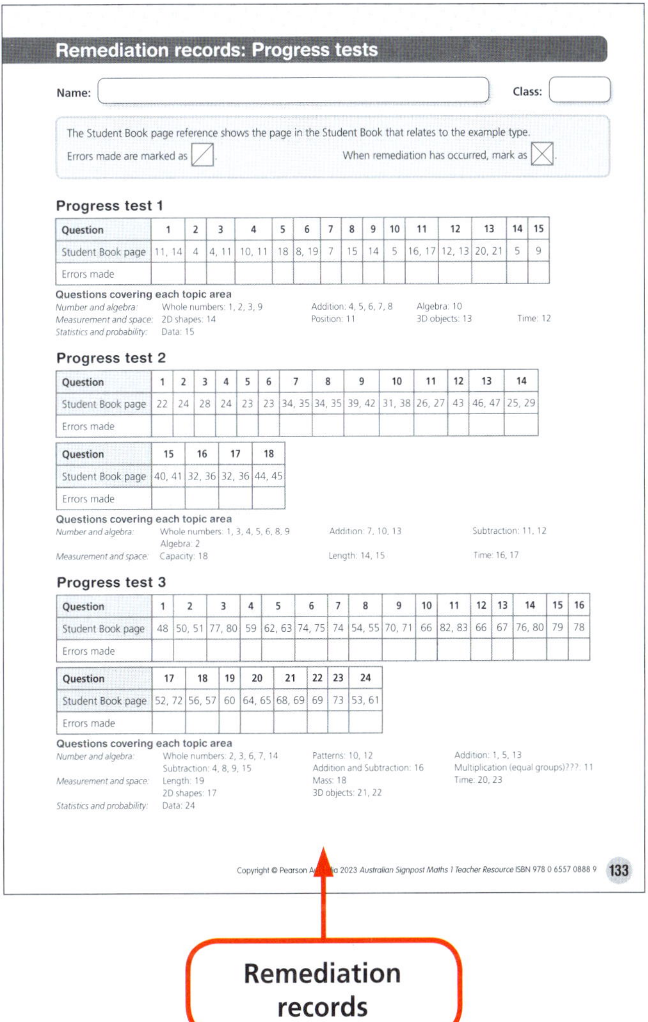

**Remediation records: Progress tests**

Name: Class:

The Student Book page reference shows the page in the Student Book that relates to the example type.

Errors made are marked as ⧄. When remediation has occurred, mark as ☒.

**Progress test 1**

| Question | 1 | 2 | 3 | 4 | 5 | 6 | 7 | 8 | 9 | 10 | 11 | 12 | 13 | 14 | 15 |
|---|---|---|---|---|---|---|---|---|---|---|---|---|---|---|---|
| Student Book page | 11, 14 | 4 | 4, 11 | 10, 11 | 18 | 8, 19 | 7 | 15 | 14 | 5 | 16, 17 | 12, 13 | 20, 21 | 5 | 9 |
| Errors made | | | | | | | | | | | | | | | |

**Questions covering each topic area**

*Number and algebra:* Whole numbers: 1, 2, 3, 9 Addition: 4, 5, 6, 7, 8 Algebra: 10

*Measurement and space:* 2D shapes: 14 Position: 11 3D objects: 13 Time: 12

*Statistics and probability:* Data: 15

**Progress test 2**

| Question | 1 | 2 | 3 | 4 | 5 | 6 | 7 | 8 | 9 | 10 | 11 | 12 | 13 | 14 |
|---|---|---|---|---|---|---|---|---|---|---|---|---|---|---|
| Student Book page | 22 | 24 | 28 | 24 | 23 | 23 | 34, 35 | 34, 35 | 39, 42 | 31, 38 | 26, 27 | 43 | 46, 47 | 25, 29 |
| Errors made | | | | | | | | | | | | | | |

| Question | 15 | 16 | 17 | 18 |
|---|---|---|---|---|
| Student Book page | 40, 41 | 32, 36 | 32, 36 | 44, 45 |
| Errors made | | | | |

**Questions covering each topic area**

*Number and algebra:* Whole numbers: 1, 3, 4, 5, 6, 8, 9 Addition: 7, 10, 13 Subtraction: 11, 12
Algebra: 2

*Measurement and space:* Capacity: 18 Length: 14, 15 Time: 16, 17

**Progress test 3**

| Question | 1 | 2 | 3 | 4 | 5 | 6 | 7 | 8 | 9 | 10 | 11 | 12 | 13 | 14 | 15 | 16 |
|---|---|---|---|---|---|---|---|---|---|---|---|---|---|---|---|---|
| Student Book page | 48 | 50, 51 | 77, 80 | 59 | 62, 63 | 74, 75 | 74 | 54, 55 | 70, 71 | 66 | 82, 83 | 66 | 67 | 76, 80 | 79 | 78 |
| Errors made | | | | | | | | | | | | | | | | |

| Question | 17 | 18 | 19 | 20 | 21 | 22 | 23 | 24 |
|---|---|---|---|---|---|---|---|---|
| Student Book page | 52, 72 | 56, 57 | 60 | 64, 65 | 68, 69 | 69 | 73 | 53, 61 |
| Errors made | | | | | | | | |

**Questions covering each topic area**

*Number and algebra:* Whole numbers: 2, 3, 6, 7, 14 Patterns: 10, 12 Addition: 1, 5, 13
Subtraction: 4, 8, 9, 15 Addition and Subtraction: 16 Multiplication (equal groups)???: 11

*Measurement and space:* Length: 19 Mass: 18 Time: 20, 23
2D shapes: 17 3D objects: 21, 22

*Statistics and probability:* Data: 24

Copyright © Pearson Australia 2023 Australian Signpost Maths 1 Teacher Resource ISBN 978 0 6557 0888 9 133

Cross-references

Answers

Remediation records

# Number lines / chart

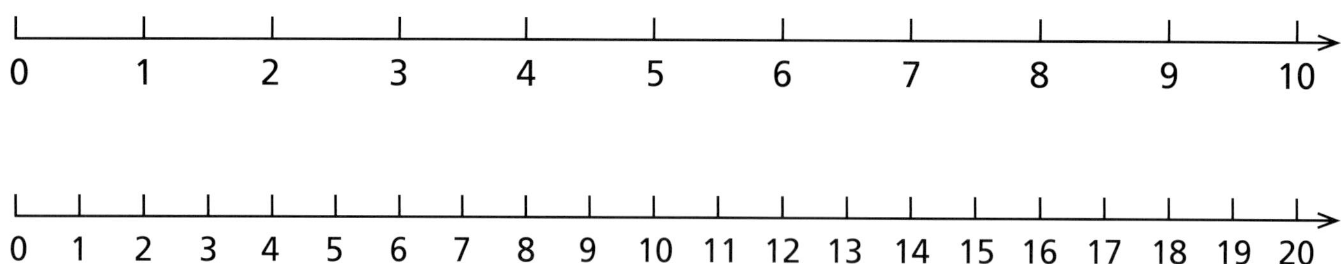


| 1 | 2 | 3 | 4 | 5 | 6 | 7 | 8 | 9 | 10 |
|---|---|---|---|---|---|---|---|---|---|
| 11 | 12 | 13 | 14 | 15 | 16 | 17 | 18 | 19 | 20 |
| 21 | 22 | 23 | 24 | 25 | 26 | 27 | 28 | 29 | 30 |
| 31 | 32 | 33 | 34 | 35 | 36 | 37 | 38 | 39 | 40 |
| 41 | 42 | 43 | 44 | 45 | 46 | 47 | 48 | 49 | 50 |
| 51 | 52 | 53 | 54 | 55 | 56 | 57 | 58 | 59 | 60 |
| 61 | 62 | 63 | 64 | 65 | 66 | 67 | 68 | 69 | 70 |
| 71 | 72 | 73 | 74 | 75 | 76 | 77 | 78 | 79 | 80 |
| 81 | 82 | 83 | 84 | 85 | 86 | 87 | 88 | 89 | 90 |
| 91 | 92 | 93 | 94 | 95 | 96 | 97 | 98 | 99 | 100 |

## Extra support page 2 Number bond houses

| 10 | |
|---|---|
| 1 | 9 |
| 2 | 8 |
| 3 | 7 |
| 4 | 6 |
| 5 | 5 |
| 6 | 4 |
| 7 | 3 |
| 8 | 2 |
| 9 | 1 |

| 9 | |
|---|---|
| 1 | 8 |
| 2 | 7 |
| 3 | 6 |
| 4 | 5 |
| 5 | 4 |
| 6 | 3 |
| 7 | 2 |
| 8 | 1 |

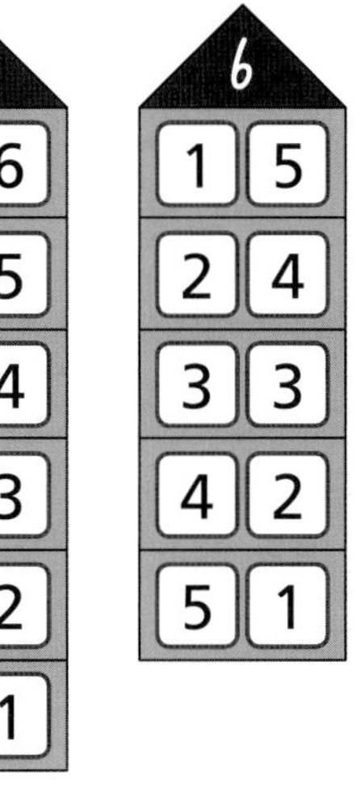


| 7 | |
|---|---|
| 1 | 6 |
| 2 | 5 |
| 3 | 4 |
| 4 | 3 |
| 5 | 2 |
| 6 | 1 |

| 6 | |
|---|---|
| 1 | 5 |
| 2 | 4 |
| 3 | 3 |
| 4 | 2 |
| 5 | 1 |

| 5 | |
|---|---|
| 1 | 4 |
| 2 | 3 |
| 3 | 2 |
| 4 | 1 |

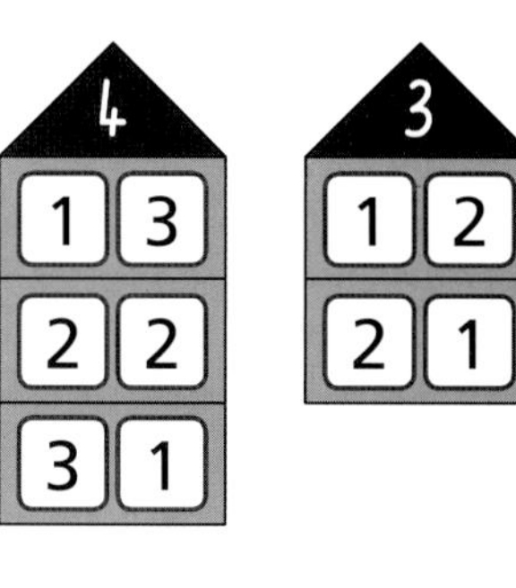


| 7 | |
|---|---|
| | 1 |
| 5 | |
| | 3 |
| 3 | |
| | 5 |
| 1 | |

| 8 | |
|---|---|
| 7 | |
| | 2 |
| 5 | |
| | 4 |
| | 5 |
| 2 | |
| | 7 |

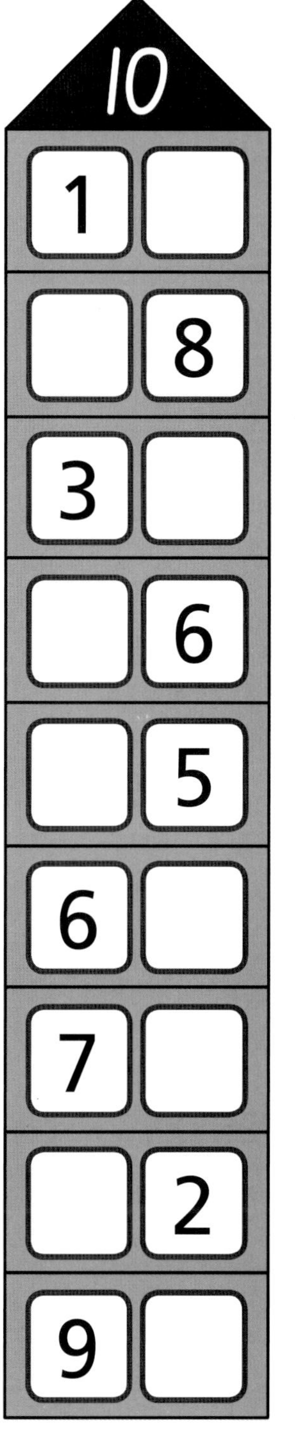


 • *AUSTRALIAN SIGNPOST MATHS 1* • ISBN 9780655708759

## Extra support page 3 Number bonds (addition)

Say the number bonds in a line, giving the answers as you go.
Line A would be 7 = 1 + ■, 6 = 3 + ■, 9 = 3 + ■, 8 = ■ + 5.

**A**

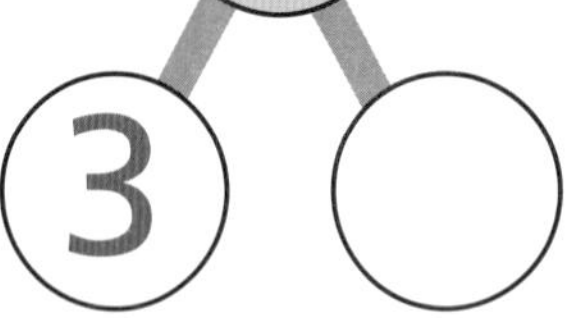

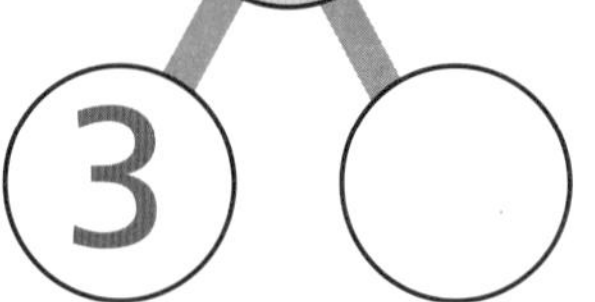

| Whole | Part | Part |
|---|---|---|
| 7 | 1 | |
| 6 | 3 | |
| 9 | 3 | |
| 8 | | 5 |

**B**

| Whole | Part | Part |
|---|---|---|
| 4 | | 1 |
| 4 | | 3 |
| 4 | | 2 |
| 10 | | 5 |

**C**

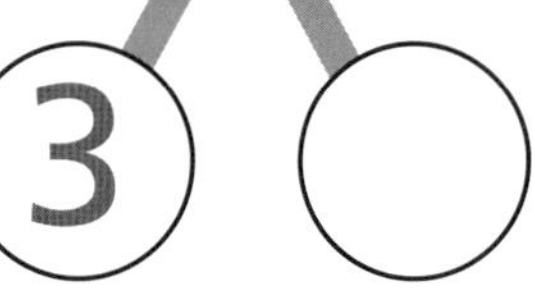

| Whole | Part | Part |
|---|---|---|
| 10 | 1 | |
| 10 | 2 | |
| 10 | 3 | |
| 10 | 4 | |

**D**

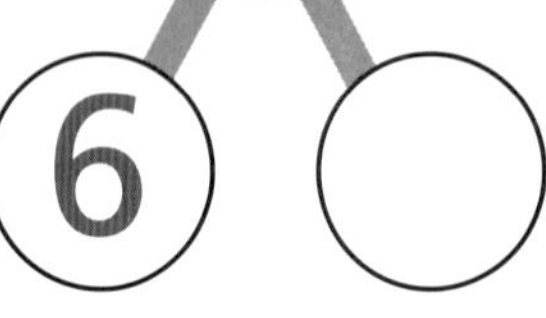

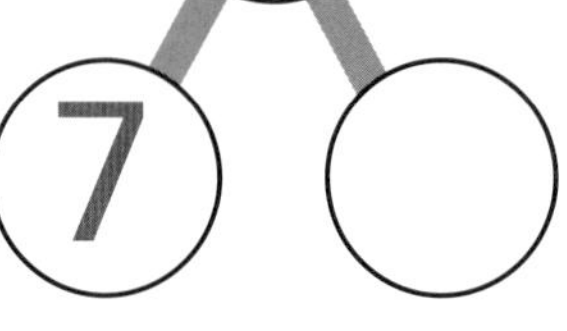

| Whole | Part | Part |
|---|---|---|
| 10 | 5 | |
| 10 | 6 | |
| 10 | 7 | |
| 10 | 8 | |

# Addition and subtraction facts

## Addition (Say the answers to each line as quickly as possible.)

| | | | | | | |
|---|---|---|---|---|---|---|
| **A** | 2 + 2 | 3 + 7 | 6 + 3 | 6 + 0 | 5 + 2 | 3 + 3 |
| **B** | 5 + 3 | 3 + 2 | 2 + 8 | 4 + 2 | 1 + 7 | 4 + 6 |
| **C** | 5 + 5 | 8 + 2 | 6 + 4 | 4 + 4 | 7 + 2 | 9 + 1 |
| **D** | 4 + 3 | 5 + 4 | 7 + 3 | 6 + 2 | 6 + 6 | 7 + 7 |
| **E** | 9 + 2 | 8 + 4 | 4 + 7 | 7 + 9 | 9 + 6 | 5 + 6 |
| **F** | 7 + 6 | 2 + 9 | 7 + 4 | 3 + 8 | 5 + 7 | 9 + 9 |
| **G** | 3 + 9 | 8 + 8 | 9 + 7 | 6 + 8 | 5 + 9 | 4 + 8 |
| **H** | 8 + 6 | 4 + 9 | 8 + 7 | 5 + 8 | 7 + 5 | 6 + 7 |
| **I** | 7 + 8 | 8 + 9 | 8 + 5 | 6 + 9 | 9 + 5 | 9 + 8 |

## Subtraction (Say the answers to each line as quickly as possible.)

| | | | | | | |
|---|---|---|---|---|---|---|
| **A** | 6 – 6 | 5 – 4 | 3 – 0 | 6 – 1 | 6 – 4 | 9 – 3 |
| **B** | 9 – 1 | 9 – 5 | 6 – 4 | 5 – 1 | 7 – 5 | 6 – 2 |
| **C** | 6 – 3 | 5 – 3 | 9 – 2 | 9 – 7 | 5 – 2 | 3 – 2 |
| **D** | 9 – 6 | 4 – 2 | 7 – 3 | 5 – 5 | 6 – 5 | 9 – 4 |
| **E** | 8 – 3 | 8 – 2 | 7 – 2 | 9 – 8 | 3 – 2 | 4 – 3 |
| **F** | 12 – 5 | 15 – 6 | 12 – 6 | 10 – 2 | 10 – 1 | 14 – 9 |
| **G** | 10 – 2 | 12 – 9 | 16 – 9 | 13 – 4 | 11 – 3 | 13 – 8 |
| **H** | 16 – 7 | 14 – 8 | 10 – 7 | 12 – 4 | 10 – 4 | 11 – 4 |
| **I** | 10 – 3 | 13 – 7 | 10 – 5 | 14 – 7 | 16 – 8 | 10 – 8 |
| **J** | 15 – 7 | 10 – 6 | 12 – 7 | 17 – 9 | 11 – 6 | 13 – 9 |
| **K** | 14 – 6 | 17 – 8 | 13 – 5 | 14 – 5 | 13 – 6 | 11 – 7 |
| **L** | 12 – 8 | 15 – 8 | 12 – 3 | 11 – 5 | 15 – 9 | 18 – 9 |

# Extra support page 3 Addition facts to 20

| + | 1 | 2 | 3 | 4 | 5 | 6 | 7 | 8 | 9 | 10 |
|---|---|---|---|---|---|---|---|---|---|---|
| 1 | 2 | 3 | 4 | 5 | 6 | 7 | 8 | 9 | 10 | 11 |
| 2 | 3 | 4 | 5 | 6 | 7 | 8 | 9 | 10 | 11 | 12 |
| 3 | 4 | 5 | 6 | 7 | 8 | 9 | 10 | 11 | 12 | 13 |
| 4 | 5 | 6 | 7 | 8 | 9 | 10 | 11 | 12 | 13 | 14 |
| 5 | 6 | 7 | 8 | 9 | 10 | 11 | 12 | 13 | 14 | 15 |
| 6 | 7 | 8 | 9 | 10 | 11 | 12 | 13 | 14 | 15 | 16 |
| 7 | 8 | 9 | 10 | 11 | 12 | 13 | 14 | 15 | 16 | 17 |
| 8 | 9 | 10 | 11 | 12 | 13 | 14 | 15 | 16 | 17 | 18 |
| 9 | 10 | 11 | 12 | 13 | 14 | 15 | 16 | 17 | 18 | 19 |
| 10 | 11 | 12 | 13 | 14 | 15 | 16 | 17 | 18 | 19 | 20 |

- Learn the addition tables with answers up to 10. (**2 + 5 = 5 + 2 = 7**)
- Learn the addition tables with answers up to 20. (**7 + 6 = 6 + 7 = 13**)
- Learn your doubles and halves.

| **Numbers** | 1 | 2 | 3 | 4 | 5 | 6 | 7 | 8 | 9 | 10 |
|---|---|---|---|---|---|---|---|---|---|---|
| **Doubles** | **2** | **4** | **6** | **8** | **10** | **12** | **14** | **16** | **18** | **20** |

**4 + 4 = 8** **Double 4 = 8.**

| **Numbers** | 2 | 4 | 6 | 8 | 10 | 12 | 14 | 16 | 18 | 20 |
|---|---|---|---|---|---|---|---|---|---|---|
| **Halves** | **1** | **2** | **3** | **4** | **5** | **6** | **7** | **8** | **9** | **10** |

**Half of 10 = 5.**